Social Work with Abused and Neglected Children

Social Work with Abused and Neglected Children

A Manual of Interdisciplinary Practice

Edited by
Kathleen Coulborn Faller

THE FREE PRESS
A Division of Macmillan Publishing Co., Inc.
NEW YORK

Collier Macmillan Publishers
LONDON

The Free Press
A Division of Macmillan Publishing Co., Inc.
866 Third Avenue, New York, N.Y. 10022

Collier Macmillan Canada, Ltd.

Library of Congress Catalog Card Number: 81-66328

Printed in the United States of America

printing number

1 2 3 4 5 6 7 8 9 10

Library of Congress Cataloging in Publication Data
Main entry under title:

Social work with abused and neglected children.

Bibliography: p.
Includes index.
1. Child abuse. 2. Social case work with children.
I. Faller, Kathleen Coulborn. [DNLM: 1. Child abuse.
2. Social work. WA 320 S678]
HV713.S62 362.7'1 81-66328
ISBN 0-02-910280-4 AACR2

Contents

Preface and Acknowledgments

Social workers are key professionals in the management of cases of child abuse and neglect. The general skills social workers have are of vital importance to this work, but specialized knowledge and expertise are also necessary. While child abuse and neglect training is available in some schools of social work and can sometimes be obtained in continuing education programs, often what is available is not timely or sufficient. This manual is designed to provide social workers with essential knowledge for working with abusive and neglectful families. It is meant to meet the needs of persons working in child protection, but it should also address the concerns of a much broader network of social workers, which includes anyone involved in working with children.

Beyond providing the tools specific to social workers, the major emphasis of the book is on the importance of collaboration with other professionals for adequate case management. Social workers cannot do the job alone, nor can any other profession. It is essential for each profession to understand the orientations of others and what constitutes good practice in the various disciplines involved with abusive and neglectful families. Thus social workers must understand what physicians can do, how to collaborate with psychiatrists and psychologists, and the various legal roles in cases of child abuse and neglect. It is our hope that this manual will meet these goals.

The manual was prepared through the collaborative efforts of members of the Interdisciplinary Project on Child Abuse and Neglect.

While individuals are given credit for separate contributions, many others were involved in reading drafts and offering suggestions. Further, many of the ideas are not "owned" by the individuals expressing them, but come out of group experience and joint efforts.

The Project is made up of faculty from the Schools of Social Work, Law, and Medicine at the University of Michigan. It is our belief that to adequately address the problem of child abuse and neglect, a range of professions must be involved and must work collaboratively. Each profession represented by our faculty (and other disciplines as well) has a unique role to play in child abuse and neglect, but without a coordination of efforts, that contribution will not be maximized.

The Project's functions are several: (1) traditional classroom teaching to students in the several professional programs from which our faculty come; (2) providing clinical and practice experiences to students of law, social work, psychiatry, and medicine who wish to have direct case experience in child abuse and neglect under our supervision; (3) enhancing the knowledge base about child abuse and neglect through ongoing clinical practice in our various disciplines and by engaging in research; (4) training practitioners in the field who are handling or will handle child abuse and neglect cases; and (5) advocacy for program change to improve the delivery of services to maltreating families. This capability to be involved on many levels and in different areas has been crucial in the production of meaningful material for the manual.

This unique project was made possible by the very generous funding provided by the Harry and Margaret Towsley Foundation. The Foundation provided a three-year grant through the University of Michigan Law School, but also involving participation from the School of Social Work and the Medical School, to develop and carry out a multidisciplinary project to address the needs for training professionals to work with abused and neglected children. Part of the program the Foundation sponsored was the writing of the social work manual.

This ambitious project could not have been carried out without the support of the schools involved—Social Work, Law and Medicine—and particularly the Dean of Social Work, Phillip Fellin, and two Law School deans, Theodore St. Antoine and Terrance Sandalow.

In addition, the contributors wish to express gratitude for their guidance and support to the Executive Committee of the Interdisciplinary Project on Child Abuse and Neglect (IPCAN), a group of senior faculty members in the three schools: Professor David Chambers and Associate Professor Steven Pepe of the Law School; Assistant Dean Dee Kilpatrick of the School of Social Work; Professor Andrew Watson of the Law School and Medical School; Associate Professor of

Pediatrics Nancy Hopwood; and Paul Glasser, formerly Professor in the School of Social Work and currently Dean of the School of Social Work at the University of Texas at Arlington. Of the current and former members of the Executive Committee, we wish to express particular appreciation to Paul Glasser, Andrew Watson, and David Chambers for reading drafts of parts of the manual and offering suggestions.

Other people were also extremely generous in reading parts or all of the manual and providing input: Dr. Ray Helfer of the Department of Pediatrics and Human Development at Michigan State University and Doctors Judi Kleinman and Ann Thompson of the University of Michigan Department of Psychiatry, who wrote portions of the manual related to psychiatry but also read and offered useful criticism of the social work part. Further we would like to thank Dr. Sallie Churchill of the Social Work faculty, who read the entire manual and offered valuable comments. The book could not have been completed without the facilitative efforts of Judith Stone, M.S.W., who was formerly Project Coordinator. Moreover, without the willingness of numerous agencies in the communities surrounding the University of Michigan to allow ourselves and our students to practice, the manual would not have the currency it does.

Finally, we would like to thank Betty Scheffler, Colleen Baranek, and Jackie Kuczborski, who patiently typed numerous drafts of the manual, and the editors from The Free Press, Gladys Topkis and Eileen DeWald.

KATHLEEN COULBORN FALLER

About the Contributors

M. Leora Bowden, M.S.W., was formerly Director of Social Work at Mott-Womens-Holden Unit of University Hospital and part-time on the Interdisciplinary Project on Child Abuse and Neglect (IPCAN) staff. Currently she is Director of the National Burn Institute in Ann Arbor, Michigan.

Donald N. Duquette, J.D., is a Clinical Associate Professor in the University of Michigan Law School. He is Co-Director of IPCAN and Director of the Child Advocacy Law Clinic, the clinical unit for law students. His other duties include consultation to social work students, training of community professionals, and legal advocacy for children.

Kathleen Coulborn Faller, M.S.W., Ph.D. candidate, is a social worker and psychologist. She is a lecturer in social work at the University of Michigan, Co-Director of the Interdisciplinary Project on Child Abuse and Neglect, and Director of a research project entitled Child Abuse and Neglect: The Family and the Community. Her duties include traditional classroom teaching, clinical supervision of social work students, clinical consultation with law students, training of practitioners in the child abuse and neglect field, and research into the causes of child abuse and neglect.

H. Mark Hildebrandt, M.D., is a pediatrician, Clinical Associate Professor in the University of Michigan Department of Pediatrics and Communicable Diseases, and formerly, a member of the staff of IPCAN. He was founder of the University Hospital Suspected Child Abuse and Neglect Team and its Director from 1971 to 1979. He is in private practice and a consultant to the Family Therapy Project, Child Abuse and Substance Abuse, in the University of Michigan Department of Psychiatry.

Carolyn Okell Jones (B.S.C. with honors, with a Home Office Letter of Recognition in Child Care) is a social work lecturer and practitioner from England who worked for seven years in the original Battered Child Research Department of the National Society for the Prevention of Cruelty to Children. During 1977–78 she was a Visiting Assistant Professor in the University of Michigan School of Social Work and a member of the IPCAN staff. Currently she is employed by the Open University, Milton Keynes, England, as a member of a small team developing a course on Conflict in the Family.

Judith Kleinman, M.D., is a faculty member of the Department of Psychiatry and a member of IPCAN staff. Her duties with IPCAN include case assessment, case consultation to law students and social work students, and training of practitioners working in the field of child abuse and neglect. She also is an adult and child psychiatrist in private practice.

Sally Russo, M.A., M.S.W., was a student in social work administration who did a field placement with IPCAN. Currently, she is a social worker in the Children and Youth Services of Delaware County, Pennsylvania.

Judith B. Stone, M.S.W., was Project Coordinator for IPCAN for three years. Currently, she is Project Associate for Region V Adoption Resource Center located in Ann Arbor, Michigan.

Janet Stubbs, M.S., is a child psychologist. She was a clinical instructor in the Department of Pediatrics and Communicable Diseases, and part-time on the IPCAN staff. Currently, she teaches in the Department of Psychology at Bridgewater State College, Bridgewater, Massachusetts.

Ann E. Thompson, M.D., is a child psychiatrist. She has been part-time on the faculty of the Department of Psychiatry at the University of Michigan and a member of the staff of IPCAN. Currently, she is in full-time private practice in East Lansing, Michigan.

Marjorie Ziefert, M.S.W., A.C.S.W., was formerly a member of the faculty of the University of Michigan School of Social Work and of the IPCAN staff. Presently she is teaching at Eastern Michigan University.

PART I

Overview

1

Definition and Scope of the Problem of Child Maltreatment

Kathleen Coulborn Faller and Sally Russo

What Is Child Maltreatment?

There is no clear-cut consensus on a definition of child maltreatment. In fact there is not even agreement about the appropriateness of this term. Some professionals think society should only be concerned with child abuse; the term "maltreatment" also includes the more nebulous neglect cases. Others prefer the term "child mistreatment" (Giovannoni and Becerra, 1979) or unusual parenting practices (Helfer and Kempe, 1976). Still others continue to use the attention-getting phrase "the battered child" (Helfer and Kempe, 1980).

Whatever term is used for the problem, in order for social workers to respond in a professional and competent way to it, they must have some way of differentiating child maltreatment from acceptable ways of managing children and from other problems in functioning. In the first instance, this is not a simple matter because how the problem is defined will vary depending upon the context in which it is viewed. In the second instance, child maltreatment is often seen as one of a constellation of interrelated family problems, making it difficult to separate out.

Because a major goal of this book is to make social workers aware of how other professionals approach child abuse and neglect, it is worthwhile examining how the problem is defined in the range of contexts relevant to an interdisciplinary approach.

Perhaps the easiest definition to grasp is the medical one. The medical professional focuses on the physical condition of the child. She/he looks for certain patterns of fractures, cuts, bruising, or other physical injuries which tend to exist if an injury is inflicted. When neglect is the concern, the physician looks for physical signs of malnutrition or exposure to unhealthy environmental conditions, or a physical condition indicating failure to seek necessary medical or dental care.

An examination of how medical knowledge developed in this field well illustrates the physiological orientation. The first major medical attention to child abuse occurred with the identification of the battered child syndrome in the 1960s (Helfer and Kempe, 1968). This condition was diagnosed when young children had multiple fractures at various stages of healing, detectable on x-ray, and no medical condition which would account for them. Such findings are regarded as diagnostic of child abuse. Similarly, Caffey's syndrome (Caffey, 1946) is defined as the concurrence of retinal hemorrhages and subdural hematomas in infants. These two types of injuries are detectable by x-ray and ophthalmoscope and are caused by shaking of a child to the point that it sustains a whiplash type of injury. (See Chapter 2, "Types of Child Abuse and Neglect," for a further discussion of medical definitions.)

In notable contrast is the legal approach to child abuse and neglect. The law is interested in child maltreatment when it becomes necessary for the state to interfere in the private affairs of the family because of parental malfeasance. An underlying assumption is that intervention is to be avoided, that families have the right to privacy and parents ought to be free to raise their children as they see fit without the interference of the state except in unusual circumstances.

However, there is some variability in this general orientation because we have fifty separate states, each with its own set of statutes addressing the problem, and most states have at least three separate statutes which address the problem. These are (1) a child maltreatment reporting law, (2) a criminal statute, and (3) a juvenile code which specifies the conditions under which a juvenile court can intervene for the purpose of protecting the child.

Under reporting laws, the primary intent is to bring cases of suspected child maltreatment to the attention of a mandated social agency so that they can be investigated and appropriate intervention can be offered, usually with the voluntary cooperation of the family. The federal government encourages uniformity in reporting laws by having certain federal funding contingent upon having laws which comply with a federal model statute.

The following definitions are from the Michigan Child Protection Law, which meets the federal definitional requirements:

> "Child Abuse" means harm or threatened harm to a child's health or welfare by a person responsible for the child's health or welfare which occurs through nonaccidental physical or mental injury, sexual abuse, or maltreatment.
>
> "Child neglect" means harm to a child's health or welfare by a person responsible for the child's health or welfare which occurs through negligent treatment, including the failure to provide adequate food, clothing, shelter, or medical care.

These definitions are broad and include not only actual harm to the child but threatened harm. The expectation is that soon all states will include in their reportable conditions both neglect and abuse, emotional as well as physical maltreatment, and sexual abuse.

Criminal statutes have a different intention as they are to be used to prosecute perpetrators, usually parents. The penalty, if convicted, is a fine or a jail sentence or both, and states will vary in whether the crime is a misdemeanor or a felony or can be both. The following examples are from the Colorado and Michigan statutes:

COLORADO

Article 13

40-13-1 Child—Health or Life Endangered

> It shall be unlawful for any person having the care or custody of any child, willfully to cause or permit the life of such child to be endangered, or the health of such child to be injured, and willfully or unnecessarily to expose to the inclemency of the weather, or to abandon such child or to torture, torment, cruelly punish or willfully and negligently to deprive of necessary food, clothing or shelter or in any other manner injure such child.
>
> Any person who shall be convicted of violating any of the provisions of section 40-13-1 . . . shall be fined not exceeding $100.00 or be imprisoned in the county jail not exceeding three months, or both in the discretion of the court, upon conviction of a second or any subsequent offense shall be fined not exceeding $200.00 or be imprisoned in the county jail not exceeding six months. (Fraser, 1973)

MICHIGAN

28.330 Exposing Child with Intent to Injure or Abandon

28.331 Cruelty to Children: Neglect and Abandonment

28.313(1) Torturing Children

> Any parent or guardian or person under whose protection or control any child may be, who tortures such child, shall be guilty of a felony

> and may be punished by imprisonment for *not* more than 10 years. (Fraser, 1973)

Finally, juvenile courts are involved when custody of the child is to be taken, that is, when the intent is to make the child either a temporary or permanent court ward. The following are the provisions of the juvenile code of the state of Michigan under which court jurisdiction can be taken for "neglect" of children:

> Jurisdiction in proceedings concerning any child under 17 years of age . . .
>
> (1) Whose parent or other person legally responsible for the care and maintenance of such child, when able to do so, neglects or refuses to provide proper or necessary support, education as required by law, medical, surgical or other care necessary for his health, morals, or who is deprived of emotional well-being, or who is abandoned by his parents, guardian, or other custodian, or who is otherwise without proper custody or guardianship; or
>
> (2) Whose home or environment, by reason of neglect, cruelty, drunkenness, criminality or depravity on the part of a parent, guardian or other custodian, is an unfit place for such child to live in, or whose mother is unmarried and without adequate provision for care and support. (Fraser, 1973)

The more onerous the penalties the law may employ, the greater is the focus on parental intent (e.g., "willfully" in the Colorado criminal statute and "when able to do so" in the juvenile code) and on parental behavior. Harm to the child becomes much less of a focal point. This contrasts markedly with medical definitions, which focus on the medical condition of the child.

Further, statutory definitions are somewhat vague and general. This vagueness is a source of some controversy, particularly in the legal profession, where it is felt that the lack of precision is an invitation for individual subjectivity and for overintrusion into families' lives. Some would prefer a definition which focuses on consequences for the child (Newberger and Bourne 1977; Wald, 1976). Others have argued on the opposite side, that such generalities are essential, for the state could not possibly anticipate the many and varied ways parents may mistreat their children.

Finally, we come to a definition from the social-psychological perspective. Professionals in the mental health field tend to focus more on the causes of maltreatment and to employ a more interactive definition. Therefore, the emphasis on maltreatment as an intentional, willful parental act is lost to a dynamic explanation of the behavior. Within this general approach among mental health professionals, there have been two conflicting theories: there are persons who see the problem as one caused mainly by parental inadequacy and those who look to the environment for the major contributing factors. Those in the first group see intrapsychic problems (and sometimes interpersonal ones) as key. Thus the parent may have a mental illness or may have been inadequately parented, or marital strife may be the crucial cause. In contrast, those who regard environmental factors as paramount note the correlation of child maltreatment with poverty (Gil, 1973, Gelles, 1970, Straus, 1978) or minority status (Gil, 1973, Gelles, 1970). They also point out that there are cultural norms which support the use of violence against children (and other family members). Straus and his colleagues state that a marriage license is a hitting license (Straus, Gelles, and Steinmetz, 1980). Further, family sociologists note that standards for how much physical punishment is appropriate to control children's behavior have changed over time. Thus what was acceptable childrearing practice 50 or 100 years ago is no longer acceptable (Giovannoni and Becerra, 1979). (See Chapter 3, "Causes of Child Abuse and Neglect," for more extensive discussion of these issues.)

Mental health professionals usually include in a definition of maltreatment harm to the child resulting from parental mistreatment. However, they do not customarily limit themselves to physical harm, but are also concerned about psychological damage. They would assert that in most cases the psychological impact is more lasting than the physical damage.

Where does this diversity of definition leave us as social workers trying to act in a professional way in response to situations of child maltreatment? First, it is essential for us to understand these varying perspectives if we are to work collaboratively. Second, it gives us some guidelines for arriving at a working definition for the social work profession. Four requirements must be met for a situation to be defined as one of child maltreatment. First, there must be some definable parental behavior, directed toward the child. This may be an act of commission (abuse) or omission (neglect), and it can be either physical or mental. However, it is important to be able to identify a specific instance or instances when the behavior occurred. For example, a worker should think "child neglect" if a parent leaves a three-year-old unsupervised several times for over an hour, but not so if the parent merely seems uninterested in the child.

Second, there must be some demonstrable harm to the child. This may be a physical injury or condition, or it may be evidence of psychological damage, or both. The psychological harm may be dramatically obvious, for example, with children who are self-destructive or have dramatic developmental lags (such as no speech at three years of age), or more subtle, as with low self-esteem. There will be a few cases where no actual harm has yet occurred but the parents' history and prognosis are such that harm will very likely occur. Examples of this are parents with chronic mental illness that does not respond to treatment and affects specifically the ability to parent, or the parent who has killed a previous child.

Third, a causal link needs to be established between parental behavior and the harm to the child. This is an important point because it is tempting to define all children who have emotional problems as having been maltreated by their parents, especially when parents do not cooperate with voluntary mental health intervention. If the definition of maltreatment is stretched this far, it will no longer have any meaning.

Finally, the social worker needs to feel that the maltreatment is sufficiently serious to warrant intervention. Many, many times parents inflict minor abuse or neglect. That is, a parent may yell at a child or smack a child as punishment, but it serves no positive end to define these situations as child maltreatment. (For a more extensive and thoughtful discussion of this issue, see Giovannoni and Becerra, 1979.)

How Pervasive Is the Problem of Child Maltreatment?

It is clear that child abuse and neglect are present in society today in alarming proportions, but precisely how extensive the problem is is not known. We have two major sources for judging incidence: reporting statistics and research studies. Until recently, our only information came from reported cases of child maltreatment, and even this data collection was sporadic and lacked uniformity.

Beginning in 1976 a National Central Registry was established so the problem could be more adequately tracked. The 1978 data (American Humane Association, 1980) from cases reported to the National Central Registry show 614,291 reports of abuse and neglect. Most of these are reports of families, not of individual victims. This is an increase of 200,000 cases from 1976, the first year in which these national statistics were collected. It probably does not represent more maltreatment of children, but rather an improvement in reporting. Of substantiated reports, 60.5 percent were of neglect only, 33.4 percent were abuse only, and 6 percent were families with both abuse and neglect. Of substantiated cases, 6.2 percent were of sexual abuse. Boys and girls were equally as likely to be victims; however, boys were more numerous among younger victims and girls among adolescents.

Poor and poorly educated families are overrepresented in reported cases, as are minorities. Of reported families, 27 percent are black or have a Spanish surname, while these groups represent only 16 percent of the national population. Mothers are more likely to maltreat than are fathers, 60 percent of perpetrators being female. However, against this statistic should be balanced the fact that in 45 percent of cases "broken family" was an identified stress. Other factors which had marked correlation were family discord (42.2 percent of cases), insufficient income (35.9 percent), continuous care of children (22.1 percent), lack of tolerance (30.2 percent), and loss of control during discipline (25.2 percent). The analysis shows that certain factors are more highly correlated with neglect (insufficient income 44.1 percent, family discord 38 percent, inadequate housing 28.3 percent) and others with abuse (lack of tolerance 48.5 percent, and history of abuse as a child 29.1 percent). Alcohol dependence is found equally in both abuse and neglect (approximately 14 percent).

We now have an additional source of statistical data on child maltreatment, a study of a representative sample of intact American families. (Straus et al., 1980). Thus this is a survey not of reported cases, but of the extent to which family members use violence in resolving their disputes.

The study estimates that 6.5 million children are stabbed, shot, kicked, beaten, punched, burned or hit with an instrument by their own parents (Straus, 1978). These findings do not include parental neglect, which is at least twice as prevalent as abuse, or emotional abuse and neglect or sexual abuse.

Like the National Central Registry analysis, Straus et al. found child abuse in all social classes but overrepresented among the poor. This confirms that poor families are more likely to maltreat their children, the reporting bias aside. However, when socioeconomic status was controlled for, blacks were not more likely to abuse than whites.

Other findings of this study are also of interest. Like the Central Registry data, this survey indicates that mothers are more likely to abuse than fathers. However, unlike the Central Registry cases, this study included no single-parent families. Unemployed fathers are much more likely to abuse their children than are fathers who are employed. Similarly, housewives are significantly more likely to abuse their children than working mothers. Further interesting statistics are that parents in large cities abuse their children more than those living elsewhere, and the Midwest has the highest incidence of child abuse while the South has the lowest.

These data are useful in giving us a general picture of the extensiveness of the problem and of some of the demographic characteristics relevant to child maltreatment. However, they cannot be a substitute for looking at the dynamics of individual cases because in reality there are not only many factors which can contribute to child maltreatment but also many different types of child abuse and neglect.

PART II

Identification

2

Types of Child Abuse and Neglect

Kathleen Coulborn Faller, M. Leora Bowden, Carolyn Okell Jones, and H. Mark Hildebrandt

Introduction

Social workers in a variety of medical and nonmedical settings need a working knowledge of the physical and behavioral characteristics of child abuse and neglect. This knowledge will be invaluable to those working directly with physicians and with other professionals on abuse and neglect cases. Social workers also need to be alert to signs of abuse and neglect because they may encounter these conditions in situations where they will need to make a preliminary assessment of the child in order to know whether to refer a case to protective services and/or to a physician. Alternatively, in some cases the social worker or protective services worker will be making the diagnosis without the need of a pediatrician, and thus must know what to look for.

Some general guidelines regarding types of abuse and neglect will be noted. Then material on a range of injuries and conditions will be presented.

General Information

There are certain "red flags" signaling abuse or neglect that are useful for the social worker to understand. First, an important indicator is an explanation given by the parents for an injury or condition of the child that does not fit the facts. Other times parents will claim to be unaware of how the injury occurred or offer no explanation. For instance, they may say, "The child fell," when clearly it has suffered a high-impact injury, or they may bring in a malnourished child and say they did not know the child was underweight.

Another sign is that some maltreating parents are excessively anxious given the condition of the child. Others seem remarkably unconcerned and may seek to talk about their own personal problems. They may bring the child to the hospital and then vanish. Often they do not visit the child if it is hospitalized.

In addition, it is not unusual in a case of maltreatment for there to be a delay in seeking medical treatment. The normal concerned parent will bring a child straightaway to a doctor if it has been injured. Because the maltreating parent is fearful of being detected, he/she may not do this, but may wait hoping the injury will heal itself.

Finally, children who are harmed intentionally often experience mistreatment repeatedly. They are likely to present with multiple injuries at various stages of healing and scars. While it may be plausible that a child will be injured accidentally a single time in a suspicious manner, it is much less likely the child will have been hurt in such a way several times.

Some additional orienting information about child abuse and neglect is useful for the social worker to know. First, cases involving serious harm to the child represent only a small percentage of the cases of child maltreatment. The most common types of abuse are minor cuts and bruises, and the most prevalent kind of neglect is the lack of adequate supervision.[1] Most situations do not require medical treatment. The more serious injuries are found in younger children, infants, and preschoolers.[2] This is partly because their small size makes them vulnerable to greater damage than older children from a given blow. Also, however, young children do not often come into contact with persons outside the family, persons who are likely to report abuse or neglect. Thus infants and toddlers may receive minor injuries which heal without requiring medical treatment, so that the only injuries coming to public attention are serious ones that need medical care.

A second point is that the neglect is reported between two and five times more frequently (depending upon what study is looked at) than abuse.[3] However, more information is available on abuse, and it has been more extensively studied. This is because abuse is much more readily diagnosed and more dramatic than neglect. Neglect, in contrast, tends to be gradual in onset, and multifaceted yet nebulous and difficult to document. Further, a single instance of neglect is not as

likely to be harmful. Therefore the problem must usually be a chronic one before intervention is justifiable.

As a rule abuse and neglect are differentiated in that abuse is regarded as an act of commission and neglect as one of omission. That is, the abusive parent actively harms the child, while the neglectful parent fails to provide for some of the child's basic needs. Although this is a useful distinction in most cases, in some situations the harmful effects to the child will be identical. For example, a child may be seriously injured or killed as a result of a fall from a second-story window whether the parent pushed the child out or left the window open and the child unattended.

Further, it is often simplistic to think of families as abuse cases or neglect cases. Increasingly we are seeing families where several kinds of maltreatment occur simultaneously or consecutively (and there may be other social problems as well). Sometimes one child is the victim, and sometimes more than one; sometimes one is abused and another neglected.

With this general information we will move to a discussion of injuries that are commonly seen in abused children and of conditions which may result from neglect. We will describe types of injuries, indicating how nonaccidental injuries can be distinguished from accidental injuries. Then we will note when certain conditions are likely to be a consequence of neglect.

Abuse

Bruises, Abrasions, Lacerations, and Scars

Impact injuries can cause bleeding on any body surface or internally. Bleeding into the skin and surrounding tissue is called a *bruise* or *contusion*. If it is extensive, it is called an *ecchymosis*. A swelling caused by a collection of blood in the space between muscles and skin or between the brain and the skull is called *hematoma*. *Petechiae* are small, flat, reddish-purple dots caused by small hemorrhages in the skin, and they occur after an impact to the skin, after straining or suffocation (head only), and as a result of vascular fragility or obstruction of tiny vessels by bacteria.

Children commonly sustain bruises in the course of their regular activities (after reaching nine months, the age of mobility). They and their parents may not be aware of how these bruises came about. However, accidental bruises are usually located on bony prominences such as the shins, the knees, the elbows, and sometimes the forehead.

Abrasions are superficial wounds in which an area of the skin has been scraped or scratched. A *laceration* is a definite cut or jagged opening in the skin. It may occur when a child falls against a hard object or surface, causing the skin to be cut between the bone and the hard surface. Otherwise, lacerations may occur when the skin is struck by a hard or sharp object. Lacerations are commonly a result of accidental falls, although frequent injuries or child–child injuries may reflect inadequate supervision.

There are several types of bruises, abrasions, and lacerations that should arouse the suspicion of child abuse. It is quite uncommon for children to have accidental bruises on their buttocks, the back of their legs, or their back. If a child falls accidentally, it is more likely to fall forward than backward. Bruises on the mouth, cheeks, vulva, penis, and rectal area should be considered inflicted or nonaccidental. Bruising around the mouth and injuries inside the mouth in infants are very likely to be inflicted. Bruises behind the ear are seldom sustained in a fall but are frequently noted when someone is struck on the side of the head. Bruises on the stomach, under the arm, and on the chest should also be considered nonaccidental. (See Appendix C for skin map of nonaccidental and accidental injury sites.)

Nonaccidental bruises may be detected by the shape of the instrument that has caused the injury. Outlines of fingers, hands, sticks (linear), belts (parallel, linear marks), or cords (loop injury with abrasions in the curve of the loop) are commonly noted in child abuse. *Grasp marks* on the upper arm or fingertip bruises on the arms or chest from forcibly holding a child down may also be seen. Human bites leave bruises in crescent and/or oval shapes that may appear as a curved line or with an imprint of individual teeth. Linear parallel lesions or scratch marks on any part of the body can be the result of fingernails being drawn across the body surface. Likewise, thin linear or possibly parallel marks or crescent-shaped marks can appear as a consequence of a whipping. They are likely to be found along the back, thighs, or buttocks several days after a whipping with a belt, switch, or cord after the initial contusions have faded and left marks where the skin was injured.[4]

Scars, marks, or *blemishes* on the skin are a residual from an earlier injury to the area. These marks can be temporary or permanent depending on the severity of the original injury and the healing capacity of the individual. All children have scars and blemishes of various sorts. Again, it is a large number and certain shapes that should arouse suspicion. Scars in unusual areas or of unique shapes are suspect. Round scars that may be from cigarette burns or crescent-shaped scars along the flank or buttocks from belt marks must be explored. Similarly, scars from large burns and lacerations that were never medically treated should arouse concern. Finally, when a child has scars as well as fresh injuries, or injuries at several stages of healing, a careful history should be taken.

Burns and Scalds

Burns that cause only redness such as sunburn are called *first-degree burns*. *Second-degree burns* lead to blistering and heal within one to three weeks depending on size. *Third-degree burns* destroy the entire skin thickness and require healing from the outside in for small areas (under one inch diameter) taking about one month, or requiring skin grafting over large areas. Burns result from exposure to flame, hot liquid, steam, electricity, or chemicals. The severity of a burn injury is determined by the depth of the burn, the amount of body surface involved, and the age of the individual burned. The younger the child, the more serious even a small burn becomes. It is very difficult to distinguish accidental from nonaccidental burns; therefore a detailed and accurate history is essential. About 10 percent of child abuse injuries are burns.[5]

The most common type of accidental burn is one that occurs when a toddler pulls hot liquid over himself. Children may be burned as a consequence of neglect, because they have been left unsupervised with matches or electrical appliances or a gas heater; or a parent may intentionally burn a child by immersing the child in hot water or by placing the child in contact with hot objects such as stoves, heaters, matches, or cigarettes.

Patterns of burn injury that have been identified in abuse cases include:

1. Cigarette burns, circular lesions about 5 mm in diameter on various parts of the body—face, hands, arms, abdomen—at various stages of healing
2. Burns on the buttocks and perineum, especially in children who are in the process of being toilet-trained or who may have a problem with bedwetting or soiling clothes
3. Contact burns that come from a part of the body being pressed to a hot source such as a stove or space heater, leaving a pattern of the heating element or protective grill
4. Burns from placing the child's hands palms down on electric coils of a stove to "teach" the child not to play with the stove, or from burning the child with matches to "teach" him/her not to play with matches

Immersion burns with clean edges should be considered suspicious. So should ones where the explanation for the immersion burn suggests the child doing something he/she is physically incapable of doing. For example, if a toddler is said to have burned his/her buttocks and perineum in the bathtub but does not have feet and ankle burns, the explanation simply does not fit the injury. A parent's report that a child was placed in a tub of hot water that the parent did not know was hot enough to scald the child should be regarded with suspicion. Water of 111° will burn small children in twenty minutes, 127° in thirty seconds, and 140° in three to five seconds. The upper level of comfort is considered 110°. Few adults would plunge into water which was 110° or more. If they put a hand in the water, they should realize it is too hot. To put a child in water of that temperature indicates parental abuse or impaired judgment suggesting child neglect.

Hot liquid that is thrown at a child will result in a splash area that spreads against gravity. The main portion will be burned most deeply, but there will be areas where the liquid flows away from this portion. One should consider whether the splash marks reflect the direction of the reported falling liquid, if such is the explanation offered.

A last clue to keep in mind is that abused children who have been burned often have evidence of other injuries such as broken bones or multiple bruises and lacerations and/or malnutrition. They may have a history of other hospitalizations for injury or failure to thrive or have siblings who have a history of hospitalizations for burns or other injury.

Fractures and Joint Injuries

Common medical terms used to describe broken bones or fractures include:

1. *Greenstick fracture*, one in which one side of a bone is broken and the other bent
2. *Multiple fracture*, a situation in which there are two or more lines of fractures in the same bone
3. *Open or compound fracture*, a fracture in which there is an external wound leading to the break
4. *Spiral or torsion fracture*, where the bone has been twisted until it breaks
5. *Subperiosteal fracture*, a crack through the bone without alteration in its alignment or contour, but leading to increased calcium depositations by the periosteum, the calcium-producing tissue covering bone.

6. *Dislocation* refers to the displacement or separation of a bone from a joint

A fracture should be suspected if there is pain, swelling, and discoloration over a bone or joint and should be proven by x-ray. Broken bones and joint injuries in all parts of the body have been found to be the result of child maltreatment. However, the most common nonaccidental fractures are of the long bones, that is, the arms, legs, and ribs. Multiple fractures at various stages of healing in a child are regarded as diagnostic of child abuse.

Formation of callus (a bony substance which forms over a bone injury) and its absorption over time reflect the healing process and are evident in x-rays. Old fractures are visible on x-rays for several months because of callus formation, and can be distinguished from newer injuries. However, exact dating of the injuries is difficult because every individual heals at his/her own rate, determined by factors of nutrition, health, and severity of injury.

Broken bones occur infrequently in small children. Babies under one year seldom have accidental injuries which cause broken bones because they are not active enough to do things that would result in a broken bone, and/or they have parents who protect them from falls and accidents. This is not to say that accidents do not happen or that infants and children never fall in an awkward position that results in a broken bone, but it is rare.

However, when a child does sustain a broken bone, there are usually signs of severe pain, loss of function, swelling, and discoloration in the area. It is extremely unusual for a normal child to sustain a broken bone and express no discomfort. Therefore parents are not likely to lack knowledge of an accident or to delay seeking treatment. In child abuse cases, parents frequently deny knowledge of old fractures identified by x-rays and commonly do not seek care for an inflicted injury until the child's condition becomes frightening. They also deny any accident or awareness of an accident that could have led to a fracture. Some children who have been abused or neglected have a condition called *agnosia*, the loss of or absence of an ability to recognize stimuli, including painful stimuli. However, there will still be swelling and a response to a broken limb, even if it is only refusal to use it, without complaining of pain.

The most common type of fracture that occurs in toddlers is the greenstick variety. Abuse should be suspected when the accident described to explain the fracture is minor or when the parent denies awareness of the fracture. A spiral fracture may occur when a child is jerked with considerable force or when a limb is twisted.

Swollen joints and apparent strains are rarely caused naturally in young children. Irritation or damage to the cartilage and the periosteum may occur when children are roughly handled or shaken. When toddlers and infants are grasped by the hand and lifted off the ground, injury to the elbow can result, and the dislocation of the shoulder. However, this is so common an injury that it should not automatically be considered abusive.

Physical conditions that lead to fragile bones and swollen joints in children are usually associated with serious illness. Children with cancer, hemophilia, sickle cell disease, juvenile rheumatoid arthritis, or kidney disease may have swollen joints and brittle bones as a result of their disease or chemicals used in treatment of their disease. However, these causes are easily detected. Osteogenesis imperfecta is a rare genetic defect that causes bones to break easily in children. It can be readily diagnosed through appropriate x-ray.

Head and Brain Injuries

All head injuries have to be considered as potentially very serious because of possible damage to the brain and central nervous system. Common medical terms used to describe injuries to the head and brain include the following:

1. *Skull fracture*, a break in the bone of the skull. Skull fractures are also usually labeled according to their location of *frontal, parietal, or temporal.*

2. *Depressed fracture*, when the bone fragments have been pressed down into the skull cavity. Such an injury requires a severe blow, such as might occur in an automobile accident, a fall from a third-story window, or an inflicted blow with a blunt instrument.

3. *Concussion*, which causes headache and vomiting with or without loss of consciousness. It occurs as a result of violent jar or shock as whiplash or inflicted injury. The bone is not usually broken.

4. *Hematomas* (collections of blood) which form around the surface of the brain as a result of a concussion type of injury or a skull fracture. *Epidural hematoma* refers to the blood that rapidly collects beneath the skull and above the dura (the dense connective tissue surrounding the brain) when a fracture ruptures an artery over the brain covering. Signs, such as vomiting, loss of consciousness, and one-sided weakness, are evident shortly after the injury. *A subdural hematoma* is blood which slowly collects between the dura and the brain surface following a severe shaking or jolt which breaks veins between the brain and the skull. The gradual increased pressure inside the skull may result in vomiting, some listlessness, or seizures several days after the in-

jury, and there will usually be increased head circumference in infants whose skull bones have not fused. Subdural hematomas occur with or without a skull fracture. A parent may shake or slap an infant, who does not have head control, and cause subdurals. Older children, who have head control, must be shaken or slapped more severely for such an injury to result. Ironically, parents often seriously harm their children by shaking them, even though they have chosen this form of discipline in order not to hurt the child.

5. Bleeding in the retina, or *retinal hemorrhage*, is clinical evidence of concussion or whiplash injuries. A hemorrhage is the escape of blood from the vessels. The retina is in the back of the eye, and a doctor can look through an eye-examining instrument and observe the retina for bleeding. Retinal hemorrhages are another type of injury which can result from a blow to the head, shaking, or slapping.

Residual effects of head injuries can be severe brain damage, paralysis, loss of sight, and loss of hearing. Injury to the brain and head is the most common cause of death from child abuse. Mild head injury may also cause poor developmental and cognitive functioning. The signs are difficulty in thinking and processing information and lack of gross and fine motor control, that is, the child may appear clumsy and awkward, display poor coordination, and have difficulty manipulating hands and fingers.

Internal Injuries

Internal injuries are very serious and require surgical exploration to determine their existence. These include injuries within the abdominal and chest area of the body. Just as the outer skin can develop bruises, the internal organs can be damaged and develop hematomas, lacerations, and tears as a result of a blow.

Crushing injuries to the chest which may damage the heart or lungs usually are accompanied by fractured ribs. However, a blow to the abdomen may show no skin injury although the liver or spleen may be damaged and bleeding; or there may be a bruise within the wall of the intestinal tract leading to obstruction.

Damage to an internal organ can cause the child to develop symptoms of a serious illness. Complaints of pain, fever, vomiting, bloody stools and urine, respiratory distress, drowsiness, and nonresponsiveness may be seen.

Internal injuries can occur when an adult hits or kicks an infant or child in the chest or abdomen, or if the child is thrown against a protruding surface. Such injuries may also be the result of serious accidents, such as automobile accidents, being hit by a car, a sledding accident, or falling out of a window. In these latter instances, it is necessary to explore the possibility of negligence or lack of supervision.

Sexual Abuse

Children have been sexually misused and abused for centuries. Only recently have society and the helping professions been willing to recognize and deal with the problem. Most sexual abuse and misuse of children leaves no physical evidence. For example, an adult masturbating a child would not leave any physical signs unless force was used. It is for this reason that a comprehensive social and psychological examination should be done. (The reader is directed to Chapter 11, "Sexual Abuse," for further elaboration of this process.)

There are some physical findings, however, that do raise the question of sexual abuse. The most obvious evidence of sexual abuse, and most frequently overlooked, is pregnancy in young females age ten to fourteen. Adolescent pregnancy is generally attributed to peer activity, and in most cases that is true. However, if the girl is very young or refuses to identify the father, or the family seems at a loss to explain the pregnancy, one should consider the possibility that it resulted from sexual relations with a family member or adult family friend. This person might be a father, brother, uncle, brother-in-law, or close family friend or acquaintance. One should ask the victim "Is there any chance you could be related to the baby's father?"

Genital infections in young girls should be considered evidence of sexual contact: gonorrhea, syphilis, venereal warts, and genital herpes are sexually transmitted. The disease organism in such cases has such a short life outside a warm moist area (vagina, mouth, penis) that it is extremely difficult to be infected other than by direct sexual contact.

Signs of physical trauma such as bruises, lacerations, contusions, or bite or sucking marks may be found on the inner thighs, genitals (vagina or penis), or anal region. Abnormal or bloody discharge from the vagina, penis, or rectum may also be symptomatic of trauma from sexual abuse.

A frequent concern in cases of suspected sexual misuse with females is whether sexual intercourse or vaginal manipulation can be documented. Unless there is actual trauma, it is extremely difficult to be definite because the tissue around the vaginal opening can stretch some without injury. It is also difficult to determine what the vaginal area was like prior to the incident. In addition, through the process of activity, play, and sexual play, such as masturbation, children by themselves may change the appearance of their hymen and vaginal opening. They are, however, unlikely to hurt themselves in this process.[6]

Behavioral signals of sexual abuse may include excessive masturbation, attempts at sexual interactions with peers and adults, and intimate knowledge about sexual matters beyond the child's developmental level. Sexually abused children may also present with school failure, running away, and emotional disturbance. A child's report of being sexually exploited should be believed. It is extremely rare for a child to make up such a story. However, children may state that nothing happened when it did, out of shame, to protect the perpetrator, or because they are afraid of what will happen if they tell.

Injuries and Harm to Children Resulting from Incidents of a Questionable Nature

Poisoning

A child who repeatedly ingests toxic substances or ingests illegal drugs, psychotropic medication, or substances that most people would not ingest should make one think of neglect in the form of inadequate supervision or abuse. A careful history may reveal that dangerous agents, medicine, or drugs are left in the child's reach or that there is much disorganization in the house, with inadequate concern for the welfare of the child or children. Curious and exploring toddlers frequently ingest what they find, but most parents will prevent a recurrence after a child has been brought to the hospital with an accidental drug or poison ingestion. The child who comes in with repeated toxic ingestions is not being adequately protected and should be considered neglected.

Occasionally children are given medication or substances to put them to sleep to keep them quiet. This is negligent treatment. Parents may also give them adult dosages not realizing that this can be harmful. In some instances people under the influence of drugs think it might be amusing to see a child under the influence of such drugs as PCP or LSD, not realizing that the dosage and reaction in children are significantly different from those in adults. In other instances, the adult may encourage the child to take medication or ingest toxic substances as a part of a delusional system or as part of an unconscious desire to be rid of the child.

Some toddlers who are emotionally and nutritionally deprived may eat dirt, paint chips, or other debris, a condition called *pica*. These children should be medically examined for lead intoxication and nutritional deficiency and growth problems. Children with the syndrome of psychosocial dwarfism (described later) frequently are described as having bizarre eating habits such as increased thirst, with large fluid intake from normal sources as well as from toilets and drainage ditches, or eating large amounts and then vomiting.

DROWNING OR NON-ACCIDENTAL IMMERSION

Occasionally a child may be drowned by a psychotic parent, by being held under water or being left unattended in water too deep for safety. It is neglectful to allow a small child to wander unattended by a river, a lake, a pond, or a backyard swimming or wading pool. It is also neglectful not to take adequate precautions when children are learning to swim or have limited capability.

GUNSHOT OR STAB WOUNDS

With the number of handguns and weapons in households, it is not surprising that a fair number of children sustain gunshot wounds. What is surprising is the number of parents who do not keep such weapons under lock and key or leave a loaded weapon in a drawer. Sometimes parents or siblings have reported that prior to the "accident" a child who shot another sibling had threatened to shoot that sibling. Yet the parents took no steps to seek help for the children or to remove the weapons.

Stab wounds should also be assessed very carefully. The angle of the wound, the depth, or the placement may indicate the injury was inflicted by an adult. Such an assessment needs to be made when the adult asserts the child inflicted the wound on himself or that another child was the perpetrator.

FALLS

It is extremely difficult to determine whether a fall down stairs or out a window was accidental where there are no witnesses. One can get some sense of the cause of the injury by evaluating the likelihood of the child initiating the particular type of accident. For example, a child is not likely to fling himself down the stairs head first or to fall out of a window too high up to be accessible. Furthermore, with a falling injury, one must consider the possibility of neglect as well as abuse.

MISCELLANEOUS

Frostbite in children may result from their being locked out of the house in freezing weather.

When children present with sharp foreign objects in parts of the body, abuse should be considered (although these could also be a consequence of neglect). Examples might be foreign bodies in the ear (glass, for example), needles stuck in children's hands or feet, objects in the vagina or anus. These conditions are fairly unlikely to occur accidentally. When they are inflicted, the perpetrator is usually quite disturbed.

Hanging or choking injuries should be carefully examined. These are sometimes the result of dangerous games unsupervised children play. Other times they are inflicted by an adult, who may or may not blame other children.

Situations where children set fire to other children or engage in dangerous or bizarre behavior that injures another child should always be evaluated. These incidents suggest serious pathology in the family. They may occur because a family conflict is being played out by the children. One should also consider the possibility that an adult injured a child.

Emotional Abuse

Emotional abuse can be defined as parental behavior which leads to psychological as opposed to physical harm to the child. It is necessary to identify both the specific behavior of the parent and the resultant demonstrable harm or emotional disturbance in the child. Furthermore, parental behavior must be chronic and must take a variety of forms. Parents who persistently tell their children that they are evil, bad, or worthless or that they are hated are emotionally abusing them. Other behaviors include threatening to send a child away or send the child to foster care or locking a child in a room, cellar, or closet for long periods. Dramatically scapegoating one child while favoring others is emotional abuse—for example, a parent who required one child to eat on the floor out of a dog's dish while giving the others especially good meals.

The kinds of symptoms emotionally abused children are likely to exhibit include bedwetting, difficulty sleeping, ticks, low self-esteem, developmental lags, school failure, hyperactivity, aggressive behavior, bizarre behavior, and inability to form intimate relationships.

Some degree of emotional abuse probably accompanies most instances of physical abuse. In order to intervene in a case where emotional abuse is the only form of abuse, careful documentation must be made of parental behavior and consequent damage to the child. It continues to be an area where child-protective agencies are reluctant to become involved and where intervention which may lead to removal of the child from the abusive environment is rare. There have been only a small number of terminations of parental rights where emotional abuse has been the only complaint.

Neglect

Growth Failure—Inadequate or Inappropriate Nutrition

Abused and neglected children often are below average in height and weight and cognitive development. This is because a child's growth and development are highly sensitive to both physical and psychological stress.

There are three separate diagnoses under the more general condition of growth failure: *nutritional deprivation, failure to thrive*, and *psychosocial dwarfism*.

1. *Nutritional deprivation* occurs when a parent cannot or does not provide a child with adequate or proper food or drink. These children may appear emaciated due to inadequate calories and dehydrated, or have a puffy face and feet and a large belly. Parents who starve their children in this manner are quite disturbed.

2. *Failure to thrive* (FTT) is a less extreme form of malnutrition and is a condition found in infants. These children's weights are below the fifth percentile; that is, when compared with the general population of their age, 95 percent of babies weigh more than they do. Frequently their length is shorter than average, too. Medical evaluation is necessary to exclude defective digestion, heart disease, or metabolic disturbances, which can also lead to FTT.[7]

We think that children with nonorganic FTT (not caused by a physical problem) may not grow because they are not fed enough or because they are not nurtured appropriately and experience parent figures as stressful. In some cases both causal factors are present.

A parent can fail to adequately nourish a child for a variety of reasons. He/she may not be aware of how much a child needs to eat and not feed the child enough. Sometimes a parent who has little money may dilute baby formula more than directions specify in order to make it go farther and thereby undernourish the child. Other times the parent's feeding technique does not mesh with the child's pattern. For example, the parent may jiggle the bottle while it is in the baby's mouth or rock the baby excessively, preventing if from sucking. If the problem is one of parent's lack of knowledge, supportive teaching usually will be well received and will remedy the deficiency.

Parents also fail to feed their infants adequately when they do not care about them, that is, when there is lack of attachment, or when they feel hostile toward or competitive with them. Those parents may be oblivious to cries of their infants, or the infants may not be very demanding and thus be ignored. In some cases the FTT infant is the third or fourth child in the family. The mother appears to lack the resources to give enough care to all of the children, and the least demanding, the FTT infant, is overlooked.

In addition, some infants who develop FTT are difficult to feed. They may have a poor suck, they may not seem interested in food, or they may vomit or ruminate, These difficulties may arise from physical problems or be of psychic origin.

We think that there are also some infants who have adequate caloric intake but fail to grow and develop because of a hostile or stressful home environment. Such hypotheses are hard to validate because one usually relies upon parental reports about food intake, and these may or may not be accurate. However, we do have studies of institutionalized infants who were fed adequately but did not thrive because they lacked nurturing human contact.

Children who have FTT will gain up to a pound a week on an adequate diet in the hospital, though this rapid gain may not start for two or three weeks. Infants who have physical problems which may affect growth should be distinguished from those with psychosocial growth retardation alone. However, there may be a psychosocial component in FTT infants with medical problems because they are often more difficult for caretakers to accept or love than normal children.

3. *Psychosocial dwarfism* (PSD), also known as hyposomatotropinism, deprivational dwarfism, and abuse dwarfism, is a syndrome characterized by emotional deprivation, environmentally induced growth impairment, abnormally low growth hormone secretion, and a variety of behavioral disorders. These symptoms cease when the child is removed from his/her family environment. Psychosocial dwarfism has been diagnosed in children as young as eighteen months and as old as sixteen; thus one of the ways it is differentiated from FTT is by the age of the group involved. Diagnostic clues of PSD are height below the fifth percentile and retarded skeletal maturation; weight slightly below what one would expect for the height; and a bizarre eating pattern such as voracious appetite, indiscriminate eating, or stealing of food. Abdominal distension and unusual thirst are also common. Pain insensitivity (agnosia) with or without a history of self-injury, night wanderings, and failure to sleep may also be found. The children may exhibit hyperactivity and/or extreme passivity with fatigue. Both enuresis (lack of bladder control) and encopresis (fecal soiling) may be present. These children usually have disturbed interpersonal relationships, language delay, or immature speech patterns.

We understand very little about the family dynamics leading to psychosocial dwarfism. However, these children seem to live under severe psychological stress, possibly causing them to burn up a lot of calories. Also, in some cases psychosocial dwarfs seem to be getting a message from the family that it is bad or dangerous to grow up and better to remain small.

Further, methods of intervention with psychosocial dwarfism have not been studied in any detail. What information is available indicates that the family patterns which lead to the development of long-term growth impairment are extremely resistant to change. Hopwood and Becker reported on thirty-five children with PSD seen over several years.[8] Only one of the children had catch-up growth while living with the biological parents. Catch-up growth initiated in the hospital and in foster care continued in only one child when returned to the home environment. The children who did best were those who were young and were separated permanently from their families of origin. As this is contrary to what helping professionals are usually taught about how to deal with impaired parent–child relationships (that the family should be helped to stay together), it is extremely difficult to get mental health workers as well as courts and families to accept a recommendation of permanent separation.

Diagnosis of growth failure and inadequate or inappropriate nutrition requires the combined expertise of a multidisciplinary team which can explore both organic and nonorganic etiologies simultaneously.

Physical Neglect

Physical neglect is failure to provide adequate shelter, clothing, and physical care (including adequate nutrition), leading to harm to the child.[9]

To justify intervention, the condition needs to be chronic and have documentable harmful effects on the child. This type of neglect may in fact be a consequence of parental poverty rather than lack of concern and thus may necessitate the provision of financial and other concrete assistance. The diagnosis of physical neglect is confirmed when adequate income is present or provided and the neglect situation persists.

To illustrate, if a parent continues to live in a dangerous and filthy house after being given money to move and spends the money on drink, the parent is being neglectful. Similarly, the caretaker is being negligent when a child is continually without an adequate coat in the winter, when clothing funds are available.

Abandonment and Failure to Provide Adequate Supervision

If parents walk out on their children, turn the children out of the house, or leave them alone for long periods of time, their behavior is regarded as neglectful. There are no hard and fast rules about when leaving children unsupervised is acceptable and when it is neglectful. Factors which must be considered are the length of time the parent is away, the age of the child and its maturity, whether a child must supervise younger children, whether an arrangement has been made for a neighbor, friend, or relative to be "on call," and whether the parent can be contacted to return.

Nevertheless, there are some general guidelines which can be used in evaluating the risk of the situation. Children under three should not be left unsupervised. Children three to seven can only be left alone for brief periods. Children eight to ten might be all right for two to five hours provided there is someone "on call" for them. A child needs to be at least eleven to be capable of baby-sitting for younger children. However, there is likely to be subcultural variability in this area. Poor and minority children may be socialized by necessity to take care of themselves and others earlier and thus not to become overwhelmed in situations which would traumatize a white middle-class child.

Parents may also be neglectful if they leave children in the supervision of an adult who is likely to harm them or who is incapable of providing adequate care. For example, parents may be found neglectful if they leave a girl child in the care of an adult who in the past sexually molested the child and sexually abuses her again or with an aged or ill adult who is unable to protect the child who then is injured.

Medical Neglect

Medical neglect is failure to provide adequate care for a child's medical problems. Although standards will vary from community to community, parents are defined as medically neglectful only when failure to provide the care results in serious or life-threatening consequences for the child. Some parents may not attend to their child's medical needs because they fear they will not be able to pay the medical bills or because they do not fully understand the need for the care, It is the professional's responsibility to see that the family receives the medical benefits for which it is eligible, and the professional must also see to it that the family understands the importance of the medical procedure. If when these conditions are satisfied the parents still do not provide medical care, then they are being neglectful.

Educational Neglect

Educational neglect is failure on the part of parents or caretaker to see that a child attends school (or an alternative educational setting): for example, a parent consistently fails to get the child up on time, dressed, etc., so that the child can get to school; or a parent keeps a child home to baby-sit or to provide the parent with company so that the child falls behind grade level.

The situation is defined as educational neglect only when the child's behavior is under the parent's control. Therefore, it applies by and large to younger children, under the age of eleven. With older children the situation might be more accurately defined as truancy. In such a case the child might refuse to get up, get dressed, etc., despite the parent's efforts, or the child might leave the house presumably to go to school and go somewhere else. While such guidelines are useful, it must also be recognized that educational neglect is an interactive problem. For instance, it may begin with the child staying home for a legitimate reason, illness for example, and the child's presence at home becoming reinforcing for both parent and child. In some cases children may worry about the parent who is left at home and become truant to take care of the parent.

Another prerequisite for the behavior to be defined as educational neglect is that it be chronic and frequent. The child must miss several days per month on a regular basis. What this means is that accurate documentation is crucial. Action should also be taken before the child gets so far behind that the school experience is an unpleasant one.

Emotional Neglect

Despite the fact that it is designated as reportable in many child protection laws, emotional neglect, like emotional abuse, is difficult to define. Thus very few cases which are purely emotional neglect are reported. A general definition is failure to provide emotional support to a child necessary for its health and well-being, such as lack of adequate nurturance (love, caring, support), the failure to provide appropriate social or cognitive stimulation, and the failure to help the child with problems. As with emotional abuse, it is necessary to document resultant harm to the child.

Types of parental behavior can best be understood with examples. The parent who does not nurture adequately is the one who leaves an infant in a crib continually, taking the child out only for feeding. Further, the feeding process does not include cuddling, cooing, or other social interaction. Lack of stimulation might be failure to provide a toddler with toys or things to play with, keeping such a child in a playpen all the time, and again failure to interact with the child. An illustration of the last type of emotional neglect would be a parent who persistently fails to respond to a child's fears and worries which are so severe that the child cannot sleep at night.

Harmful effects on the child may be the same as those found in emotional abuse: developmental lags, problems in developing intimate relationships, etc. However, withdrawn and self-stimulating behaviors are common and aggression is not. An infant may appear depressed or apathetic or may indulge in autistic behavior patterns. Some children are more vulnerable constitutionally than others. Thus the same parental neglect will be harmful to vulnerable children but will not have an impact or have a milder impact on less vulnerable ones.

One of the most difficult jobs for the professional social worker is to make the decision whether to intervene and attempt to improve the home situation when there is unusually high risk, or not to intervene in the absence of harm to the child. Intervention may be indicated to attempt to alleviate harm, but may violate the rights of privacy when the harm is not substantial.

Notes

1. American Humane Association, *National Analysis of Official Child Abuse and Neglect Reporting*.
2. *Ibid*.
3. *Ibid*.
4. Schmitt, "The Physician's Evaluation."
5. *Ibid*.
6. Orr, "Limitations of Emergency Room Evaluations of Sexually Abused Children."
7. Helfer, "The Special Problem of Failure to Thrive."
8. Hopwood and Becker, "Psycho-social Dwarfism: Detection, Evaluation, and Management."
9. Sussman, "Reporting Child Abuse: A Review of the Literature."

3

Causes of Child Abuse and Neglect

Kathleen Coulborn Faller and Marjorie Ziefert

Introduction

Today when we refer to child abuse and neglect, we are referring to a wide range of behaviors. These behaviors include actual physical harm, emotional abuse or neglect, sexual maltreatment, and medical or educational neglect. We find a continuum of maltreatment from mild to extreme, and we include chronic problems as well as intermittent and single incidents. Because we are not talking about a single pattern of child maltreatment, we usually do not find the source of the maltreatment in a single cause. Different personal and environmental dynamics lead to different types of abuse and neglect. Further, in a given family only one type of maltreatment may be present or several may exist simultaneously.

It is useful to divide the factors which may be instrumental in abuse and neglect into three categories:

1. Individual-parent factors
2. Family-related factors
3. Environmental factors

The interplay of two or more of these factors is often the cause of abuse and/or neglect. It therefore must be the goal of sound, interdisciplinary evaluation and treatment planning to look at the wide variety of interacting factors. We must then explore the relative significance of each factor and plan appropriately to deal with problem areas on individual, family, and environmental levels. The concept is illustrated diagramatically by Figure 3-1. It suggests that it is the interaction of various factors, represented by the arrows, which causes child abuse and/or neglect. Relative importance of various factors is illustrated diagramatically by Figure 3-2. In the interest of clarity we will present each of these variables as a separate phenomenon, again imploring the reader to integrate the variety of factors so as not to make diagnosis simplistic and perhaps inadequate to do appropriate planning.

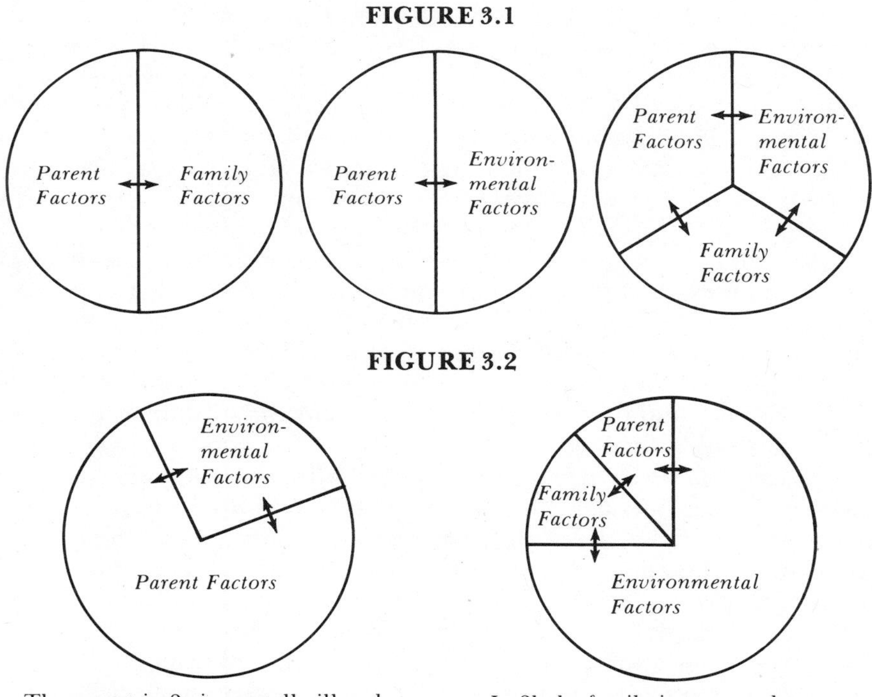

The parent in 2a is mentally ill and therefore the parent factors are of overriding importance.

In 2b the family is poor, and poverty with its concomitant conditions are crucial.

Individual-Parent Factors

Abusive and neglectful parents fit no single psychiatric diagnostic category, and as a rule they are not very different from the general population. However, there are some personality characteristics found frequently in maltreating parents. In addition there are special abuse or neglect situations where parents do have mental illness. And finally there are a number of parental problems which play an important part in abuse and neglect.

Common Personality Characteristics

We will describe identifiable personality characteristics frequently found in maltreating parents. Maltreating parents frequently experience feelings of low self-esteem.[1] They may think that they are worthless, incompetent, or bad as people. Some neglectful parents neglect themselves as well as their children, and these patterns continuously remind them of what worthless people they are. When parents abuse their children, the behavior is frequently an effort to exert some control and thereby enhance the parents' feeling of well-being, but it also has an adverse effect because the maltreatment reinforces the feelings they have about themselves as being bad and worthless.

Another common characteristic in maltreating parents is excessive dependency.[2] In diagnosis, however, one must be careful to differentiate the client who experiences crises or problems and appropriately reaches out for help from the person who has excessive dependency needs which exhaust the personal resources of individuals attempting to help her/him. Typically, overdependent parents have not matured and differentiated themselves from their own parents, and they may expect other adults to satisfy their unmet needs. They see other individuals as potential fulfillers of their own wants rather than as persons to be valued as individuals.

They experience serious difficulties with the very demanding tasks of parenting. They may expect to be cared for and nurtured by their children. They have children and raise them to get their own needs met, and the child's care becomes secondary. Therefore, the parents neglect their children, or when children make normal or sometimes excessive dependency demands upon the parents, the parents cannot cope appropriately and lash out at the children.

Other characteristics found in some abusive and neglectful parents are certain deficits in superego functioning. One is impulsivity. All persons experience aggressive and sexual feelings toward persons they are close to (and even toward persons they do not have intimate relationships with). However, impulsive parents translate these feelings into action. They lack the capacity to channel or control these desires and needs. Thus their anger may lead directly to assault on the child, or alternatively they may be so caught up in impulsive patterns that they fail to consider the child's needs. Similarly, sexual feelings toward their children may become translated into sexual encounters, or sexual feeling toward other adults may lead to sexual behavior which fails to take into account the children's needs.

Abusive parents may also have rigid superego structures. Sometimes these parents keep very tight control on their own aggressive or sexual feelings. That is, they view having such sentiments toward their children as unacceptable and deny they exist. What can happen is that these feelings may suddenly erupt into abusive behavior. Other parents with rigid superegos have fixed ideas about how things should be and are unable to tolerate child misbehavior or child interference with their own wishes. Consequently, when those things happen, the parent punishes or attacks the child.

Other parents have quite a different problem; they have deficient consciences, particularly with reference to mistreating their children. They appear to lack an appropriate level of empathy toward the child and rationalize abusive behavior.

Psychopathy

It is important to differentiate parents just described (who are said to have "holes in their superegos") from parents who are psychopaths. These latter are a small percentage of abusive parents (under 5 percent), but children in the care of such a parent are at considerable risk.[3]

Psychopathic parents have not had the early experience of loving, consistent parenting and have not been able to compensate for this lack in later life. Thus they do not form loving attachments, but rather develop exploitive relationships. Because they have missed an early nurturing experience, they have grossly distorted superegos. When they have harmed a child, they show no genuine remorse about what they have done to the child. Differential diagnosis of true psychopathy is difficult because deviancy resulting from other causes is often confused with it, and psychopathy represents the extreme end of a continuum of personality disorder. Maltreating parents more often present with some psychopathic traits than with true psychopathy. Psychiatric and/or psychological evaluations are often necessary to make the determination.

True psychopaths are extremely difficult to work with and have little potential for providing a nurturing risk-free environment for their children. Some will benefit from being hospitalized or placed in some other very structured setting where they may become depressed and then the depression is treated. However, such programs are not very common, and it is often impossible to get psychopathic parents to see the need for hospitalization.

Depression

Perhaps the most prevalent of individual factors in neglect is depression.[4] Parents who are depressed seem always sad, show little animation, rarely smile, complain of being overwhelmed, and may show evidence of inability to cope. In severe cases they may spend the day in bed, not get meals together, or pay little attention to their child's behavior and appearance. It is important to differentiate between parents with chronic depressive personalities and ones with situational depressions and cyclical depressive syndromes. Both a history of the individual's past functioning and a knowledge of recent life events will help to differentiate between the two.

Types of situational depressions to be alert for are postpartum depression, and depression precipitated by the death of a loved one, the removal of children, or desertion or separation. Situational depressions will respond to changes in the circumstances leading to the depression, short-term therapy, community supports, and antidepressant medication. In addition, manic-depressive syndrome and severe cyclical depressions are likely to respond to medication.

In contrast, in chronic depression parents do not seem in such acute distress. However, the prognosis is less hopeful, and the illness does not respond to medication. In working with such a person, it is important to assess other aspects of functioning for potential strengths and to devise an intervention plan which can compensate for deficits in parenting capacity.

Parents who struggle against depression may be continually irritable and harsh with their children. In addition, because we hypothesize depression has its source in repressed anger, they may intermittently strike out and abuse their children.

Psychosis

Psychosis is found in only about 5 percent of the parents who abuse and/or neglect their children.[5] However, it is potentially one of the most dangerous situations for a child. If the child is a part of the parent's delusional system (e.g., the child is seen as possessed by the devil or the child is seen as potentially harmful to the parent), there is high risk of abuse. Neglect is sometimes the result of a parent's being totally consumed in his or her own inner psychic world and delusional system to the point of not being aware of the child's presence or needs. Sometimes professionals fail to appreciate the fact that when these parents are not psychotic, they have good relationships with their children and nurture them adequately. However, constant supervision or removal of the child from the parent's care is necessary when the parent is actively psychotic. Psychiatric treatment, perhaps including antipsychotic drugs, is the intervention of choice for the parent. When the active psychosis is reduced, the child may well be able to be returned or to live unsupervised with the parent.

In addition, in neglect it is common to find a parent who is not clearly psychotic but whose reality orientation is borderline; that is, he/she may drift in and out of psychosis, may have brief psychotic episodes, or may have certain areas of functioning in which thought process is psychotic. The condition is usually chronic with some fluctuation. Such parents may also abuse alcohol or drugs in an attempt to handle their distress. A psychiatric assessment is needed to determine the workability of the parent, and the attachment between parent and child must be evaluated. If these are both positive, then supportive services should be provided to relieve the parent of some of the child-caring burden.

Mental Retardation

Although retarded adults can be nurturing and caring parents, they often lack the skill and knowledge to rear children adequately. Thus they may be abusive or neglectful parents because of their limitations. A psychological evaluation is usually necessary to assess whether they have the potential to care for children. Then, if they do, concrete help and the teaching of parenting skills are very useful in maintaining children with a retarded parent. However, it is also necessary that the parents be willing to accept help and acknowledge their deficits. Supportive services may be required indefinitely but are often a better alternative than the destruction of a family where there is a strong bond between parent and child.

Substance Abuse

Parents who are either drug-addicted or alcoholic are very high risk for abuse or neglect. Sometimes the abuse is a result of loss of impulse control while on drugs, particularly alcohol, and reflects underlying anger. Neglect is more common in drug abusers who become immobilized or semiconscious or pass out, and are unable to perform everyday tasks while high. In both instances there are underlying causes of the substance abuse and usually other factors besides substance abuse involved in the child abuse or neglect. However, before the parent is amenable for treatment of other difficulties, she/he must deal with the substance abuse problem. Substance abuse treatment programs will be the most successful way of addressing the addiction.

Parent's Childrearing Experience

Many abusive and neglectful parents develop inappropriate childrearing patterns because of their own childhood experience. In evaluating parents, one probes for instances of early deprivation and evidence of having been abusively or neglectfully raised. Examples of the types of deprivation to look for are early death of a parent, early placement or frequent placement, chronic parental alcoholism or mental illness, and parental rejection. In assessing whether parents were abused or neglected as children, one asks parents suspected of abuse or neglect what discipline techniques and child-caring practices their parents employed while raising them. However, caution must be used because acceptable childrearing methods have become much less coercive over the years. Therefore, just the fact that parents were physically punished as children does not mean they were abused and that this is why they are harming their children as adults.

The negative childhood experiences described above are usually part of the upbringing of the parents described thus far in this chapter who display fixed personality characteristics or mental illness which makes it very difficult for them to nurture adequately. However, they are also found among maltreating parents who function much more adequately. This latter group are often ignorant of children's developmental needs and lack knowledge of other methods of discipline and child management than those used upon themselves as children. Thus they may attempt to toilet-train a child before it has sphincter control or may expect a child to clean up after itself when it is only two, because they lack knowledge.

When parental ignorance is a major dynamic, parents will respond to supportive teaching. Although classroom parent education may be useful in some instances, often a more appropriate method is small-group experiential learning or one-to-one nonthreatening modeling and practicing. Such services may be provided by professionals, but recently there has been noted success using paraprofessionals and volunteers from socioeconomic circumstances similar to the parents' to assist parents in improving their skills.

Parents whose main problem is ignorance can be distinguished from those whose personality characteristics are a major factor in their capacity to respond to supportive teaching. When it is the parent's personality which is of concern, supportive teaching will only be useful as an adjunct to therapy.

Social Isolation

Clinicians working with abusive and neglectful families have noted that many families seem cut off from their social environment.[6] Many do not have telephones and transportation. They shun contacts with neighbors and do not participate in community activities. Moreover, they are resistant to the efforts of professional helpers and agencies.

It is hypothesized that this isolation means that they do not have ongoing reciprocal relationships with friends, neighbors, and relatives to relieve them of the everyday burdens of childrearing. In addition they have no companions to share their concerns and problems with, and their worries may get blown out of proportion. Finally, in times of crisis, they have no one to turn to, and abuse and neglect can occur.

Researchers have taken these clinical findings and have begun to look at them using control groups of nonmaltreating families. Preliminary results add the following: Some studies show the target families to be isolated from informal networks, particularly from relatives. However, they appear to be heavily involved with formal network resources (professional helpers and agencies). But with the latter, often there is a failure on the part of service providers to coordinate their activities, and families find the services are not the ones they feel they need the most. Families in one study stated that they wanted more concrete services (housing, jobs, money) and less therapy.[7]

Again, the therapist needs to carefully examine both the extent of the isolation and its possible causes. Do economic conditions preclude mobility? Does a parent have realistic fears of neighbors, relatives, or agencies? Are the interpersonal skills of the parents such that they don't socialize readily? Or are there underlying personality characteristics in a parent which make it very difficult for him/her to develop relationships with others?

Several innovative intervention strategies have been developed that deal specifically with social isolation. One is a parent aide or lay therapy program which uses paraprofessionals or volunteers to serve as friends to isolated parents. Second, Parents Anonymous, a self-help group for abusive and potentially abusive parents, has as a major function combating the social isolation of these parents.

Family Factors

Child abuse and neglect occur within the context of the family. Therefore it is logical that the family dynamics play an important role in what happens. Some of these have been explored extensively by experts in the area, child factors for example. Others we know less about, the role of stepparents for instance.

Parental Collusion in Maltreatment

In two-parent families, when abuse or neglect occurs, both parents have a role in the dynamics of the maltreatment. Studies vary but suggest that either father or mother is likely to be the active mistreater and that both parents are actively involved less frequently. However, the passive parent is usually instrumental in the active partner's maltreatment. The passive spouse may give covert permission, for example by approving of the abuse as a mode of punishment for misbehavior, by agreeing with the abuser that the deed for which the child is being punished is very bad, or by designating the active abuser as disciplinarian in the family. In neglect, the passive parent (usually the father) may well be in complete agreement with the active parent's value system which rationalizes neglect or he may fail to pick up the slack when the active neglecter becomes overwhelmed and cannot parent appropriately.

Or one parent may take the other parent to task for the way that parent allows the children to behave. This kind of dispute can lead to either parent abusing the children. Finally, ongoing marital disputes can consume parents' energy and time so that the children are neglected.

Scapegoating

Children may also get caught in parental and family conflicts and become the focus of the anger and aggression. When there is a marital dispute, often the child becomes enmeshed in this conflict and traditional generational boundaries are blurred. Thus the antagonism between the spouses is displaced onto the child as abuse and neglect. In some instances parents may bury their own disputes by focusing on the child's problem. In others the weaker spouse, usually the wife, may not be able to retaliate against the stronger spouse and may take this anger out on the child(ren).

Sometimes one child is singled out as the scapegoat because that child reminds the parent of the disliked partner, of the parent him/herself, is the wrong sex, or reminds the parent of a stressful period in the parent's life. In addition, it is common to find that the scapegoated child is defined as bad in contrast to a good child in the family, and sometimes the "good child," fearful of maltreatment, is actively involved in helping the parent see the scapegoated child as bad. Family therapy is the intervention of choice in such situations.

Stepparents and Reorganized Families

Research and clinical data suggest that stepparents or live-in partners who are not the parents of the children are more likely to maltreat children than natural parents. Such findings are logical from a common-sense standpoint because stepparents are usually less attached to the children than natural parents. In cases of sexual abuse, the incest taboo is attenuated or nonexistent. Further, frequently there are resentments on the children's part of a new partner and jealousies and competition among all parties involved.

Single-Parent Status

We find single parents overrepresented among abusive and neglectful parents.[8] It is not clear how much this is a consequence of reporting biases and how much it is because single parents experience more difficulty in childrearing. Aid to Families with Dependent Children (AFDC) mothers are exposed more to public agencies who might report them than are mothers supported by their spouses. But be that as it may, we must not ignore the real strains inherent in single-parent status. Unless the parent has help from outside the family, he/she must perform the domestic functions of two parents and, in addition, provide for the financial support of the family. Because the single parent sometimes cannot manage the responsibilities of two parents, some of these responsibilities go unmet. If they are in the area of childrearing, then the parent can be defined as neglectful. Alternatively, the strain of trying to perform two roles may lead to abuse. Problems are likely to exist in terms of meeting children's needs for both nurturance and control. In the adequately functioning two-parent family, parents get a lot of nurturance from one another and do not have to rely upon the children for it. A problem frequently seen in maltreating parents is relying upon the children for nurturance and love. In addition, getting support from their spouses makes parents better able to give to their children.

The single parent may also be at a disadvantage in disciplining children. It is easier to exert control over the children if two people are doing it rather than one. In addition, collaboration on what the limits should be and what kind of punishment should be used can be very helpful. Without this, the single parent may not have the energy to control the children, may overreact to children's behavior and punish excessively, or may alternate between these two responses.

Adolescent Parents

The adolescent mother has a child while she is still a child, and the disruption of this developmental stage can be problematic for both the adolescent and her offspring. Becoming a parent at such a young age is even more problematic if the adolescent is single. Impulsiveness and irresponsibility characteristic of adolescence can be disastrous in a parent. Thus adolescent parents are high risk for both abuse and neglect. Further, many adolescents become pregnant with the hope that the baby will provide the fulfillment lacking in their lives. They want something to love them and to love often because they have not been adequately loved as children. Because of this motivation they may not be attuned to the baby's needs, but only to their own. Moreover, they may be sorely disappointed by the absence of rewards from parenting and may become overwhelmed by the responsibility. These circumstances can lead to either abuse or neglect.

The Extended Family

The relationship an extended family has with the nuclear family is an important influence on the functioning of that family. The extended family has historically been the source of emotional support, of the learning of childrearing skills, and of economic resources in times of crisis. Problems arise when these relationships are dysfunctional or nonexistent. In families where abuse and neglect occur, there is very often a history in the previous generations of maladaptive interaction between parent and child. One sometimes finds, in abusive families, meddling relatives who are overly critical, dislike one partner in the marriage, make overwhelming additional demands on the parent, or generally add to the stress that already exists. A common pattern in single-parent families where maltreatment occurs is to find mothers who disapprove of their daughters or who are in competition with them. These mothers then become involved with their daughters in an unproductive way when they become parents.

In neglectful families it is more likely that the extended family will be absent either physically or emotionally, increasing the loneliness and isolation of the parent. Thus the extended family is not available to aid the family in times of stress, nor does it relieve the everyday burden of parenting by assisting on a regular basis. It is notable that the research shows black families are no more likely to maltreat their children, despite the fact that they experience greater stress than white families, because they are able to depend upon their extended family.[9]

In treatment, one attempts to work with this network of people so that they will provide more functional support for the family and not be so disruptive.

Child Factors

Certain factors related to the child or children put them at greater risk for abuse or neglect. Although it is important not to "blame the victim," it is also clinically naive not to evaluate this factor because the more efficacious way to intervene may be to address the special difficulties the child presents.

Temperamental Factors

Infants are born with particular temperaments. At one end of the continuum is the child who is extremely active, hyperresponsive to stimuli, and difficult to soothe and calm. At the other end is the baby who is markedly placid, sleeps most of the time, and is minimally responsive to outside stimuli.

The very active child is likely to present difficulties for any parent and therefore is at greater risk for abuse than other children. The extremely placid child may be at risk for neglect because it does not demand care. Further, some parents may worry that the baby is too unresponsive and that something is wrong with it. However, beyond the problems infants at the two ends of the continuum present, an important concern is whether the baby's temperament fits with parental expectations and capacities. When these are out of synchrony, there may be risk for maltreatment. A typical risk situation is one where the parent's first child was very placid and next the parent has an active child who seems abnormal and unmanageable.

Physical Factors

Very often the physical condition of the child plays a contributing role in her/his mistreatment.[10] The child may be born with a problem which makes him/her more difficult to care for and therefore at risk. Some of the conditions which render children vulnerable to maltreatment are prematurity, colic and feeding problems, and birth anomalies, such as intestinal malformation, hearing defects, and cleft palates or lips. Children who suffer brain damage at birth and/or are born retarded may also be targets for mistreatment.

Children with these problematic conditions may require a higher level of care than an ordinary infant. When that care is not provided, the parent is defined as neglectful. Alternatively, the experience of caring for such a child may be frustrating and cause the parent to harm or reject the child.

Further, these children may be less responsive to comfort and nurturance because of their special conditions, and their problems may necessitate a separation from the parent. (A premature child may have to remain in the hospital after its mother goes home, and a defective child may require surgery.) Such factors can interfere with bonding between parent and child. Bonding, or attachment, is a phenomenon of major importance in inhibiting maltreatment of children. Proper attachment compels parents to nurture and care for children even under difficult circumstances, such as when the parent is tired or stressed. A parent trying to handle a child who is hard to care for and with whom there is incomplete attachment is more likely to abuse or neglect the child. Early identification (at birth) and supportive services or therapy can do much to ease the burden upon the parent of an exceptional child and facilitate bonding between parent and child.

PROBLEMS WITH OLDER CHILDREN

Problems with older children which may lead to their maltreatment are conditions such as hyperactivity, aggressive behavior, stealing, truancy, running away, and sexual acting out. We often find parents have played an important role in producing the child's condition. For example, later mental retardation or hyperactivity may be a consequence of being abused or neglected. Conditions such as withdrawal, aggressive behavior, stealing, or sexual acting out may arise because of the nature of the parent-child interaction. For instance, withdrawal may be rooted in rejection by the parent, and we know that children who are aggressive have been handled aggressively at home.

Problems of this type, in which parental behavior is maintaining child deviancy, vary in severity and therefore in prognosis. Some can be efficaciously treated using family therapy or a strategy which focuses on parent-child interaction.

In other instances, the interaction is too pathological and/or the child is too much at risk and must be removed from the home, sometimes permanently. Even then the child and foster or adoptive parents may need supportive treatment. Often the child's problematic behavior persists or is exacerbated after removal because maladaptive patterns are the only way the child knows to relate. Thus we sometimes see abuse and neglect of these children in foster care.

Environmental Factors

One of the best ways to understand how environmental factors lead to abuse and neglect is to view them as stresses on the family. A stress is a condition, change, or problem with which a family has difficulty coping. Many of the factors discussed thus far can be regarded as stresses, and therefore considering child maltreatment as arising from stress encompasses more than just environmental factors. Mental illness, not knowing how to raise children, marital discord, and having a problem child are conditions which make coping difficult. However, there are other situations not yet discussed and essentially environmental which are stressful for families and lead to maltreatment. For example, stress may result from environmental changes, such as natural disasters or an economic depression; or it may originate outside the family but focus directly upon it, such as an incarceration, a truancy petition, or a job loss; or it may originate with intrafamily relations, as is the case with runaways or unwanted pregnancy.[11]

Research has shown that families in which child abuse and neglect occur are subject to a greater number of stresses and are less able to cope with them than normal families.[12] Either or both of these factors may cause these families to maltreat their children. A useful way to categorize the type of stress these families experience is as follows: chronic stressors, situational stressors, and precipitating stressors.

Chronic Stressors

A chronic stressor is a long-standing problematic condition with which the family must cope. Abusing and neglectful families may have to deal with a number of these. Some of the most characteristic chronic stressors will be discussed to illustrate their impact upon the family.

Being a Parent

The experience of being parents is a chronic stress for most people but more so for maltreating parents. They may be unready, ignorant, or too young to deal with dependent infants who cannot verbalize their needs. In addition, the problem of parenthood frequently is exacerbated for them by having several young children close in age. As discussed earlier, if children have special problems such as prematurity, colic, physical defects, retardation, or hyperactivity, the situation is even more difficult for the parents. Similarly, being a single parent produces a situation of chronic stress.

CHRONIC ILLNESS

Having a chronically physically or mentally ill family member or a parent who is a substance abuser is another kind of chronic stress. The constant worry and extra care this member requires may exhaust the family's financial and emotional resources. Further, the ailing person, particularly when this member is a parent, cannot carry out his/her share of family responsibilities, and others must take them over. Again, the tension which results from this chronic stress can lead either to maltreatment of children or failure to respond to their physical and emotional needs. (The way illness operates here is separate from its instrumental role in causing the sick person to maltreat a child.)

POVERTY

The most widespread chronic stress which can lead to abuse or neglect is poverty. Sociologists who have looked at the demographic characteristics of families reported for abuse and neglect have found a high correlation between being reported as an abusing or neglectful parent and being poor.[13]

Further, they find among reported cases high rates of conditions commonly associated with poverty, such as poor housing, frequent eviction, inadequate nutrition, insufficient clothing, frequent illnesses, poor medical and dental care, unemployment and underemployment, and inadequate education. These problems lead to high levels of tension in the family which may get diffused into child abuse. Moreover, poverty rather than parental neglect may be the cause of parental failure to provide adequate nutrition and physical care. Or alternatively, neglect may be secondary to being overwhelmed by the conditions of poverty. That is, a parent may be immobilized by his/her circumstances to the point of not being able to care for his/her child.

Because child abuse and neglect are also found among the more affluent, there has been disagreement among experts about whether poverty leads to child maltreatment or being poor means one is more likely to be reported for abuse or neglect. Poor people tend to use community agencies, which are more prone to comply with the child abuse and neglect reporting laws. The poor take their children to emergency rooms and public health facilities for medical treatment. Persons of means will take their children to private pediatricians, who are much less likely to report suspected abuse or neglect. Similarly, poor people receive treatment for emotional problems, which may be connected to child maltreatment, from public agencies likely to be sensitive to reporting requirements. Middle-class parents go to private therapists, not likely to report. The poor are exposed to additional community agencies, likely to report: the financial assistance office, medicaid officials, the food stamp office, and employment services.

Moreover, many experts would argue that professionals required to report find it easier to believe abuse or neglect by poor people than by their own socioeconomic class, and that thus they are more likely to report poor persons.

Notwithstanding these arguments, recent research supports the first set of hypotheses: that poverty is an important cause of child abuse and neglect. Gelles[14] has looked at the incidence of abuse and neglect among a representative sample of the national population (not of reported cases) and has found a linear relationship between income and maltreatment. The lower a family's income, the more likely they are to mistreat their children. An interesting related point is that the relationship between education and maltreatment is not linear; it is curvilinear. That is, parents with very low and very high education are less likely to abuse their children. Another finding of this research is that black families are no more likely and perhaps less likely to abuse their children than their white counterparts, despite the fact that they experience the additional chronic stress of racial discrimination.

It should be stressed that poverty is not a necessary cause of child maltreatment. Many poor families care for their children quite adequately, and some families of adequate means maltreat theirs.

The appropriate intervention, the elimination of poverty and concomitant conditions, may or may not be within the grasp of persons working with the family. For some families, employment (or job training and employment) may alter the circumstances. Likewise, improved housing may transform the quality of the family's life including that of the children. Sometimes providing families with public assistance, food stamps, or medicaid can improve noticeably their functioning. Unfortunately, however, often the resources one can provide are woefully inadequate or inappropriate for the family's situation, and poverty, with its accompanying ills, cannot be alleviated. Therefore, while the worker may first focus on the family's poverty, attention must also be devoted to helping them handle the stresses better and not taking them out on the children.

Situational Stressors

Situational stressors are recent changes in the family's social circumstances. Generally, these are changes for the worse, but they may sometimes be changes for the better (for example a promotion) to which the family cannot accommodate.

Many situational stressors are economic. Loss of employment by a parent can be stressful and produce a crisis. This is particularly troublesome when it is the husband who loses his job. Male status depends largely on job status. Therefore, loss of employment leads to loss of self-esteem and consequent stress. Further, the husband is suddenly spending far more time with the children, and thus they are more available to be abused when he is unemployed. Likewise, a change in work may be stressful, even if it is for the better. The wage earner must learn to cope with new routines in a new work situation.

A wife's going to work may entail stress for the family in several ways. Suddenly she has two jobs (employee and housewife) and usually without gaining much assistance in domestic responsibilities. Second, her going to work may adversely affect her husband's self-esteem. It may signal to him his failure to fulfill his economic role. This is particularly true when the husband's unemployment is instrumental in the wife going to work. In such a situation, the increased level of tension may lead either parent to strike out at the children. Moreover, the fact that the wife now has two jobs instead of one may cause her to neglect her childrearing responsibilities.

Other kinds of economic factors can increase the level of stress in a family. Incurring a debt, as when having to buy a new car or new appliance or having medical bills, may be difficult for a family to cope with. Moving or buying a house is also likely to increase family tension.

There are also situational stressors which are the result of changes in family composition. Events such as the birth of a new baby, wanted or unwanted, relatives moving in with the family, or the death of a family member may be difficult for the family to manage. Clinicians have also noted abuse in situations where in-laws were visiting or about to visit.[15]

Further, desertion, separation, or divorce may be an important factor in child maltreatment. Marital dissolution means the major child care responsibility falls to the partner who has custody of the children. The role overload, as well as the tension produced by the situation, may be instrumental in abuse or neglect.

Precipitating Stressors

Precipitating stressors are incidents which trigger maltreatment. They are, so to speak, the straws which break the camel's back. It is more usual for a precipitator to cause abuse, but it can also lead to neglect, in the form of abandonment or withdrawal from parenting responsibilities.

A substantial proportion of precipitating stressors are perceived or actual child misbehavior. Often malfunctioning parents have unrealistic expectations for their children. They may attribute malice, stubbornness, or belligerence to an infant. This perceived misbehavior may precipitate punishment which does serious and permanent damage because the baby is so small. Alternatively, parents may emotionally and physically neglect babies because they think they might spoil them. In addition, problematic behaviors such as persistent crying, excessive activity, undesirable eating patterns, or lack of compliance in toilet training may precipitate abuse or neglect.

Somewhat older children may be overdisciplined because they fight with one another, physically attack an adult, damage property, or otherwise misbehave. This kind of conduct may also cause parents to give up and withdraw or abandon their children.

Incidents unrelated to children's behavior may also trigger maltreatment. The breakdown of the family automobile, stove, refrigerator, washing machine, or TV may play such a role. Likewise, a fight with the spouse or someone else in the household may precipitate abuse or neglect.

A Culture or Subculture That Supports Violence

Having reviewed a wide range of causes of child abuse and neglect, it is important to put them in their larger social context. Experts who have looked at child abuse and neglect within this context point out that social values support the use of violence to achieve desired ends and more specifically support coercion against children. As a society we sanction utilizing military force in the international arena and police forces on national, state, and local levels. Particularly we allow the use of violence and coercion against poor and minority people.

Related to this are social norms which assert that to spare the rod is to spoil the child. Moreover, recently the Supreme Court has declared that it cannot outlaw the use of corporal punishment in the schools. This gives powerful permission to physically harm children. Further, although there has been some improvement during this century, children are often treated as second-class citizens and lack a political voice. This has meant that their dire needs are often overlooked in developing programs and policies. In this social context, it should not surprise us that some parents use physical punishment with their children to the point of child abuse or that parents ignore their children's basic needs.

In some segments of our society the use of violence to control children (and for other ends as well) receives more support than in others. Research indicates that lower-class parents are more likely to condone the use of corporal punishment than middle-class parents.[16] In addition, some religions may directly or indirectly justify the use of severe physical punishment for misbehavior. The child may be perceived as evil or possessed by the devil, and it is felt drastic measures are necessary to remedy this.

Some parents from such subcultures are loving parents as well as parents who use harsh physical punishment, and can adopt other methods of discipline, while others use normative supports to justify the expression of angry and hostile feelings toward their children.

If we are to address this cause of child abuse, we must change society's attitude about violence as a legitimate tool for dealing with problems. Particularly we must reverse public acceptance of the use of force against children.

Conclusion

We have described a wide range of factors which can be contributing causes of child abuse and neglect. What should be clear is that there can be a high level of variability in what factors are important in any given case. In some cases parents will be mentally ill, and even a normal placid child will suffer maltreatment at their hands. In others parents will be perfectly adequate until their marriage develops problems. Some factors can be universal stressors on individuals. Other stressors will be idiosyncratic. There will be families who experience a great deal of stress before it reflects upon the way they handle their children. In others the first aspect of functioning to deteriorate under stress will be their parenting.

What this discussion suggests is that there is no simple or universal dynamic in child abuse and neglect. Efforts to construct such a theory would blur important distinctions which exist in different types of cases and thus would be of little utility in designing intervention.

Notes

1. Steele, *Working With Abusive Parents from a Psychiatric Point of View.*
2. *Ibid.*
3. Spinnetta and Rigler, "The Child Abusing Parent: A Psychological Review," pp. 296-314.
4. Polansky, DeSaix, and Sharlin, *Child Neglect, Understanding and Reaching the Parent.*
5. Steele, *op. cit.*
6. Polansky, Chalmers, Buttenweiser, and Williams, "The Isolation of the Neglectful Family."
7. Giovannoni and Becerra, *Defining Child Abuse.*
8. Gelles, R., "Child Abuse as Psychopathology: A Sociological Reconstruction," pp. 611-621.
9. Straus, "Family Patterns and Child Abuse in a Nationally Representative American Sample."
10. Herrenkohl, "Research in Progress."
11. Hanson and Hill, "Families Under Stress," pp. 787-792.
12. Justice and Justice, *The Abusing Family.*
13. Gelles, *op. cit.* Gil, *Violence Against Children.*
14. Gelles, R., "Research in Progress," Straus, *op cit.*
15. Justice and Justice, *op cit.*
16. Walters and Stinnett, "Parent-Child Relationships: A Decade Review of Research," pp. 99-140.

PART III

Intervention

4

Assessment

Kathleen Coulborn Faller

There are several different types of questions a social worker might be asked to address in assessment: Did the child abuse or neglect occur? If so, what are (or were) the specific dynamics leading to the maltreatment? Is the child safe in the home or at risk? If the child must be removed, what is an appropriate placement? What interventions or treatment should be utilized? If treatment has been taking place, is it helping the family change? Is it safe for the child to return home? Can treatment be terminated? If treatment is not being successful, should something different be tried? Should the child be removed from the family, or is it appropriate to seek termination of parental rights?

Clearly, the social worker must understand what questions he/she needs to address in the assessment. However, there are some basic areas and a basic approach which should be employed in all such evaluations. It should also be pointed out that under ideal circumstances the social worker will not have the responsibility for the entire assessment alone, but will divide it up and be able to share the responsibility with other mental health professionals.

The assessment must look at the individuals—both parents and children—and how they function as individuals. Second, the worker must be concerned with parent-child interaction and family dynamics. Finally, it is important to evaluate practical difficulties and environmental problems which impinge upon the family and diminish the capacity of parents to function. Because many of the families will be poverty-ridden, multiproblem, minority-status families, the worker must be sensitive to these issues. Care must be taken to take into account these characteristics and to reach out to establish alliances with the individuals and the family. Otherwise they will not be candid enough to allow the worker to do a valid evaluation.

It is important to allow enough time for all necessary aspects of functioning to be adequately assessed. Further, it is very useful to do at least part of the evaluation in the home. Beyond this, the worker must attempt to gain an understanding of the individual and family functioning over time, particularly because the assessment time may be a time of crisis for the family and it may be functioning less well than usual. This can be done by taking a good social history, probing for times of better coping, and by seeing the family on a number of occasions over time.

As a rule, the worker will use the same assessment tools employed in other types of evaluations and will cover areas examined in the traditional social history (see Appendix B, "Social History Outline"). However, there are some specific dimensions of individual parent and child functioning, as well as some particulars of parent-child interaction, which deserve special concern in cases of suspected or substantiated child abuse or neglect. The dynamics of these dimensions are discussed at length in Chapter 3 of this manual, "Causes of Child Abuse and Neglect." Therefore they will only be outlined here.

A. Parent functioning (for each parent in a two-parent family)

   1. Probe for a good early nurturing experience (which will suggest the capacity to nurture) versus early deprivation. Early deprivation is correlated with severe abuse and/or lack of attachment and neglect of a child.

      a. Death of parent or sibling.

      b. Separation or divorce of parents.

      c. Abandonment, having been placed in foster care, in an institution, or with relatives or friends (the more moves, the more detrimental).

      d. Having an alcoholic, drug-addicted or criminal parent.

   2. Get a thorough history of how parent was disciplined as a child and his/her feelings about those methods. Parents are likely to repeat the methods used on them.

   3. Indicators of psychopathology.

      a. Psychosis.

i. Fixed delusions involving the child make the child high risk for abuse.
ii. Psychosis or borderline states can lead to child neglect.

b. Psychopathy or sociopathy—a parent with one of these disorders will lack true empathy and the child will be at high risk for maltreatment.

c. Depression—most commonly associated with neglect, but may also lead to periodic aggression.

4. Capacity or lack thereof to handle aggressive and/or sexual impulses.

5. Evidence of a rigid personality.

6. Existence of excessive dependency needs.

7. Does the parent understand child's developmental needs and have realistic expectations for the child, or is there a lack of knowledge about children and unrealistic expectations?

8. What discipline methods does the parent state he/she uses and in what circumstances? What can be observed in terms of discipline?

B. Child's functioning.

1. Health of the child.

a. Unusual problems—present or past—making the child hard to handle or care for.

b. Is current health care adequate?

2. Other physical problems—birth defects, physical anomalies.

3. Behavioral problems.

a. Aggression.

b. Stealing.

c. Emotional problems.

d. Withdrawal.

4. Developmental difficulties.

a. Developmental lags.

i. Gross motor

ii. Fine motor
iii. Language
iv. Height and weight

b. Toilet training.

c. School and other achievement problems.

d. Mental retardation.

C. The quality of interaction among family members.

1. Do family members engage in eye contact and normal physical contact with one another (e.g., mother cuddles infant, holds toddler comfortably on lap, puts arm around older child; child seeks comfort from parent, stays close to parent), or is there absence of eye contact and appropriate physical contact (e.g., parent does not touch child, is physically rough with child; child avoids parent, is wary of parents)?

2. Do family members have positive things to say about one another (e.g., child does well in school, minds mother, takes care of little sister) or mention negative characteristics (e.g., child is belligerent, bad, ugly, unmanageable)?

3. Do they speak civilly or yell and become angry and upset?

4. Is the parent able to protect and manage the child (e.g., keep the child from falling off the examining table, prevent the child from getting burnt on the stove)?

5. Are family members able to engage in appropriate activities together (e.g., parent works a puzzle, plays with doll house, helps child get undressed for examination)?

D. Environmental difficulties and stresses which can contribute to child abuse and neglect (see section "Environmental Factors" in Chapter 3).

1. Chronic stresses and long-standing conditions which absorb much of parent's energy.

2. Situational stresses—recent changes in the family's situation.

3. Precipitating stress—trigger incidents which lead to abuse or neglect. (A useful strategy for eliciting these data is to ask the family what a typical day is like, hour by hour, then ask them to describe the day the abuse occurred.)

Assessment

A careful assessment of individual factors (parent and child), family factors, and environmental stresses is essential to arriving at an intervention package which will address the specific needs of the family. This may take a day, a week, or longer, or the worker may need to engage in ongoing assessment making use of new information on the family as it becomes known and observing the effects of intervention on the family.

5

Treatment Planning, Process, and Progress

Kathleen Coulborn Faller, Marjorie Ziefert, and Carolyn Okell Jones

Treatment efforts should recognize and build upon the strengths of the family and should focus upon those areas where problems in functioning are found—that is, individual difficulties, problems in family functioning, or crisis generated by environmental issues. The worker must also be aware that problems from these three areas interact with one another.

Where there are many areas of environmental stress, these should serve as the primary focus of intervention. Some stresses may be alleviated completely, for example poor housing and unemployment. For others, like having a retarded or physically handicapped child, special services will be available to the family in the community. And for some stresses, such as marital difficulty or crying children, the practitioner will help the family acquire better coping skills.

It is important in the treatment process to support the family's adaptive behavior and constantly reinforce them when they improve in order to build upon their strengths while at the same time providing help for their deficits. The worker should also recognize unique characteristics of families, be they ethnic, racial, or traditional, and understand these and value them.

It is also crucial that the treatment goals be carefully considered and realistic. Specifically, for some families the expectation may be minimal or even no change. The intervention will be focused on maintaining and supporting the family, and it may need to be in place for a very long time or indefinitely. For instance, if the parent is retarded yet nevertheless loves the child, an intervention might be to improve child-caring skills somewhat but basically to maintain that affective relationship and supplement the parent's capacities.

With other families more change can be expected. However, the worker needs to use "minimal sufficient level of child care" rather than "optimal functioning" as a goal, as with most families optimal functioning will be an unrealistic goal. Further, it is necessary to distinguish aspects of family functioning which are related to the health and welfare of the child from other aspects of family functioning. Those which affect the child's care are first-order considerations in treatment of child abuse and neglect cases and other family problems are second order.

In addition, in planning intervention, there must be clarity about how long the treatment will take or should be tried and what specific changes should be expected. Some families will respond rapidly, but a substantial number will require longer intervention. It is useful to have a time for reevaluation specified when the plan is put into place. In many cases the worker will learn what methods will help a family by trial and error. Moreover, the worker must expect to revise the treatment plan a number of times. He/she must be willing to exhaust all strategies which might potentially be helpful before concluding the family is not workable and it is unsafe for the child to remain with or return to the family.

While all clients, regardless of what they say, will be somewhat resistant to therapists' attempts to help them change, abusive and neglectful clients present particular challenges in their resistance to intervention. They usually have not sought help but have been told they need it. For a fair number coercive intervention may actually be therapeutic; that is, they need the pressure of protective services or the court to enable them to focus on the problems. Others may have the opposite reaction. Some parents may actually recognize that they have problems in parenting but be too defensive to admit this when initially encountering a protective services worker or other mental health worker. Other parents genuinely will not see the problem as society sees it. Thus they may be passively resistant or openly hostile. They may miss appointments and come late, or they may refuse to allow the worker to enter their home or walk out of a treatment session. Or they may undermine attempts to work with them or may become rigid in their denial, feeling that if they persist, the worker will eventually accept their interpretation or go away. Alternatively, because they are in a state of crisis, they may make excessive demands upon the worker's time. Their reaction to intervention will be influenced by past experiences with helping persons or agencies. These encounters may well have been negative, and often such parents have difficulty making discriminations among agencies and professionals.

Thus dealing with abusive and neglectful parents necessitates special strategies and greater flexibility than the traditional agency usually provides. Early in treatment the therapist must acknowledge and deal with the client's angry feelings or passive resistance. Workers often have to visit clients rather than expect them to come into the office. Workers must be prepared to try to establish contact many times and be tolerant of missed appointments and angry outbursts.

They must be willing to deal with the client's frequent emergencies. If the worker is to be seen at all as helpful, he/she must help the family through their crises. Beyond that, we know that these times of family disequilibrium are the times families are more amenable to change. If the worker is not there to facilitate movement at that time, the crisis is likely to be resolved in the family's usual dysfunctional way and the opportunity lost. This may mean giving the client one's home as well as office phone number or developing an on-call system in one's agency.

Frequently families will see their problems in terms of very concrete difficulties: (1) lack of adequate money for food or clothing, (2) no funds for household furnishings, (3) poor housing, (4) no transportation, (5) no money for medical care, (6) trouble brought on by the school, the court, the police, etc.

If a worker is to establish a relationship with the nonvoluntary client, the worker must begin where the client is, with the concrete problems the client presents. This may mean engaging in very mundane activities such as helping the client deal with the public assistance system and finding or providing transportation for the client. The worker may have to act as advocate for the client or at least as a supportive person in dealing with schools, courts, etc. Such activities are indispensable if the worker is to develop a trust relationship with the parent, and a trust relationship is likely to be central to helping the parent change.

Further, we know that the stress caused by these very concrete problems plays a central role in child abuse and neglect. Once these issues are addressed or alleviated, the parents may function quite adequately. Even when this is not the result, it is still paramount that concrete problems be dealt with either prior to or concurrent with any therapeutic intervention. It is unrealistic to expect parents to focus on their interaction with their child if they do not know how long they will have a roof over their heads.

It is crucial that the worker recognize that the protective service and/or treatment interventions may be crisis factors for the family.

Thus initially professional involvement may exacerbate the family's problems rather than alleviate them. While for most families the fact that someone is observing their parenting will initially prevent further maltreatment, in a few families the children will be at greater risk. Further, the worker should be aware that the protective services effect is short term and the family is likely to return to its maltreating pattern unless other changes are made.

It is important to determine what specific type of treatment makes most sense to an individual or family before moving ahead. For example, a person without the capacity for introspection will not derive much from dynamic psychotherapy, and such an experience may preclude the possibility of engaging him/her in other types of treatment. Often intervention which emphasizes behavioral change rather than insight is more useful. For example, behavior modification, problem-solving modes, and structural manipulations may hold greater promise than psychotherapy.

Frequently the persons who are easy to engage in treatment are the mother-child(ren) configuration. Left out may be the husband, live-in partner, or boyfriend. This person's role in the family may or may not be pivotal. Often enough he is the abuser, and the therapist, in such a case, may pursue a treatment goal of strengthening the mother so she will protect the children from him. This kind of lopsided intervention can have complications. It may lead to family break-up. The treatment is also vulnerable to sabotage by the absent partner, who may be the stronger member.

When a family has many problems, it may seem appropriate to use several different services. This not only allows for responding with expertise to a variety of problems but can facilitate monitoring of children and prevent one worker from being overwhelmed by the responsibility of the totality of the family's situation. Against this have to be weighed the coordination problems of many providers and the impact on the family of having to talk to several people about its problems. Since many maltreating families are deficient in their capacity to form primary relationships, an important therapeutic goal is likely to be allowing them the opportunity to compensate for this deficit. This cannot be done if they are involved with too many helpers. One strategy which can be useful is to have a primary therapist who works on the relationship aspect of functioning and secondary service providers whose relationships are less intimate. However, for some families intimate relationships will be too threatening, and an appropriate strategy may be the employment of several different professionals.

Moreover, in child-protective social work it is important to continually refocus on the child. The worker must keep in mind what is called the child's sense of time. What may be a short time for an adult may be a very long period in the development of a young child. This must be recognized so that children do not remain in harmful environments or in the limbo of foster care awaiting the improvement of their parents. Not only must the physical safety of children be the worker's concern but also their emotional health. Therefore, not only must children be included in the family treatment plan but sometimes they need treatment in their own right. (See Chapter 7, "Characteristics and Needs of Abused and Neglected Children.")

It is necessary to be aware of the impact of court intervention on the family, particularly when the child is removed and/or there is serious question about whether the child will ever be returned. This difficulty is exacerbated by adjournments and long intervals between hearings. Unfortunately intervention plans may be "frozen" in the meantime, because the court will make the plan as part of disposition. Court appearances and the legal process itself may contribute to the family dysfunction and tension. Thus the social worker must work with the court and attorneys involved to make the court work for the social goals of the case rather than against them.

Further, while some families will have a positive response to court coercion, others will become extremely angry at workers and even more difficult to work with. Often they react by criticizing foster parents and by attempting to turn the child against helpers and foster family. It is easy for the worker to lose touch or avoid the family during the court process and placement. However, workers should go out of their way to maintain contact with the family and should attempt to support and empathize with them and explain, perhaps repeatedly, what is happening and the rationale behind the intervention.

Many different reactions may be seen in family members to placement of a child. For example, parents and/or remaining siblings may go through all the stages of guilt and mourning including distress and depression, anger, and indifference. They may find it hard to bring themselves to visit the child because the situation is so painful; they may even close ranks and totally reject the child; or they may attempt to replace the "lost" child by conceiving another very quickly.

In the relatively small percentage of cases in which criminal proceedings are initiated against the parent(s) that result in a jail sentence, professionals should remember that this is typically only a short-term method of intervention. A parent will receive little or no effective help in jail and on release will be free to return to his/her family or commence another relationship and produce more children.

If treatment is unsuccessful, the worker may be able to play a key role in getting parents to relinquish a child voluntarily. When this cannot be done and termination is achieved through the court process, it is easy to lose contact with the parents. Continued professional intervention is guaranteed for the child until a satisfactory permanent placement can be found. However, all too often any attempts by professionals to continue to work with the parent(s) are quickly abandoned in the face of hostility and resistance. This is a critical time when the parent might be helped to build a new life, change patterns of interaction with remaining children, or become better prepared for children still to be conceived.

When the children have been temporarily removed, it is important to have some guidelines as to when it is safe to return them. First, gradual return with the parents having the child for progressively longer time periods is preferable to a sudden abrupt return. It has three advantages. It allows professionals to monitor the safety and care of the child as parents have the child for increasing periods of time. Second, parents have a better chance to adjust to the responsibility of again caring for the child. Third, children are likely to have become attached to their substitute caretakers and will be more traumatized by a sudden switch in custody (which they are likely to experience as rejection) than by a gradual reduction in their contact with substitute caretakers.

A number of criteria have been developed by workers in the field to help determine when it is safe to return a child home and/or to phase out treatment. Many of these depend on the worker's ability to qualitatively assess the ambience of the family as well as on more readily observable changes. These criteria include:

1. A reduction in social and environmental stress experienced by the family, e.g., improved housing and employment status
2. Changes in the parents' individual functioning, including signs that they have found more ways of getting satisfaction and pleasure in their lives and that they are less socially isolated from their community and able to use available resources
3. Changes in the parents' (caretakers') interpersonal relationships and functioning. These may include the break-up of a very stressful relationship or the permanent exclusion of a very disturbed partner from the home. Alternatively the worker may note demonstrations that conflict between the partners can be handled more openly and constructively, acknowledgment of what makes for dangerous situations with the child, increased recognition of one another's problems, and ability to give mutual support at times of stress
4. Improvement in quality of contact between parents and the separated child (and siblings remaining in the home), including implementing suggestions/advice given on child management, a more consistent nonpunitive use of discipline and

ability to set fair limits, greater acceptance of the child as an individual with needs, desires, rights of his own, more realistic expectations of the child's abilities, increased enjoyment of the child, and more positive modes of interacting

5. Reduction in the child's provocative behavior, signs that the child is able to respond to parental overtures without fear and the ability to elicit positive parental responses
6. The development of a trusting relationship between the parents and the worker(s) to the point where the parents can turn to worker(s) (parent aide, etc.) at times of stress
7. Amelioration of relationships with extended family, neighbors, and friends so that they are supportive rather than problematic and some assistance can be gotten from such persons in times of stress
8. The availability of an acceptable form of relief from the child such as day care once he/she is returned home if this is indicated

The progress of treatment and strategy for termination will depend a great deal upon the family in question. Families with a high degree of variability in functioning come to our attention for abuse and neglect.

Some families will be open to and eager for treatment. Often families will engage quickly in treatment, learn rapidly, and make considerable change in a short time. These families are liable to be those who have experienced several situational stresses which impaired their functions. They can usually be satisfactorily treated within the time constraints of protective services intervention (within about six months to a year), but with the door left open in case other problems arise.

Other families will engage in a constructive way with the treatment persons, acceding to them expertise in certain areas and making good use of them for assistance and emergency help in those areas. However, they will maintain control over other areas of functioning. For example, a single mother might agree to having help in developing better discipline techniques but refuse help in dealing with her employer.

Still other families will throughout treatment keep the worker at arm's length. Often they continue to say they don't need treatment and challenge attempts to change their ways of functioning. They will nevertheless make changes either at the urging of the therapist or on their own. Often these are structural changes such as not allowing a parent to care for the children when he is drunk or assigning an older child the responsibility for helping a younger one with school work.

Such alterations can have a far-reaching impact on family functioning and can make the environment safe for children and more nurturing.

These latter two types of families are likely to be more attached to the therapist than they are willing to admit, although they will also have social supports from other arenas. Therefore treatment and concrete services should be gradually withdrawn, with monitoring of the impact.

Families with unmet dependency needs are likely to initially resist engagement, but with persistent therapeutic efforts often become quite dependent. This is desirable at the intermediate stages of treatment because the family members need the nurturance the therapist or therapeutic team can provide. Further, it will enable the therapist to get them to use better ways of coping. However, at a point toward the end of treatment, the therapist will need to gradually enable them to become more independent. This is done by, for example, getting them to begin resolving marital disputes themselves rather than have the therapist act as mediator, or by having them go alone to deal with the school rather than have the worker accompany them. In addition, the therapist begins scheduling sessions farther apart and monitors carefully the effect of withdrawal of intervention. The door should always be left open for such families in case they need help in the future.

A final point needs to be made (and emphasized) about treatment outcome with abusive and neglectful families. Therapy, without measures to address the concrete and practical problems of families, is unsuccessful. It leads to unacceptably high rates of severe reincidence (30 percent in one study; Cohn, 1979). Thus the worker cannot be successful by merely "doing therapy." Concurrent must be the provision of concrete services such as help with housing, day care, and employment assistance.

6

Resources for Intervention

Kathleen Coulborn Faller

A range of resources can be useful in working with cases of child abuse and neglect. Some will be services which most communities have and which can be adapted to working with child maltreatment problems. There are others which will be created to deal specifically with child abuse and neglect. Roughly speaking, these resources can be classified as treatment modalities and concrete or practical services, some of which are basic and some of which have a teaching component. What follows is a description of these types of resources and what their utilities are for abusive and neglectful families.

Treatment Modalities

Individual Therapy

Individual therapy may be employed for either parent. There are many types of individual therapy. It can focus upon the here and now or the client's past experience or both. It can emphasize insight or changes in behavior. It can be of long or short duration. If the worker is referring the client elsewhere for treatment, it is important to know or find out what the orientation of the agency or individual is, determine that the service fits the client's needs, and let the client know what to expect.

For adults, individual therapy is indicated in instances where the parent evidences psychopathology which must be addressed in order for him/her to parent adequately. There will be situations where it seems clear that the overriding problem is the disturbance of the parent. In such cases it may be possible to address it with individual therapy alone. In other instances the worker may regard other family members as also disturbed or as contributing to the pathology of the maltreating parent. In these cases, individual therapy may be used in conjunction with other therapies, such as marital or family treatment.

Individual therapy may also be indicated for the child in certain circumstances. In fact, it is probably needed much more often than it is employed. Too often the parents' problems are addressed with the assumption that once the parents improve, their handling of the children will improve, and the children's symptoms will disappear. This does not necessarily happen. Adults may improve in their own functioning but not in their handling of children.[1] Further, some children are so damaged that individual therapy is necessary. Indications of the need for individual treatment of children are marked withdrawal, noticeable nervousness and anxiety, marked aggressiveness, persistent sleep difficulties, encopresis or persistent enuresis, self-mutilation and attempts at suicide, and developmental lags and marked learning difficulties.

One of the problems of providing treatment, particularly to very young children, is that there will be few professionals with skills for the population. Another consideration is whether the therapy will be appropriately perceived by parents and child. Sometimes parents will regard therapy for the child as a confirmation of their view that something is wrong with the child, or alternatively will be jealous of the child for receiving that attention.

Another pitfall to beware of is the possibility that the child's therapy may be out of synchrony with the rest of the family's treatment. Treatment goals may diverge, or what is more common is that children make progress more quickly than parents are able to accommodate. For example, the formerly compliant withdrawn child begins to express anger or perhaps merely to explore more, and the parents cannot tolerate the change. In such a situation, the child is even more vulnerable to abuse than before.

Therapy Focusing on Parent-Child Interaction

In some communities the worker will have available alternatives to individual treatment for parents and children. Therapy may be available which focuses on the *parent-child interaction*. While part of the treatment involves teaching parents how to enjoy, nurture, and manage their children, it also focuses on why parents have difficulty in doing these things. It therefore deals with parents' experiences with their own parents, allowing for ventilation, interpretation, and the development of insight.

An indication for this type of treatment is the suggestion of deprivation or trauma in the parent's background which is interfering with the parent's relationship with the child. Further, if the parent's perception of the child seems inaccurate, such treatment may be useful. Finally, if the parent's central difficulty is with the child rather than embedded elsewhere in the family system or secondary to other practical problems, therapy focusing on the parent-child interaction may be indicated.

Marital Treatment

There is a correlation between child maltreatment and marital discord, and often the abuse or neglect is a consequence of this conflict. When this is so, it suggests *marital treatment* as the therapy of choice. Marital treatment may be eclectic or from a particular theoretical perspective. Some treatments focus upon improving verbal and nonverbal communication. Others attempt to explore how the current marital dysfunction relates to the past experiences of both partners. Some therapists use a very practical problem-solving approach, aiding the couple in identifying their areas of conflict and helping them generate and carry out solutions to these difficulties. In addition behavior modification is sometimes used to treat marital discord. With this approach, the therapist facilitates exchanges in which each partner rewards the other for desired changes in behavior. Ideally, one tries to match the therapy with the desire and capacities of the couple. Practically, one may not have this choice. In such a situation, the best guideline is that the therapist has a good reputation and has been successful with couples like the one the worker is referring.

In deciding when marital treatment is most appropriate, one needs to look at the individual parents and at the role of the marital discord in the family dynamics. If one partner is very disturbed, probably individual treatment for that person should be tried first or prescribed in addition to marital or family therapy. On the other hand, if one judges that a good deal of the family malfunction occurs because the parents can't cooperate, the most parsimonious intervention may be marital treatment. Frequently children exploit or become pawns in marital discord. If the parental relationship becomes more harmonious or if the parents can agree to leave the children out of the conflict, abuse and neglect can be alleviated.

Family Therapy

In situations where child maltreatment is more centrally imbedded in the family dynamics, *family therapy* may be indicated. For example, in situations of abuse or neglect often one parent or one child is scapegoated. One frequently finds the maltreating parent is given covert permission to abuse or neglect the child by the other parent. In other instances it is the lack of support and assistance to the mistreating parent which is instrumental in the maltreatment. Similarly, when there is a child who is defined as disobedient, belligerent, or out of control, often the child is so defined in contrast to a good child; or the only way the misbehaving child gets any attention in the family is by acting out.

A considerable advantage of family therapy is that it allows all family members to receive treatment simultaneously and for them to make changes together. This inhibits the sabotage of changed behavior (which is a problem in other types of treatment) by those not included in the therapy. However, it also requires a powerful therapist who will not be overwhelmed and coopted by the family.

Because of the instability in family composition of some abusive and neglectful families, it may be difficult to decide who to include in the therapy. That is, the crisis of protective services involvement may result in the child or children being placed elsewhere, or one partner leaving the household, or someone, usually a friend or relative, intruding in the family decisions or coming to stay. These kinds of changes in family composition may preclude family therapy.

Group Therapy

Group therapy is another treatment which can be very useful for abusive and neglectful parents. These parents tend to be socially isolated and distrustful of professionals. The experience of meeting others with similar problems and participating in treatment where they don't have to deal with a therapist alone can be very beneficial.

Although a variety of group therapy approaches have been employed with maltreating parents, Parents Anonymous,[2] the self-help group for abusive and potentially abusive parents, thus far is the most efficacious. It was begun in 1969 through the efforts of a former child abuser (Jolly K.), with the assistance of her social worker. It now is a national organization with a grant from the Office of Child Development in the Department of Health, Education, and Welfare to expand to 200 chapters and later to 800.

Like other self-help groups, the members themselves are responsible for supporting and assisting one another. They do this by working on mutual problems during the course of weekly meetings, by serving as crisis contacts for one another between meetings, and by other activities helpful to the group.

The groups have one and sometimes two professional sponsors who serve as resource persons. In addition, Parents Anonymous encourages its participants to seek treatment in addition to their counseling as needed. PA groups are showing themselves to be a very effective intervention strategy for parents who are willing to become involved.

However, because it is limited to parents with whom abuse is the problem and because parents must define their problem in terms of their mistreatment of their children, the audience is a limited one.

Group therapy can also be useful for children of all ages. Frequently children have difficulty engaging in a one-to-one relationship with an adult but can benefit from peer support and therapeutic group process. A wide range of groups from activity groups to group psychotherapy have usefulness for abused and neglected children. These may exist in schools or child guidance clinics or may be part of public recreation programs. Frequently, group therapy is the treatment of choice for maltreated adolescents who would not come to individual treatment.

Parent Aides

A recently developed and successful technique is the employment of *parent aides*, or lay therapists.[3] These are persons without professional training who work with one or a few abusive or neglectful families in the clients' own homes. Frequently the parent aides are volunteers.

Their functions vary, but they usually include serving as a supportive, nurturant figure for the parents and teaching them more appropriate parenting skills. They are also likely to do such things as help the family improve its economic functioning, for example, by guiding them through the financial assistance bureaucracy; ensuring they get appropriate medical and psychological services; transporting them to appointments when necessary; and providing any other assistance which might enhance the family's functioning. Thus parent aides are very useful with families who are socially isolated.

The most appealing asset of parent aides for maltreating parents is that aides *choose* to help the family instead of being paid to. However, recruiting volunteers to work in abuse and neglect may be difficult. They can sometimes be the central mode of intervention, but when families have many problems in addition to social isolation, other services and treatment must also be provided. In addition, for parent aides to be effective, they require good support and supervision.

Concrete Services

Basic

Often child abuse and neglect are a function of lack of adequate material resources. Either abuse or neglect may be related to frustration because of material deprivation, and some types of neglect are more a consequence of lack of resources than parental malfeasance.

Financial Assistance

Therefore for some families *financial assistance*, such as AFDC, General Assistance (GA), or Social Security Insurance (SSI), may improve their ability to function and parent. Similarly, adjustments in their current grants may be helpful. Public assistance only allows for the bare necessities, so any underpayment can cause much hardship. In addition, workers may be fortunate enough to have material resources beyond these, available in the community. These might be free clothing or furniture or special funds to pay utilities or rent.

While financial assistance may alleviate the family's hardship, it has definite limits. In fact it only provides families with the bare minimum. Therefore even with all their entitlements, families live a very spartan life. Further, it does not, as a rule, provide for financial emergencies of the sort abusive and neglectful families tend to experience. Finally, to subsist on public assistance presupposes skills at money management many of these families do not have.

Employment and Education Services

The family's poverty may also be a consequence of poor education, poorly paid employment, or unemployment. We know that child abuse is correlated with unemployment of fathers. It both increases the level of stress in families and increases the amount of time fathers spend with their children. In such circumstances, *education services* and *employment services* may be indicated. If a parent can complete high school or a training course, then she/he will be more able to earn a decent living, which can both alleviate the stress of poverty and allow sufficient income to provide for the children. In addition, such increased capacity improves self-esteem, and when parents feel better about themselves, they have more to give to their children. Employment services such as job counseling and placement can have the same effect. While one might question the efficacy and feasibility of getting mothers of young children to work, a recent study[4] indicated that the highest rate of abuse was among mothers who did not work. Unemployed fathers in that study were found to abuse their children at a rate 62 percent greater than working spouses.

MEDICAL ASSISTANCE

Medical assistance is another concrete service which may do much to alleviate conditions which lead to maltreatment. Families may not seek adequate medical care because they cannot afford it. If the children are the family members requiring the care, failure to provide it is defined as medical neglect. Moreover, parents who are unwell are at a disadvantage in caring for the children. Finally, having excessive unpaid medical bills can lead to tension, which may precipitate abuse or neglect. Thus there are many ways medical care and assistance can be useful in situations of child maltreatment. However, one must recognize that frequently the quality of medical care provided to poor families is second rate. They may have to wait for service and may be looked down upon by medical staff. Further, although Medicaid pays for many medical services, it does not pay for all.

HOUSING SERVICES

Lack of adequate *housing* may be an important variable in family malfunction, and moving the family to better quarters may notably improve the quality of family life. Crowded quarters can increase the level of family tension and be instrumental in abuse. Housing which is dilapidated, with conditions dangerous to children, may cause a parent to be reported for neglect. Further a comfortable living situation produces an emotional equanimity conducive to adequate parenting.

However, we must acknowledge possible difficulties in getting maltreating families rehoused. If they are on public assistance, the rent allowance may not be sufficient to pay for adequate housing. Also sometimes these families have poor references or many children, so that it takes considerable effort to find them a suitable place to live.

Despite their imperfections, the importance of the concrete services described thus far should not be underestimated. We should emphasize that problems in parent-child interaction may be, to varying degrees, a result of problems related to material resources. Further, abusive and neglectful families frequently regard these latter as their major problems. A recent study asking families on protective services rolls what sorts of services they needed and felt lacking revealed that they desired concrete services rather than therapy. Their workers, on the other hand, wanted more therapy, not more concrete services. For the worker, providing concrete services may be crucial for the therapeutic relationship, even if the worker feels these are not the family's major problems. Some families cannot deal with the parent-child problems until more basic needs have been met. Further, if the worker responds to these requests from the family, this suggests to the family that the worker is genuinely concerned with what they define as their problems and they will be more likely to trust the worker.

Concrete Services with a Teaching Component

There are other types of concrete services which have a larger teaching component and a lesser material component. These include day care, homemaker services, visiting nurse service, and instruction in parenting.

Day Care

Most of the interventions employed in situations of abuse and neglect are directed toward the parents. *Day care* is one which focuses on the child while providing benefits to both child and parent.

For the child, it can furnish a place of safety and a situation where the child's physical condition can be monitored. It can also afford exposure to alternative adult role models who are nuturant as well as fair and consistent in discipline. Further, if the child's home environment is deficient in terms of age-appropriate stimulation, the day care setting can provide cognitive, interpersonal, and motor experiences to compensate for the home.

For the parent, day care can furnish needed relief from the constant and overwhelming task of parenting. Having this alternative can allow the mother to develop for herself an existence differentiated from her children. In addition, some day care centers provide opportunities for parent participation. Parents may work in the centers, or there may be groups for parents. This type of participation combats the isolation often experienced by maltreating parents, and it exposes them to alternative ways of viewing and caring for children.

So far I have discussed the benefits of day care in general. In addition two specialized types of day care are of great utility in situations of child maltreatment. The first is an emergency day care service. Ideally such a facility should be open twenty-four hours a day seven days a week, so families can use it on the spur of the moment, on a regular basis or in time of crisis. In the latter instance, being able to use the service can relieve the stress being experienced and assure that the child does not become its target.

The second special kind of day care is therapeutic day care. Such settings vary in structure, but their basic goal is to allow children who have been damaged by parental maltreatment to receive treatment to undo this harm.

Unfortunately day care is not as available as it should be. Many communities have no emergency or therapeutic day care, and the number of hours children can remain may be limited. Often facilities are not licensed for children under two and a half, because of the belief that children under this age should not be away from the parents for long periods. However, such young children are the ones most severely damaged in situations of abuse and neglect. Sometimes, in the absence of therapeutic day care, children with problems in functioning are placed in regular day care, and they overwhelm the staff. Also parents may resist the children's attendance. Thus, while day care is one of the most useful interventions we presently have, it does not always have the desired effect.

HOMEMAKER SERVICE

Homemaker service is another concrete intervention which can serve a variety of functions. Optimally the worker should have available homemakers, trained to work with maltreating families, whose involvement can range from moving in with the family for a time and taking over the parenting functions down to something as minimal as instruction a few hours a week in adequate nutrition, child care, or cleaning. Often, being able to move a responsible adult into the home can prevent family dissolution if the children are deemed at risk or if a parent is incapacitated.

When a homemaker teaches a parent, usually this is by acting as a role model and performing the task along with the parent. For many parents this is much more appropriate than classroom learning. In addition homemakers can monitor the condition of the children.

Some problems which may arise in the use of homemaker service are the following: Often homemakers are not specifically trained to work with maltreating families, but rather provide services to a wide range of client groups. They may not know how to handle these sometimes difficult families, may be fearful of them, and may be resistant to working with them. Similarly, they are often not available to move in, and the extent of their service may be circumscribed. For example, the maximum amount of time they can give to each client may be two or three hours a week. They also may require a degree of cooperation from the client (which may not be forthcoming from maltreating parents) in order to remain involved. It is important that the worker be specific about what she/he wants the homemaker to do with the family. Otherwise the homemaker may be at a loss or may engage the client in inappropriate enterprises. Finally, the worker should be aware that the homemaker may need her/his support in dealing with the family.

Visiting Nurses

Visiting nurses can be of considerable utility in both identification of and provision of services to abusive and neglectful families. Because nurses provide a medical service, they can within the course of their activities quite naturally undress children and examine them. In addition, they observe circumstances in the home which reflect the quality of the children's care and can assess the adequacy of the children's nutrition. Their services are also useful in the treatment of sequelae of abuse and neglect and in providing preventative intervention with infants at risk because of physical problems. Some public health nurses are able to provide not only medical and nutritional services but developmental assessment and assistance to the parent in developmentally appropriate interaction with the child.

In using visiting nurses, the worker must be aware of the following limitations: Public health nurses cannot go into the home without the family's permission. The family may refuse outright or passively resist intervention by being absent or not answering the door when the nurse comes. There may also be limitations on the amount and type of service the nurse can provide because of the size of her caseload. Sometimes nurses can visit three or four times a week, but the norm is closer to once a week or every other week. Thus if the family chooses to avoid contact, it can go months without being seen by a visiting nurse. Finally, it is important for the worker to appreciate how isolated a visiting nurse may feel and support her. Like the protective services worker, she is one of the few people who goes into the home. She usually works alone and sometimes in dangerous circumstances.

Parenting Instruction

Many abusive and neglectful parents can benefit from *instruction in parenting*. Frequently they mistreat their children because they do not know alternative and more appropriate ways of rearing them. While some parents can benefit from classes in parenting, such as those taught in evening school and at some community colleges, most get more out of more intimate situations and those which afford opportunities for trying out new techniques.

Some good results have come from providing instruction in small-group settings which allow the parents to share of themselves and their experiences in childrearing. Two methodologies in particular have been used in such contexts: PET and behavior modification. PET, or parent effectiveness training, is an approach developed by Thomas Gordon and emphasizes empathic communication between parent and child and treating children as autonomous individuals.[5] Behavioral approaches teach parents how to use positive reinforcement—praise, treats, or monetary rewards—in response to good behavior and how to eliminate inappropriate behavior without relying upon physical force.

Similar types of training are also provided on a one-to-one basis by homemakers and visiting nurses, as mentioned earlier, or by social workers, including those from protective services, and paraprofessionals who go into the home. With such an approach, the worker usually explains the approach to a parent, helps the parent devise a way to use it in his/her family, perhaps models the behavior, has the parent practice it while the worker is there, and develops specifics for how to implement and follow up attempts at utilization.

In cases where the worker employs a teaching approach with families, she/he must be clear about the extent to which parents' maltreatment is the result of ignorance and how the maltreatment fits into the total family picture. Some parents will be sufficiently disturbed to need therapy in addition to or instead of instruction in parenting. In other situations the child's and parents' roles in the family system will be too entrenched to be altered by such instruction, and other interventions, like family therapy, may be necessary.

Notes

1. Jones, "The Predicament of Abused Children."
2. U.S. Dept. of Health, Education, and Welfare, *Child Abuse and Neglect; The Problem and Its Management*.
3. *Ibid*.
4. Straus, "Family Patterns and Child Abuse in a Nationally Representative American Sample."
5. Gordon, *Parent Effectiveness Training*.

7

Characteristics and Needs of Abused and Neglected Children

Carolyn Okell Jones

Much professional effort has been directed toward understanding abusive and neglectful parents and developing a variety of intervention strategies to meet their needs in the hope that the children would indirectly benefit from the therapeutic help given to the parents. Ironically, comparatively little professional attention has been directed toward the children themselves in terms of their behavioral and developmental problems and therapeutic needs after maltreatment. (This is reflected in the literature as well as in practice.) Instead there has been a tendency to view children as case-finding devices and to concentrate on their physical injuries and problems and on their physical safety.

However, as various recent research studies have indicated that intervention which is aimed primarily at the parents has insufficient impact on many abused and neglected children, in this chapter I shall focus specifically on such children's needs. Currently there is a growing awareness of the importance of looking at the treatment and placement needs of children separately from those of their parents or caretakers and increasing recognition that children cannot be left in limbo while efforts are made to alter or modify their parents' attitudes and behavior.[1]

Follow-up studies of abused and neglected children are fraught with methodological difficulties as well as the issue of to what extent the problems they present are consequences of the physical trauma per se, or other adverse environmental influences frequently associated with physical abuse or neglect. The latter are already known to have the potential to impair the growing child's development, (e.g., emotional neglect and rejection, social and/or economic disadvantage, emotional disturbance in the parents, and family instability). Additionally, professional intervention and treatment planning (e.g., prolonged hospitalization, frequent changes of foster home placement) may do damage. But in spite of the difficulties described above and the dangers inherent in making generalizations from small samples, there is a growing body of information about the characteristics of abused and neglected children which practitioners can usefully draw on. Some of this information will now be summarized. However, I should caution the reader that because the families who become known to the protective services system vary widely in their degree of pathology, the following material relates mainly to those children who are severely or chronically maltreated.

There is general agreement among researchers and clinicians that abuse and neglect do not result in a specific personality or neurological profile. Rather, abused and neglected children exhibit problems in a wide range of areas, both in developmentally related areas such as language and cognitive and motor skills and in the more emotionally related area of socialization skills with adults and peers and interaction patterns with family members. It is clear that many severe inflicted injuries will leave children with lifelong scars and deformities and handicaps including permanent neurological damage in some cases. However, there are conflicting findings on the extent to which physical or developmental deviations antedate abuse and are of a congenital nature or are the result of rearing in an abusive/neglectful environment.[2]

Characteristics of Abused and Neglected Infants and Preschool Children

Feeding difficulties are common among abused and neglected young infants. Some children have great difficulty in being satisfied; others become uninterested in feeding or constantly regurgitate their food. Many infants who are abused seem unusually irritable, engaging in excessive, high-pitched crying.

Even during the first six months the beginnings of a delay in motor and social development can be observed in some children. They have poor muscle tone and are somewhat slow to turn over, to reach for toys, and later to sit and crawl. Similarly there is often a delay in social responses such as smiling and vocalization when a parent is in view.

Reference is often made to the fact that these infants look much older than their years. They show extensive attentiveness to their surroundings; they are constantly scanning their environment and are hypersensitive to loud noises and other hidden stimuli. Some children avoid all eye contact and in a few extreme cases display "frozen watchfulness," a state similar to that of shell shock in adults. Another outstanding characteristic of abused infants (and of older children too) is their passive compliance and acceptance of whatever happens to them or is expected of them; for example, they may submit to painful medical procedures without protest, remain in uncomfortable positions without wriggling, or sit unmoving on an adult's lap. They appear very stoic, listless, apathetic children who display little affect. It seems that some children learn very young that their best hope of getting food and care in a hostile or chaotic environment where parents are preoccupied with their own needs seems to be total submission to their parents' wishes.

It is important to emphasize at this point that not all young abused children show psychological or developmental abnormalities. Some are children who seem constitutionally invulnerable. Others are children who are intermittently abused and get plenty of stimulation and attention and who display obvious signs of attachment and positive responses to their parents. Other children will persist in their attempts to receive attention from their parents with very little reward or even discouragement.

Between six and twelve months the lack of social response or variations in its quality often become more striking in abused children. They may display little reaction to being separated from their parents, and little of the usual kind of anxiety about strangers, forming indiscriminate attachments to adults at the first opportunity. Older abused children often react to actual or threatened *object loss* with intense anxiety, which is often revealed in therapy. It may take considerable time in a supportive environment for these children to play out their fear of abandonment or rejection. Frequently abused and neglected children under the age of three show a generalized apathy or passivity, a lack of activity in relationship to people and objects alike. Their capacity to play is impaired, and they appear uninterested in toys or ignorant of what to do with them. Delays in gross motor skills and poor motor coordination are common even in the absence of any neurological disorders, as are delays in speech with poor enunciation and vocabulary.

Many of the problems described above simply continue to be more pronounced among abused and neglected preschool children.

Regardless of their actual intellectual potential and their neurological status, the children's responses to psychological testing are typically highly variable and their scores on standardized tests depressed. Some children become extremely anxious in the testing situation and show fear of failure; others are hypervigilant and so preoccupied with the needs of the examiner that they cannot get on with the task in hand. A few children become negativistic and refuse to perform.[3]

It is in the preschool years that two distinct patterns of behavior and methods of coping tend to become apparent in abused and neglected children. Some children remain apathetic, compliant, withdrawn, and restricted within a passive mode of coping. Others develop a negativistic, aggressive, action-oriented way of coping. The latter group tend to engage in manic activity and have very short attention spans and extremely low tolerance of frustration. They are often extremely rough with toys and other children and may treat animals cruelly. They are often clumsy, uncoordinated children, careless of personal danger in the environment, prone to accidents, erupting in unpredictable and uncontrollable outbursts of temper. These children's problems are often so severe that professionals may suspect they are neurologically determined. However, many of these children tend to improve rapidly if they are exposed to a calm, structured environment, which suggests that they are in fact suffering from disorganizing anxiety and have learned to seek pain and provoke violence as a release from chronic tension.

School-Age Abused and Neglected Children

Excessive expectations coupled with unreasonable and unpredictable punishment as well as emotional rejection or neglect lead to the development of extremely poor self-images in abused and neglected children. Over time the childrens' only possible rationalization for the abuse or neglect of their needs is that somehow and in some way they truly are bad children or unworthwhile persons. They are often very reluctant to discuss their abuse, and may be burdened with holding in secrets about family violence for years. They will not transfer the blame to their parents or see them as bad people and will go to great lengths to make up to their parents and gratify their wishes. These children, initially at least, show considerable distrust of other adults, seem to expect punishment, disapproval, or criticism, and are very preoccupied with hearing limits defined and ascertaining what they can and cannot do in any new situations. Even with peers they may be extremely guarded in their relationships, and they may be actively discouraged by their parents from having friends and inviting other children to their homes. They may become generally isolated, lonely children who act in inappropriate ways, causing others to reject or dislike them.

They tend to have great difficulty in expressing their feelings and minimal capacity for age-appropriate pleasure, enjoyment, or playfulness. Some children display obsessive-compulsive behavior or pseudo-mature behavior including overdeveloped skills in some areas, for example a remarkable precocious solicitousness to their parents' needs from an early age. While these coping mechanisms may be highly adaptive and assets to survival in an abusive or neglectful home, they are weaknesses at school insofar as they contribute to the children's literalness and inflexibility.

It is evident that a great deal of abused and neglected children's energy is consumed in trying to create some source of order and security for themselves out of confusion and unpredictability and in struggling with their own identity problems. In addition, in many of their homes there is a lack of stimulation and their parents discourage exploration and initiative so that any sense of mastery and competence is curtailed. Hence quite apart from children who are mentally retarded as a result of serious head injuries and neurological damage, many abused children present with learning difficulties in school. Equally, children who have been physically neglected and undernourished at an early age may present with problems at school, including a reduced ability to focus on, orient to, or sustain interest in learning tasks. Moreover, it appears that children who are undernourished as well as physically abused have a particularly poor prognosis in terms of mental function and neurological integrity. One exception to children described above is a small group of intelligent children whose parents place a high value on learning abilities and school performance. It seems that these children understand that as long as they can perform and keep abreast with parental expectations, they can avoid extreme punishment. Hence they often do very well scholastically but remain socially and emotionally very limited.

Notes

1. Jones, "The Predicament of Abused Children." Martin, *The Abused Child.*
2. Martin, *Ibid.* Elmer, "Follow-up Study of Traumatized Children."
3. Martin, *Ibid.*

8

Making the Decision to Separate Child and Family

Ann E. Thompson

Making the decision to separate a child from his/her family is one of the most serious and difficult decisions made by helping professionals. We know that if this happens, most children will pay a psychological price in their developmental progress. On the most obvious level we see children signal their distress in wetting or soiling, in refusing to eat, in difficulty getting to sleep or nightmaring, by joylessness, or by being "bad," failing at school, or not achieving the skills expected of children at their age. Unspoken and frequently unseen is the fact that internally children interpret removal as a statement of their own badness and can only experience being taken from home as punishment, rejection, or abandonment. In addition, we know that placement in a foster home or institution may in fact be as detrimental as staying at home. All of these factors make it more difficult when either a short-term or permanent separation is the best solution at a given time. It places a burden on helping professionals to carefully evaluate, consider, and discriminate unique needs of the particular child and family.

A constructive decision requires information with regard to the following:

1. *The child.* What is the quality of attachment to nurturing people? What is the developmental stage of the child? What has been the effect of abuse or neglect on the child? (Health, so-

cial, affective or mood, intellectual, motor, and adaptive areas need evaluation.)

2. *The parents.* What strengths and weaknesses do they have as parents and as individuals? What is their capacity to change so as to meet the child's needs?
3. *Environmental stresses.* What are the external stresses to the family which may have precipitated breakdown of nurturing functions?
4. *Available helping systems.* What forms of assistance are there in the community for helping with the specific problems found in (1), (2), and (3)?

An assessment of the child needs first to include an evaluation of the child's psychological vulnerability to separation. This will depend upon the quality of the child's attachment to current nurturing adults and his/her developmental level. Attachment is the loving bond between the child and the parent which permits normal psychological and physical development to proceed. Attachment develops as adult and child interact in ways which can be observed. With good attachment there is prolonged eye-to-eye contact, preferential smiling, and physical contact in stroking, cuddling, and snuggling. In distress the child will confidently turn to this adult for comfort. We will see a reaction to the parents leaving and returning. In real-life situations these interactions will of course be interspersed with times of independent activity and negative behavior toward the adult.

A continuous relationship where there is good attachment is of crucial importance between three months and three years of age. This allows the child first to develop trust in another human being and then to develop a sense of him/herself as a separate, reliable person. This process of psychological separation and individuation is of itself anxiety-producing. It proceeds through a series of stages with a peak in anxiety during the phase known as the "crisis" phase around eighteen months. Most of you can probably recall how children of this age suddenly become very unhappy at being left with a babysitter they have liked previously.

There are frequently difficulties during this "crisis" time around bedtime, which is also a time requiring separation (when the child goes to bed) of adult and child. Separation of more than a few days traumatizes children at this age who cannot sustain a clear, comforting memory of the parent, cannot meet their own needs, and lack the words to express the grief and anxiety they feel at being separated. Briefly put yourselves as adults in the eighteen-month-old child's situation. Imagine yourselves in a situation where you are placed against your will, at a time totally out of your control, among total strangers in a distant place without access to anyone or anything familiar. How would you feel? The child in this situation is precipitated into depression. Energies which would normally be used for growth are turned to containing the overwhelming feelings. Between three months and three years the specific developmental tasks which will be interrupted by separation include learning the rules and behaviors of how to get along with other people (socialization). How to love and feel angry toward the same person. How to convert angry acts into angry words. During the period up to three years, the most primitive form of empathy should begin to develop ("That would hurt me and I wouldn't like it if it were me"). An early form of conscience develops along with progressive control of and responsibility for one's own body, including toilet training. From having a vocabulary of a few words at a year, at three the child will be able to talk in simple two- or three-word sentences. Thinking during this period will be an unsophisticated "primary" process, but a huge store of information about the physical, nonlogical properties of the world will be built. By three most children have a solid sense of sexual identity and will be practicing many of the roles associated with this identity. All these achievements are important and lay the groundwork for future development.

How quickly depression and the interruption of development which separation cause resolve will depend not only on the child's age but also on the quality of replacement nurturing. As the child's need for a nurturing person builds in the new placement, he/she will reattach if the capacity to love and trust has been developed previously, and if a consistent nurturing person is available. If the child should attach to the new caretaker, the trauma of breaking this attachment will be repeated when the child returns home.

My own opinion is that children should not be completely separated from their parents for more than about four or five days prior to age three, for more than a two- or three-week period prior to age five, and at no time longer than a year. Only in late adolescence can separation be accepted with more ease and be accompanied by a sense of confidence that life can continue happily. If any of you had to move while attending high school, you know placement away from friends and family at this age is still difficult and painful. The need to keep the child with his/her family must be balanced against the fact that children are most vulnerable to abuse and neglect at very young ages.

At this point we must turn to assess the parents, the stresses on them, and their capacity to use help to change within the realities of what help is available. In getting to know the parents, both their strengths and weaknesses in parenting skills and their strengths and weaknesses as individuals need to be understood.

The parents' capacity to meet a child's needs can be best assessed in the home. An excellent time to do this is during a mealtime, and as children are put to bed. At these times the child's needs are often the highest. These can be rewarding times or times of great stress. As child and parent interact, it is important to evaluate the parents' capacity to perceive the child as a separate, dependent, immature being. Do they have the capacity to respond to the child's nonverbal signals and to set firm, clear limits as well as to be psychologically available if there is genuine distress? The overriding attitude toward the child can be heard and seen as well as the parents' judgment of themselves as parents. How does the parent help the child understand what is happening? How does the parent respond to the developmental needs of the child? Does the parent express angry and sexual feelings toward the child in action? All of the factors just cited need assessment.

The strengths and weaknesses of the parents as individuals also need evaluating. What is their capacity for successful coping, for guilt, for maintaining a loving relationship with each other? What is their relationship with their extended family and the community? What are the parents' own pleasures and struggles?

The ways in which angry and sexual feelings are handled can be seen in the home interview, deduced from the child's condition and by talking to the parent about a number of areas. In inquiring about anger in regard to the child, one can ask about what the parent judges to be misbehavior on the part of the child and then ask how it is responded to. For example, "All kids make you angry sometimes. What kinds of things does Johnny do to make you angry?" What happens then? And then? And then? One can also inquire into areas of anger between parents. "What things do you fight about?" What happens then? And then? And then? Use of alcohol and/or drugs both in the past and in the present needs to be inquired about directly. We know both sexual and physical abuse are correlated with use of these substances. A more indirect but equally rich source of information with regard to anger and sexuality is to ask the parents about their own childhood and growing-up times.

Parents may resist talking about this more distant area. A statement like "Who you are now has a lot to do with what life was like for you when you were younger" helps make a sensible transition from the present to the parents' past. What was their family of origin like? How were they disciplined? What were neighborhood, school, and adolescence like? Were there people who helped their family in times of difficulty when they were little? Discussion of these difficult times provides opportunity for the helping person to make empathetic contact as the parent talks about his/her own difficulties as a child.

An important part of the assessment is review of records from schools, institutions, or hospitals, which will give essential information about those areas too painful for the parent to discuss freely. As one moves from the past toward the present, it is important to assess what stresses are causing the current crisis. Is there poor health, job loss, financial crisis, or loss of support of important relationship through divorce, death, or a move?

The amount of time for assessment will vary with each individual helper and his/her training and experience. No one in this role should be without consultation for the purpose of clarification of the data and talking through the upsetting feelings which occur in everyone working with these families. At this stage in the process many complex factors can be considered and balanced in order to determine if intervention is necessary, as illustrated by the following chart:

Intervention with Child and Family to Include Separation	Intervention with Child and Family with Intact Family
I. *Nature of abuse or neglect*	
Sadistic injury Multiple injuries over a period of time Head injury Severe neglect	Single injury
II. *Child factors*	
Child fearful or unmanageable with poor attachment Child requires exceptional caretaking Child's survival in question Serious developmental delay	Child under three years of age (however, a young child is more vulnerable to serious physical harm) Child has good attachment
III. *Parents* AS INDIVIDUALS	
Alcohol or drug addiction No areas of successful coping Sexual and/or angry feelings expressed in action No guilt Not capable of trusting relationships Family of origin unable to use help No response to trial of therapy	Areas and times of good coping with life problems Sexual and angry feelings not converted into action Capable of remorse; not only motivated by fear Extended family available to help Response to trial of therapy

AS PARENTS

Cannot perceive child's needs and/or cannot respond to them at age appropriate level	Capacity to differentiate child's needs from own needs for health, safety, stimulation, limits, love, and continuity
Child perceived as bad, as cause of family's problems	

IV. *Environment*

Multiple chronic stresses	Short-term crisis
No supports available to family	Some helping network, formal or informal
Community lacks resources to help parents improve parenting functioning	Community has infant mental health services or family therapists

If it is decided that the child needs protection and/or the family urgently needs structure in order to parent properly, one can turn to a number of solutions which leave the attachment relationship intact. The solution may be the admission of mother and child to a hospital, use of therapeutic foster homes for mother and child, or admission of the whole family to crisis houses. Sometimes extended family or friends of the family can fulfill these same needs during the acute crisis.

If these forms of assistance are not available, one may come to a decision to remove the child. This decision should be made only as an *added* step in a long- and short-term plan to help child and family. Removal should be made only with a plan for keeping the attachment relationship intact.

As we have already seen, the length of time in which one can "benefit" a child by separation without adding the additional trauma of breaking the attachment relationship is very brief. Unless removal is only part of a plan, this time will pass quickly without assessment of the parents' capacity to use help on behalf of the child. The other parts of the plan need to address the problem areas identified in the assessment period. It is important that all areas be assessed. To provide help on only one level—for example, just to change the environment with new housing—and ignore parenting difficulties based on psychological conflict is to provide pseudo-help.

If removal is necessary, there are a number of things which can help the child and parent make the transition, both into and out of a foster home.

Help for these families may be offered on the concrete level of food, housing, medical care, or whatever measures are needed to assist in finding a better solution of the precipitating crisis. Emotional support and parenting education are other levels of intervention which can be very useful. Family or individual therapy may be necessary for those families who have internal psychological problems. Where alcohol or drug abuse is involved, these issues must receive attention in order for any change to be sustained. As these supports are offered, one needs to specifically assess how they impact on the parents' capacity to nurture the child in those areas which were initially defined as difficult for the parent.

The next essential step, when there has been separation of child and family, is to evaluate how the parent is able to use help in better nurturing the child. This evaluation over time may or may not lead to a decision to terminate parental rights. At any time when it seems that this may be necessary, it should be talked about with the parents, but at the same time you should make a clear statement that you want to do everything you can to help the family grow together.

If by careful monitoring and reassessment it is shown that there is a lack of capacity to use available help or that sufficient help is not available in the particular community, the painful and difficult decision to terminate parental rights should be made on behalf of the child. The future is dismal for children left in a state of uncertainty in foster care or for children returned to families who have not changed.

The following case examples illustrate what happened to two children and their parents who were identified as needing help, were assessed, and experienced a trial of therapy. In one case the mother of a small child was able to use therapeutic intervention. In the other case the mother could not use therapeutic intervention, and termination was recommended.

CASE ONE

At fifteen months of age John was reported to protective services by his day care center because he stood stiffly for hours beside his crib and screamed in terror if a man approached him or if someone attempted to change his diapers. Often he was not picked up by his mother at the appointed time. A referral to an infant mental health worker was made for evaluation. It was learned John's young unmarried mother was a heroin addict. The times when she didn't pick him up were times when she was truly unable to care for him. In addition to day care, she occasionally took him to her parents and his godmother. The therapist learned that when John's father visited, there was sexual behavior and violence which John saw.

Observing John and his mother together, the therapist saw that there were moments of empathy, joy, and tenderness between them. John's fear was seen in how he was unable to touch a toy unless his mother first touched it. He cried, clung, and trembled when she attempted to leave the room. As the therapist observed

John and his mother together and talked to her, it was clear that John's mother experienced him as a separate individual and, except for not seeing him as frightened, was able to see his needs realistically.

She did not want to drag John down with her. When the possibility of termination was discussed with her on this first visit, along with a commitment to work with her to avoid this, she was able to quite sadly agree that termination might be best for him. The following months were months of continuous crisis, oftentimes with one step forward and three steps backward. However, long before John's mother could begin to work at the underlying core of her own problems, she was able to see John's fright and protect him by refusing to let his father come to the apartment any more. She also switched from leaving John at the day care center, where there were multiple caretakers, to leaving him with his grandmother. John's separation anxiety decreased. He played freely and became more joyful. His mother began to use a drug help program and over the next several years continued to work on her own problems.

CASE TWO

Suzie was brought to protective services at one year of age by the police, who had found her wandering on the streets. It was learned later that her mother was drinking at a nearby bar. She was placed in emergency foster care, where she settled in well and appeared normal to the worker. When the protective services worker met Suzie's mother, she learned that she was presently separated from Suzie's father. Suzie's mother told the worker of many physical illnesses for which she medicated herself. She denied, however, any drug or alcohol abuse.

The worker found it extremely difficult to understand Suzie's mother and so requested a psychiatric assessment. This showed that she had serious difficulty in thinking coherently and logically under stress. When Suzie and her mother were observed together, there was clear evidence of love and good attachment between them. It was also noted that Suzie was an extremely active child who would challenge any parent. She frequently placed herself in dangerous situations and would then fall, cutting and bruising herself. Her mother seemed unable to anticipate and act to protect her. Case work was begun, and Suzie was returned home.

Over the next three years Suzie was placed in eight different foster homes. A pattern repeated in which Suzie's mother would become stressed, frequently by a physical illness, and would then become disorganized. At times when she became upset, Suzie's mother would talk of all her problems being due to a bee poison which circulated in her blood from a bee sting several years previously. She also became terribly frustrated with Suzie and would then request foster care. After a few days Suzie's mother would request her return home, stating with real genuineness her love and need for her. Because of the organization of foster care services, the nine placements included eight different homes. There were four different protective services workers. The pattern continued in spite of a therapist of the mother's own, work with an infant mental health therapist, and day care for Suzie. Suzie's mother remained unable to limit Suzie except by bribing her or, after considerable provocation, by exploding punitively in anger. Their days were frequently spent in a darkened room with the TV on.

When Suzie was approximately three years of age, the judge who was asked to order a ninth placement in foster care ordered Suzie to be cared for in a single foster home for a six-month period. For the first time Suzie's mother admitted her drug and alcohol abuse. She went to some distant relatives in the South for detoxification, with the promise that if she could get off drugs and alcohol, Suzie would be returned to her. In this final placement, Suzie initially adjusted as a model child, except for being extremely upset at any separation from her foster family.

On Suzie's mother's return, visits were begun. On returning from these visits, Suzie would sob for long periods of time. Regression occurred in all her three-year-old skills several days after each visit. She would eat with her hands, and talk babytalk. She nightmared. When visits were extended to include an entire weekend, Suzie became so upset and unable to control her anger at the repeated abandonment that she acted it out by throwing a pregnant dog off a balcony. The dog aborted and the puppies were born dead.

The foster parents at this time began to talk about how Suzie would be a delinquent when she grew up. In addition to this being an accurate perception of the degree of Suzie's upset, it was a way of expressing anger and rejection of Suzie. In spite of this, it was decided to return Suzie home because that had been the contract with the previous protective services worker. The week before Suzie was to return home, her mother requested a delay in her return. She and Suzie's father had fought and separated, and she wished to wait. At this point the worker decided, because of the mother's incapacity to use the help available and because of Suzie's development of symptoms, that parental rights would be terminated.

In retrospect, this case not only illustrates a parent's incapacity to use therapeutic help but also demonstrates how without clear goals an appropriate decision for termination can be delayed to the detriment of the child.

In the first case, there was a severe developmental interference, and an immobilizing fear which prevented John from moving ahead with development. John's mother, however, had the capacity to separate her own needs from his and, once she understood his fear, to act to meet his needs. She was able also to use assistance in working on her own drug abuse and underlying emotional difficulties. In the second case, Suzie's anxiety was expressed in hyperactivity and by putting herself in dangerous situations. This was directly related to her mother's incapacity to see her as immature and needing protection or to perceive Suzie's needs as separate from her own. With repeated placements she became much more severely disturbed. Because of her own severe disturbance Suzie's mother was unable to use the help of an infant mental health worker to improve parenting skills or an individual therapist to work on her own problems. The decision was made finally to terminate parental rights.

It is tempting to ease one's own sense of guilt and/or pain at what is happening to a child by saying, "He'll get over it." Children are wonderfully resilient. Resolution of trauma can occur as the child's age-specific needs are met in the context of an attachment bond. For some children, however, children who are severely damaged in the first year of life, improvement may be possible but an achievement of a degree of normalcy is not possible. Most children will carry some evidence of trauma into their future lives. But sometimes surface behavior does not show the underlying vulnerability, which will surface only under stress. The following analogy may be useful for understanding this point. If one starts life with a hundred soldiers to fight the battle to maturity, the fact that twenty soldiers are used up to defend against a disruption at age two will not be apparent as long as later life battles require only eighty soldiers. If, however, ninety soldiers are needed, a breakdown will occur in functioning. Where this analogy does not fit is that it fails to portray the fact that even while the eighty soldiers are in working order, they aren't at times in very good working order.

The function most sensitive to impairment seems to be in the quality of relating to other people—the capacity to love and still be autonomous. As we have seen again and again, it is this critical capacity which is centrally involved in parenting that may not break down until children grow up and attempt to parent themselves.

PART IV

Institutional Structures for Handling Child Abuse and Neglect

9

The Child Welfare System

Kathleen Coulborn Faller and Judith B. Stone

Introduction

What is the child welfare system? It is the network of social services set up to compensate for deficiencies in parents' provision of care to their children. It includes protective services for abused and neglected children, foster care services employed not only for maltreated children but also for other dependent children without adequate living situations, institutional services for children, delinquency services, and adoption services. Some parts of the system are in the public sector, and some are in the private.

All parts of the child welfare system have some relevance to the issue of child abuse and neglect. Children who are maltreated in their early years are five times more likely to become delinquent than the general population.[1] Similarly, if the family of the maltreated child cannot be helped to change, the parents' rights will usually be terminated and the child freed for adoption. Further, abused and neglected children are more likely to need institutional placement because of special problems they have which may either be a consequence of their mistreatment or have led to their mistreatment.

However, most central to the problem of child maltreatment are protective services and foster care. Therefore the discussion which follows will focus on these two parts of the system.

The description which follows will outline the characteristics common to most child welfare systems and detail how the systems operate. In addition, we will note many of the dilemmas faced by child welfare workers and some of the problems of the system, although these problems vary from location to location.

Most social workers come into contact with the child welfare system at some time in their practice. It is common to find that social workers relate to the system on a case-by-case basis and never really understand the overall organization and function of the system. Often lack of a thorough understanding of what child welfare is required to do and, more importantly, lack of understanding of the legal limitations and resource constraints of child welfare service workers cause other community professionals to have unrealistic expectations of the system.

A first and important limitation is the training of workers. In many communities those who choose to work in child welfare are not persons who enter the system with vast professional experience. Frequently people select this work as their first experience in the social welfare field. In most communities professional degrees and/or experience are not a prerequisite for hiring. Staff learn by doing one of the most demanding jobs in the human service field.

A second fact of life is the size of the child welfare workers' caseload. While a manageable caseload might be around twenty, depending upon the difficulty of the individual cases, most workers' caseloads are higher. In general, foster care caseloads are higher than protective services loads. It is not uncommon to find a protective services load in the fifties, sixties, or seventies and a foster care load in the hundreds.[2] Because in most cases child welfare workers are dealing with nonvoluntary clients who require intensive and extensive contact for intervention to be effective, caseloads should be smaller rather than larger than the traditional social work caseload.

Third, the services child welfare workers are mandated to provide are extensive. They are supposed to deal with emergencies as well as to provide ongoing treatment to families. They must monitor situations to see that children are safe and make decisions regarding removal and return of children. Time must be spent coordinating other agencies' involvement with families, and they must prepare cases for court and appear in court. Because there is too much work, the job may not get done to satisfactory standards, and those things for which the worker will be held most accountable get priority. This means emergencies and court cases are attended to at the expense of treatment and service coordination.

The amount of paper work and number of bureaucratic constraints are often overwhelming. Frequently workers face not only the everyday stress of working with this particular client population, which is considerable but a constant battle against the child welfare system to make it bend to meet clients' needs.

Last, the worker may often be constrained and frustrated in her/his plans for a client by the absence of available resources. Other agencies in the community are often resistant to taking on clients from the child welfare system for treatment. If they are not unwilling, the worker may face long waiting lists or services which do not meet the needs of the client.

All of these problems with the system contribute to unacceptably high rates of worker turnover. Some workers only last weeks. In many communities the turnover is as high as 100 percent per year. Often those who do remain are "burned out." That is, they no longer have the energy to invest in the clients and tend to be punitive or "follow the rules" of the job or even to shirk responsibility.[3] It should be noted however, that there are *many* first-rate child welfare workers who help clients a great deal, either because they have good innate skills or have been well trained. Finally, we should emphasize that the problems are endemic to the system and are not a reflection on individual workers.

Protective Services

Introduction

In every state there is a child protective system which has a state structure and delivers protective services on the local, usually county, level. Some programs are part of the public social services delivery system, others are located in the courts, and a small number are attached to police departments.

Enabling legislation passed by Congress in 1975 created the National Center on Child Abuse and Neglect. One of the functions of the National Center is the distribution of certain federal funds to state child-protective systems. To receive funds the state system must meet certain criteria. The intent of setting these criteria was in some respects to standardize and to upgrade child-protective systems. In order to qualify for federal funds, a child-protective system must have:

1. A definition of abuse and neglect which includes physical and *mental* injury, sexual abuse, negligent treatment, and maltreatment
2. Reporting mechanisms
3. Immunity for those reporting
4. Procedures for prompt investigation

5. Treatment mechanisms that demonstrate effectiveness
6. Confidentiality of records
7. Interdisciplinary and interagency cooperation
8. Preferential treatment for self-help groups such as Parents Anonymous
9. Public education about child abuse and neglect

Certainly not all child-protective systems meet all of these criteria. However, the existence of such a set of criteria has served as a pressure toward a degree of uniformity in state systems.[4]

Reporting

In most communities reports of suspected abuse and neglect can be made either to the child-protective system or to the police seven days a week, twenty-four hours a day. Those professionals required to make reports vary from state to state but usually include doctors, nurses, social workers, and teachers. These people must make a verbal report within a specified time, usually twenty-four hours, and a written one in a short time thereafter. Other persons, not mentioned in the law, may also make referrals to protective services. Persons filing a report are usually protected against suit for reporting, and professionals may be held responsible for subsequent harm done to the child if they *fail* to report. In addition, the reporter can choose to have his/her identity remain confidential and not be revealed to the family. In turn, protective services must maintain confidentiality of the reported family, and thus is constrained in the information it can share with persons who have made a report, or with other interested parties.[5]

Most state child protection laws are written in such a way as to encourage liberal reporting. That is, persons are supposed to report suspicion, not proven cases. It is the responsibility of the protective services worker to make the determination of abuse or neglect.

Mandated reporting of child maltreatment raises certain problems. Although there are some conditions which can be unmistakenly defined as child abuse or child neglect, there are some situations where it is less clear. There is no formula, for example, which differentiates child abuse from overdiscipline. There is no uniform definition of emotional abuse or emotional neglect. It is often impossible to separate the consequences of poverty from neglect. Because of this definitional difficulty, what reporters, protective services workers, judges, and others in a community regard as abuse and neglect is somewhat subjective. Moreover, these judgments are influenced by such factors as availability and level of training of protective services workers, characteristics and severity of local social problems, and certain political factors.

Many professionals do not want to become involved in a public agency and possible court appearance, or they are concerned about the effect of their making a report to protective services on their relationship with the family. Thus there is differential compliance to the reporting requirement. Persons in the private sector, like private physicians, psychiatrists, and social workers in private practice, have low rates of reporting. In addition, often persons who have an ongoing relationship with the family, like public health nurses and persons in treatment agencies, will not report until the situation is desperate and children have to be removed. Better training about how to handle reporting with the family could help a great deal with problems professionals have in complying with this requirement.

The provision for having the reporter's identity remain confidential has some unanticipated consequences. Professionals may want to maintain confidentiality to preserve a helping relationship. While this is an important safeguard for nonprofessionals (e.g., friends, neighbors, and relatives), the professional who takes advantage of this provision may in the end do more harm than good to his clients. First the client may focus on "Who reported me?" rather than the issue of child maltreatment; moreover, the client will probably be able to guess which professional made the report. Such a discovery is likely to have a much more detrimental impact upon the relationship than honest confrontation before reporting and then support through involvement with protective services. Finally, the anonymity of the reporting person is a false security if the case goes to court. There, that person's testimony may be crucial, and he/she is likely to be subpoenaed and must testify under oath in the presence of the client.

Finally it should be noted that one very frustrating consequence of reporting is that the professional often gets no feedback from the protective services system after he/she has made the report. Because protective services cases are confidential, she/he may not be able to find out whether the allegation of abuse or neglect was true, what services are being provided, or how protective services recommends the family be treated by the reporter.

Investigation

When a case is reported, the protective services case worker who is to handle the complaint usually checks to see if there is a current or closed case on the family and checks with the Central Registry. The Central Registry exists at the state level and comprises past substantiated cases of child abuse or neglect.[6] The next step is to make a face-to-face contact with the family to gather information, usually with a time constraint (twenty-four hours, and emergency cases taking priority over less serious ones). The worker discusses the allegations with the parents, if feasible, discusses them with the child, and makes an assessment of the home environment. In this process the worker may undress the child to look for injuries and inspect the house for sufficient food, appropriate sleeping arrangements, and physical safety. The worker will also probably contact other agencies involved with the family including schools, the health department, the police, and social services and treatment agencies. The worker may also talk to relatives and friends. In most states, protective services may request a medical examination of the child, and a psychiatric or psychological examination. If the parents refuse to allow an evaluation, the worker can get a court order.

If the worker decides that the report is justified, based on his/her own observation or a medical exam, then she/he must determine whether the child is at risk in the home. If she/he thinks the child is in danger, the child can be removed to the hospital, to a shelter or foster placement, or to the home of a relative or friend on an emergency basis. As a rule, emergency removal also requires a court order.[7]

The difficulty of doing investigations in cases of suspected maltreatment should not be underestimated. The first problem for the worker is likely to be the family's response. Some families are relieved that help is to be offered, but more often families are angry and hostile, and they may also be frightened. Sometimes the angry feelings are directed at the reporting person. Other times they are focused on the child. But more often the hostility is directed at the worker. One of the most difficult parts of being a protective services worker is to maintain a helping stance in the face of hostility, verbal abuse, or other ways the family may express their feelings.

In the face of possible hostility, the worker may have to further penetrate the family's privacy by requiring a medical or psychiatric exam and by questioning other persons who might know about the family. Moreover, if the worker at any point during the investigation thinks it is unsafe for the child to remain at home, the worker must risk further antagonization by removing the child. The situation becomes even more complicated if there is a concurrent investigation by the police, as happens in some cases.

Finally, because child maltreatment usually takes place in the privacy of the family, it may not be possible to be sure whether it has occurred or not, and whether the child is at risk. Decisions must be made quickly, often with incomplete data. To be responsible for decisions in such situations is onerous.

Working in these circumstances requires considerable skill. Workers need to be honest with families about the protective services role without being hostile; they must be supportive as well as confronting; and they must maintain equanimity in very stressful situations.

Based on the investigation, the worker decides to open the case or not to open (that is, deny it). More than half of the cases are denied on this point.[8] If the worker determines that the family has problems but the case is not a situation of child maltreatment, she/he usually refers the family to other relevant resources.

Intervention

If the worker substantiates the family's need for protective services, then a plan for treatment is initiated. In some communities there are separate workers for investigation, or intake, and treatment, or ongoing work.[9] There are advantages and disadvantages to both structures. If there is one worker, the family does not have the problem of losing someone with whom they have just begun to develop a relationship and having to relate to yet another person who will delve into the intimacy of their family life. On the other hand, having a single worker may mean there is such a residue of hostility because of the investigation that forming a therapeutic alliance is very difficult.

Having worker specialization (separation of investigation and treatment functions) has been regarded by agency administrators as an efficient division of labor because workers only have to learn one role. However, precious time and energy are lost in the case transfer procedure and the effort of the new worker to familiarize her/himself with the family. Frequently, there is a hiatus in service delivery during case transfer. Further, such specialization may make the protective services job unattractive because the role is too narrow. On the other hand, some workers will find the narrow focus to their liking. Workers may prefer the investigative or the treatment role and will be uncomfortable having to do both.

The basic thrust of the treatment worker's intervention with the family depends upon what services the family was receiving at the time of referral, how cooperative they are, and the degree of risk to the child. Ideally there should have been a careful assessment and diagnosis during the investigative phase using professionals other than the child protection worker where needed. This point deserves emphasis because in emergencies the need for initial and ongoing assessment can be overlooked. In fact, sometimes no coherent intervention plan is made because the worker is so busy responding to emergencies.

The following are alternative strategies the worker might employ:

1. If during the investigation stage the worker finds the family is already productively involved with an agency in the community, the worker may choose to allow that agency to provide all or the major part of the intervention.
2. In situations where the family is cooperative and the child is not in danger, the worker may leave the child in the home (or return the child if it was removed on an emergency basis) and provide direct service to the family or arrange for service from other agencies, entities, or persons in the community.
3. In other instances the worker may need the authority of the court, which can make the child a temporary ward in its own home and order the family to cooperate with protective services.
4. In still other circumstances it may be necessary for the child's safety to remove it or continue it in placement temporarily with a foster family, friend, or relative while the worker attempts to get the family to make enough changes so it can provide minimum sufficient care for the child.
5. Finally, there will be situations in which the family is not amenable to change or able to change and the child must be permanently removed from the home.

The types of service provided directly by the protective services worker will vary depending upon the needs of the family, the size of the worker's caseload, and the availability of other services in the community. One of the strains on the current protective services system is the fact that the considerable emphasis placed upon the need to report abuse and neglect has led to a very large increase in the number of cases being reported. So far we have not seen a comparable increase in treatment services. It has been easier to get funds for detection than it has been to get money to help the families. The irony is that many families need intensive intervention in order to change, but these resources are not available.

Because of these constraints, in some instances all the worker will be able to do is monitor the family. He/she will make periodic visits and assess whether the child has been harmed or is at risk. If at any point the worker feels the situation is dangerous, he/she may remove the child if there is a foster home or placement facility available. But no real treatment will be provided by the worker to the family. This is a very cost-inefficient policy because it is far more expensive to maintain a child outside its home than to provide services to keep families together.

In other instances the worker's role will be that of case coordinator. He/she will orchestrate intervention, but most of the direct service will be provided by others. His/her role is to see that the various professionals follow through and to periodically reassess the intervention.

In some cases protective services workers will provide direct treatment. Their customary model is one of crisis intervention to deal with the emergency. What workers actually do depends upon what the family presents as problems and the skills of the worker.

In situations where the intervention is more than mere monitoring, the worker relies upon two main types of resources when making a plan: concrete services and therapy. Concrete services include financial assistance, medical services and assistance, employment services, education services, housing assistance, homemaker service, day care, and visits from public health nurses. Many different types of therapy might be employed—crisis intervention, mentioned earlier, individual therapy for parent or child, marital treatment, family therapy, therapy which focuses on the parent-child interaction, group therapy, and/or lay therapy, or parent aides.[10] (These resources are discussed in detail in Chapter 6, "Resources for Intervention.")

We know that all of these methods are useful to a degree with abusive and neglectful families. However, because protective services clients are usually nonvoluntary, the most useful services to the worker are an array of readily available concrete services and outreach services. Thus the capacity to respond to the family's need for clothing or furniture can alleviate stress, relieve neglect, and make a resistant family more trusting of the worker. Similarly, if the worker provides therapy in the family's home when the family needs it, (or can call on another treatment resource for this), failed appointments and resistance to therapy will be reduced.

Ideally the family should be constantly reassessed to determine whether the intervention is being effective and/or new problems have developed or have been uncovered. A substantial percentage of the families where abuse and neglect occur are ones with many problems. The worker alters intervention strategies in response to changes in a family's problems.

While the primary goal of protective services intervention is to protect children, its secondary goal is to keep families together. Thus the worker attempts to move the child back (if it has been removed) into the home as soon as it is safe, and maintain the child in the home whenever it is feasible.

Closing a Case

Protective services intervention is supposed to be short term, lasting from three months to a year.[11] However, some cases remain active longer because of repeated referrals to protective services, because the children continue to be regarded as at risk, because the court mandates ongoing protective services supervision, or for various other reasons.

Cases are closed for two reasons:

1. Intervention goals have been reached. This may or may not mean families are adequately functioning. Some families' problems can be treated within the protective services time constraints by the protective services worker. In other instances cases are closed when the children are no longer at risk but other problems remain. In situations like these, protective services should refer the family to other appropriate agencies and then close its case.

A problem that occurs when this is done is that families may not form an alliance with the new agency, or they may keep appointments so long as their protective services case is open and cease going when the case is closed. The agency to which they have been referred may not recontact protective services and may not have the capability of reaching out to the family.

2. Cases are closed when goals are not reached. There is a cohort of protective services cases where the intervention provided does not lead to an appropriate level of change. Sometimes the problem is that the services are too meager; other times they are considerable but not effective. Because some of these cases are not serious enough to warrant court intervention or because there is a gap between what the worker regards as problematic and what the court does, a number of these cases fall through the cracks. They may be closed outright or when referrals are made to other agencies even though the referral has little likelihood of success. This is a serious problem with which the protective services system is not yet able to deal.

In other situations, particularly where there is careful documentation of the efforts at intervention, children can be removed from the home through court intervention. (The protective services case usually is then closed and the family is transferred to another part of the social services system).

The Foster Care System

Introduction

The foster care system provides placement for children and services to families after children have been removed from their home. One of the ways it differs from the child protective system is that there is no designated federal agency (like the National Center on Child Abuse and Neglect) responsible for setting policy and attending to federal guidelines.[12] This is so despite the fact that placement services for dependent and neglected children have a longer history than protective services. The system includes foster care placements licensed by public social service departments, placements by courts, and placements under the auspices of private agencies. Frequently, private agencies have contracts with the public sector to provide foster care services. Funding for these different types of programs comes from a variety of sources. Foster care workers also place children in residential treatment centers and institutions and will monitor their progress in these facilities.

One of the problems with such diversity is lack of accountability. This has been exacerbated by the failure of the federal government to take a leadership role in developing guidelines for quality control and seeing to their enforcement. Therefore at a given time a state may not know how many children it has in foster care and other placements, how long they have been there, or demographic data about the children. Thus many children become lost in the system, remaining in foster care far longer than they need to with no permanent plan made for them. However, within the past year a new child welfare and adoption law has been passed, which may lead to needed changes.

It is estimated that there are over 500,000 children in the United States in placements, and minority children are overrepresented in placements. These numbers include both voluntary and adjudicated placements. The vast majority of children are in publicly sponsored settings.[13] Voluntary placements occur when a parent or guardian requests his/her child be placed because he/she is unable to care for the child. Involuntary placements are adjudicated. That is, the children are removed from the parents' care by court order.

Induction into the Foster Care System

Protective Services and Foster Care

The exact relationship between protective services and foster care varies from state to state and community to community. About 10 percent of protective services cases eventually go to court, and in a substantial proportion of these cases the child is removed from the home.[14] Technically, then, the child has passed into the foster care system. However, in some communities the same worker continues to work with the case. In other places the protective services worker will continue to handle the case if the child is placed for a short time, for example up to three weeks.[15] If the child remains in placement longer, the case is transferred to the foster care division and the family gets a new worker. In other communities, once the case is adjudicated and the child placed, a worker connected with the juvenile court assumes primary responsibility.

While families may harbor hostility toward a worker who has removed their children and be less angry at a new worker, much time may be wasted in this transition. It is not uncommon for the new worker to be unaware of or to disagree with the treatment plan instituted by protective services. In addition, the necessity of having to relate to yet another social worker may exacerbate the trauma of removal for both child and parents.

LEGAL STATUS

When protective services families have their children taken away, the placement is usually involuntary. That is, the child is removed from the parents by court order. However, sometimes these families will agree to place their children voluntarily either because they are unable to adequately care for them or because they have harmed or fear they will harm the children. Alternatively, they may be persuaded that placement is the only course of action. Whether such a placement is adjudicated so that the child becomes a court ward differs from locality to locality, and the length of time such a child can remain in a voluntary placement varies.

The extent of court involvement in the intervention plan when the child is a court ward will also vary. Sometimes the court will order specific treatment, medical follow-up, day care, or other services. Other times the court will allow the worker considerable autonomy in developing the treatment plan but will periodically review (every six months or so) the progress of the family. And sometimes the court will even give the worker the power to return the children when he/she sees fit without returning to court. There are also communities where there is no systematic court review or involvement after placement.

Unless termination of parental rights is anticipated immediately, some provision is usually made for parental visitation. Sometimes the exact terms are spelled out in the court order; other times they are left up to the discretion of the foster care worker. Typically visitation is weekly for up to a few hours, and it is often supervised. It may be in the home of the foster parents, in the social services office, or in the home of the parents.

Foster Parents

Families are recruited and licensed to accept foster children by either a state or private agency licensing worker. The criteria used for determining whether people will be good foster parents are illusive. Further, it is difficult to make a judgment based upon a one- or two-hour home study. Partly because of this, undue weight is placed upon the physical environment, e.g., whether the foster family has enough space for a child, whether the home meets certain fire department requirements. Consequently, the quality of foster care placements is quite uneven, some being excellent, others being unfit, and the majority falling somewhere in between.

Typically a family is licensed to take a given number of children, and foster parents may make specifications about the kind of children they want. For example, they may not want adolescents, or refuse adolescents with drug problems, or only be willing to keep a child two weeks, or require children placed with them to attend church. However, because there is a chronic shortage of foster parents, foster parents are frequently asked to keep children who do not meet the specifications of their license or preferences. Workers often have to beg families to take children and may succumb to the temptation of glossing over some of the difficulties the foster parents are likely to encounter with the child.

There are many reasons for this shortage. First, the amount of money such parents receive for keeping children barely covers the children's basic expenses. It provides for little beyond the essentials and does not allow for special circumstances. Most foster parents lose money rather than make it in the venture.

Second, many foster children are hard to manage. The move into foster care is traumatic for most children, and they experience emotional upset in the process. In addition, many children who must be placed have behavioral, developmental, and sometimes physical problems. What foster parents get in terms of support, guidance, and respite in these situations is minimal. Workers have little time to spend with them, and there are only a handful of training programs in the country for foster parents. In fact, many children who are placed in foster care need specially trained foster parents or sometimes therapeutic placements. However, few communities have these, and often very disturbed children are put with untrained foster parents.

Further, frequently foster parents become attached to the children whom they keep and suffer (as do the children) when the children are moved. If children are freed for adoption, only some localities give preference to foster parents if they wish to adopt. Moreover, while subsidized adoptions do exist, the amount granted is generally insufficient, and subsidized adoption programs are not widespread enough.

In recent years, foster parents themselves have attempted to address the problems of the system by forming a national organization and establishing state and local chapters. Among its activities are sharing of problems and ideas through regular meetings, the provision of training and written informational materials for its members, lobbying, and litigation.

Intervention

When a child is placed in foster care, the worker has responsibilities to three different client groups—the natural parents, the foster parents, and the children. Each has its own special needs.

WORKING WITH PARENTS

In working with parents, the goal of the foster care worker is to help them make changes so the child can be returned as expeditiously as possible. The foster care worker will use many of the same types of services employed by the protective services worker, and there should be a carryover in the plan which was instituted by protective services. Thus the major services employed will be concrete services such as financial assistance, housing and employment services, homemaker services, and therapy appropriate to the family's needs. The worker's aim is to help the family achieve a sufficient level of functioning so that it will be safe for them to have the child back.

If the child has remained in foster care for more than a few weeks or if the worker is not sure about the capacity of the parents to care for the child when return is contemplated, return should be gradual. In the first instance, the child may have made an attachment with the foster parents and the relationship should not be suddenly severed. In the second, gradual return will allow the worker to monitor the parents' ability to cope with the child. Return might involve first a visit during the day, then an overnight stay, next a weekend stay, and then full return. After the child has been returned, the worker will continue to be involved with the family and may provide additional service necessitated by the return of the child.

Working with parents whose children have been removed is especially difficult because the worker must deal not only with the problems in functioning which necessitated the removal but also with the parents' anger and sense of loss. Further, while removing the child may initially increase motivation to change in order to get the child back, if the child remains out of the house for some time, the desire to change diminishes. This is because without the child there, parents are not daily confronted with situations in which they have difficulty managing the child. In addition, it is hard for the worker to address problems in parent-child interaction without current examples to work from.

This limitation may lead the worker to focus on environmental changes such as a parent getting a job, an adequate place for the child to live, and day care. These changes can be observed and measured, whereas improvement in the parent-child relationship cannot. While environmental problems are important, it should not be assumed that meeting these needs will automatically lead to improved child care.

Working with the Foster Parents

The foster care worker must also work closely with the foster parents. Foster parents may need material and practical assistance, such as emergency funds for clothing or help getting the child enrolled in school. They also may need support in dealing with the child's emotional and behavioral problems and with their own feelings about the child and its parents. Unfortunately, often foster care caseloads are so high that only concrete problems get the attention of the worker. One very problematic consequence is "foster care instability." Because no one is available to assist foster parents in coping with interpersonal issues, when things become too stressful they ask that the child be removed.

In some model programs foster parents are key agents not only in helping the child but also for the parents, for whom they serve as role models and nurturant persons. However, such programs are the exception, and under ordinary circumstances there is much animosity between parents and foster parents.

Frequently parental visitation is traumatic for the foster parent and may trigger acting out by the child. Thus sometimes agency policy does not allow visitation for the first two weeks or so after placement or may prohibit visitation if it upsets the child.[16] While this may make things smoother for the foster parents and the worker, its effects on the parent-child relationship are devastating, particularly with young children (see Chapter 8). Further, research shows that frequent visits by parents is the factor most highly correlated with the return of the child to its natural family.[17]

Helping the Child

The worker's first responsibility as far as the child is concerned is to assure that the child is safe from harm. However, when the child is placed in foster care, the worker must also help the child understand and cope with what is happening. For while some children will experience being in a new safe environment as positive, children are more likely to be traumatized by the new unfamiliar environment and sense of loss of their parents. The worker's role is to tell the child in language comprehensible to the child that he/she is being placed because the parent or parents cannot care for him/her at that time and emphasize that removal is not the child's fault. Ideally as much description as possible is provided about the foster family, the length of time to expect to remain in care, and particulars about visitation. In many communities workers make an effort to allow the child to visit the prospective home before placement.

The worker may be the only consistent person in the child's life during placement, particularly if he/she was involved with the family prior to placement. Thus frequent visits to the child in the period right after he/she is put in foster care may be invaluable for the child.

The worker may also need to help the child with guilt feelings concerning divided loyalties if the child forms an attachment to the foster parents. If the child is verbal, he/she is supposed to be involved in future planning. Obviously, the older the child, the more say he/she would have.

Unfortunately, foster care workers may lack the skills crucial for working with children. They are likely to be young and inexperienced and often do not have children of their own. They may not feel comfortable even talking to children. They may be unaware of how traumatic placement is to the child. In fact, frequently they are overwhelmed by the emotional dynamics of the other persons—parents and foster parents—and never think of the emotional needs of the child.

The Course of Foster Care

Ideally, once a child is removed, intensive work should be initiated with the parents to facilitate speedy change and return of the child. If parents do not move toward more adequate functioning, the removal should be made permanent. The goal of a stable environment for children should be paramount. Children who have been abused or neglected have already experienced an unstable and hostile living environment, and this trauma is often compounded by placement and frequent moves. The only way to rectify this situation is to provide the child with a safe, stable, nurturing environment. Further, we know that such an environment is essential for emotional and cognitive development. Therefore, if the parents are not likely to provide an adequate home, the child should be placed with a relative or freed for adoption. To ensure this course of activity, workers often contract with parents around needed change and set a time limit for implementation.

Unfortunately, this kind of planning may not occur. Once the child is safe, the overriding urge to improve family functioning lessens for the worker. Moreover, if there has been a change in workers as the child comes into care, this will delay active intervention. Thus it is not uncommon for a child to be in foster placement for months to years without any permanent plan being made. And we know that once a child has been in foster care for a year, the likelihood of return is very remote.[18]

Another problem with foster care is that children may be moved from placement to placement. This can happen because the child is a behavior problem and the foster parents request that the child be moved. Foster children are sent back to the agency during family crises—for example, when the foster mother becomes ill or a new baby is born. Foster children also are likely to be relinquished if the family moves.

Foster care workers themselves may move children for many reasons. They may need the home for another child. For example, if a house is licensed for three children and only one child is in the placement, the single child may be moved to make room for three new arrivals who are siblings. Workers may also move children to put them with families who will provide them with better material or cultural advantages, or to a home more like that of the natural parents, without considering the psychic damage done by the move itself.

In the past, social workers regarded it as detrimental to the overall case plan if the foster parents became too attached to the children and therefore would move them if they thought the foster parents were becoming the child's psychological parents. Most persons in the foster care field now recognize that these close attachments are beneficial rather than harmful and do not move children for such reasons. However, workers do move children for other reasons without adequate consideration of the traumatic effect on the child, and children are allowed to linger in foster care for years without workers taking into account the psychological impact of being in such a limbo.[19]

Conclusion

While there are many problems with the child welfare system, we must remember that it is an institution which is in the process of developing. The protective services system really cannot be considered more than ten or fifteen years old. As we learn more about how to handle child abuse and neglect, new provisions are written into child protection laws and new programs for intervention are developed. Similarly, we should view the foster care system as one in a state of evolution. Whereas twenty or thirty years ago children removed from their homes would have been placed in group care facilities and institutions, today we realize that children should be placed in a homelike atmosphere. Currently we are recognizing the long-term impact of a system which may rescue children from immediate physical danger but fails to address the long-term impact of removal and to make long-range plans for the child.

In the future we can expect to see changes which will improve the system. Nevertheless, some old flaws will remain, and we will become aware of new ones.

Notes

1. Gelles, R., Conference Presentation.
2. Data gathered from talking to protective services and foster care workers in several states.
3. For a discussion of stress in Child Abuse see Copaiss et al., The Stresses of Treating Child Abuses.
4. U.S. Dept. of Health, Education, and Welfare, *Child Abuse and Neglect: The Problems and Its Management.*
5. *Ibid.*
6. *Ibid.*
7. See, for example, Michigan State Department of Social Services, *Services Manual: Protective Services.*
8. American Humane Association, *National Analysis of Child Abuse and Neglect Reporting.*
9. U.S. Dept. of Health, Education, and Welfare, *A Guide to Protective Services for Abused and Neglected Children and Their Families.*
10. *Ibid.*
11. DHEW, *Child Abuse and Neglect.*
12. Kadushin, *Child Welfare Strategy in The Coming Years.*
13. Children's Defense Fund, *Children Without Homes.*
14. American Humane Association, *op. cit.*
15. Michigan State Department of Social Services, *op. cit.*
16. Information gathered from talking to Foster Care Workers from various localities.
17. Fanshel and Shinn, *Children in Foster Care: A Longitudinal Investigation.*
18. *Ibid.*
19. For a further discussion of the foster care system, see Wiltse, "Current Issues and New Directions in Foster Care."

10

The Legal Aspects of Child Abuse and Neglect

Donald N. Duquette

Introduction

The law is an essential partner with the medical, social work, and mental health professions in identifying and responding to children who may be abused and neglected and their families. The law governs reporting of suspected child abuse and neglect and outlines the duties of the child protection agency in responding to those reports. Statutes and court rules determine the circumstances under which a child suspected of being abused or neglected may be detained in a hospital or removed from his home on an emergency basis. Child abuse and neglect laws in all states aim to facilitate the benevolent intervention in family life by professionals intending to strengthen family life whenever possible. The philosophy is to intervene helpfully in a family without causing further harm or punishing the family.

The idealistic goals of child protection laws must not obscure the fact that government intervention in family life infringes fundamental personal liberties of both parents and children, and may not fulfill its idealistic and benevolent promise. The personal freedoms of parents to have children in their care and custody and to raise them as they see fit and the correlative rights of children to live with their parents unfettered by government interference must be protected and must be set aside only under carefully defined circumstances. Families may accept intervention voluntarily. If not, however, arbitrary and unwarranted intrusion into family privacy, even with the best of motives, is a deprivation of personal freedom clearly out of place in our free and democratic society.

The court system acts as arbiter of personal liberty in child protection. By the application of laws the court must assure that the rights of the parents and children are protected and are abridged only after full and fair and objective court process. Only the court can compel unwilling parents or children to submit to the authority of the state. In the case of involuntary clients, the court controls the coercive elements of society and allows those coercive elements to be unleashed only after due process of law.

Once the government has interfered with parental rights and the child's right to be with the parent, the laws in most states require that the parents be treated fairly by the social agencies and other professionals and that the family be provided all assistance reasonable to allow them to correct existing problems so that the child may be returned to them. However, if the parents do not, or are not able to, correct the deficiencies which led to the government intervention in the first place, the interests of the child in having a permanent and stable home are served by termination of the natural parents' rights and placing the child for adoption or in some other permanent placement.

The perspective of the lawyer and judge is somewhat different from that of the other professionals involved in child protection. That perspective is often found puzzling and even repugnant to other professionals. Personal rights and liberties, their protection and their abrogation in certain cases, are the unique business of lawyers and judges. Lawyers act as advocates for one side or another. They need not pursue the solution best for all concerned in the circumstances, but must determine the client's interest and advocate for that position—zealously. Although increased use of negotiation and mediation and the lessening of adversarial tension are especially desirable in child protection proceedings, ultimately the court process is adversarial. Attorneys rely on the adversarial system to produce wise solutions, while physicians, social workers, and mental health professionals rely on trust and cooperation and find the adversarial process discomforting, foreign, and nonproductive or counterproductive in terms of the "real problems" faced by the family. In the interests of interdisciplinary understanding of the legal system, a brief description of the role of the lawyer for the government, for the parents, and for the child is offered below (see Chapter 15).

A description of the legal aspects of child abuse and neglect begins logically with the laws which mandate the reporting of suspected child abuse and neglect cases. The limited role of a reporting law or of any other law must be clear. No law is the ultimate answer to any problem. A law may prohibit child abuse or neglect, but it cannot cure it. A law may require the reporting of maltreated children, but cannot ensure it. A law may mandate the rehabilitation of parents, but it cannot rehabilitate them. A law may articulate children's rights to and needs of permanent homes, but cannot move children from foster care and make them eligible for adoption.

What laws *can* do is establish the institutional framework for the protection of children. The law can articulate a philosophy that will motivate and guide individuals within a system as they deal with the personal and unique problems of children and families.

Ultimately, the prevention and treatment of child abuse and neglect depend less on laws and more on the existence of sufficient and suitable helping services for children and parents. Prevention and treatment of child abuse and neglect depend on individual people—well-trained social workers, doctors, lawyers, nurses, psychologists, judges, foster parents—pulling together in interdisciplinary collaboration for a common goal. Laws are a necessary ally but are not a substitute for caring and well-trained professionals.

Reporting Laws

History

For many years child maltreatment was a hidden problem, relegated to understaffed and overwhelmed protective services far from public view. Only in recent years has the extent of child abuse and neglect been widely recognized. Leaders in the medical profession brought the plight of the "battered child" to public attention. Caffey in 1946 provided the first serious medical report on the problem of possible child abuse and neglect by noting the frequent correlation between subdural hematoma and fractures of the long bones in children.[1] The most conclusive and influential study was produced in 1961 by Kempe and others, who found hundreds of children severely injured by their parents. The condition was given a new medical term by the authors, "the battered child syndrome."[2]

Legislative action quickly followed. In 1962 the Children's Bureau called a conference to formulate recommendations for meeting the medical and social challenge of child abuse. The result, published in 1963, was the first proposed mandatory reporting legislation.[3] Within three years every state had enacted a reporting law, many patterned after the Children's Bureau Model.[4]

In the 1970s widespread concern about other forms of child maltreatment and an evolution of social responses to the problem led to amended child protection legislation. In 1974 the Federal Child Abuse Prevention and Treatment Act was passed, which established certain eligibility criteria for states in order to qualify for federal grants. Over forty states amended their laws to require the reporting of suspected child neglect as well as child abuse. Reporting laws were also expanded to include important ancillary provisions such as immunity for good-faith reporting, penalties for failure to report, protective custody, the abrogation of certain privileged communications, and central registries of reports received.[5]

Philosophy and Purpose

The philosophy and purpose of child abuse and neglect reporting laws are generally to discover cases of child maltreatment so that the child may be protected and rehabilitative or supportive services may be provided the family. State statutes generally provide that the purpose of the law or duty of the public social agency is to safeguard the well-being of endangered children and to preserve and stabilize family life whenever possible.[6] Most statutes focus on care and protection of children and on the provision of proper social services to their families, rather than on any punitive action against the perpetrator.[7]

A distinction must be drawn between the reporting laws with their case-finding emphasis and state statutes which allow the juvenile or family court to intervene coercively to suspend parental rights temporarily or permanently when children are maltreated or in danger. The latter set of laws are discussed under "The Court Process" later in this chapter. Nationally between 10 and 15 percent of reports of suspected child abuse or neglect result in court action.[8] Most reports of suspected child abuse or neglect are responded to without court action, presumably with the voluntary cooperation of the family. (See "The Danger of Overreaching," later in this chapter).

What Is to Be Reported?

Most state reporting laws require or permit reporting suspected child abuse or neglect and define those terms, if at all, very generally.[9] A common definition of child abuse or neglect that is to be reported is "harm or threatened harm to a child's health or welfare by a person responsible for the child's health or welfare which occurs through nonaccidental physical or mental injury, sexual abuse, maltreatment or negligent treatment, including the failure to provide adequate food, clothing or shelter."[10] Recent commentators have argued for a narrower definition of children who must be reported.[11]

Reporting laws do not require the reporting person to know with certainty that child maltreatment has actually taken place. The statutes generally mandate or permit reporting when there exists "reasonable cause to suspect" child abuse and neglect. Thus the reporting persons are not expected to investigate the matter, to know the definitions used in judicial proceedings, or even to know the name of the perpetrator. The statutes clearly are weighted toward encouraging persons to overreport rather than underreport.[12]

Who Is to Report?

The laws of nearly all states *require* certain professionals to report child abuse or neglect that they see or suspect. The class of mandated reporters encompasses professionals who are in frequent contact with children and whose training and experience should make them sensitive to the possible abuse and neglect of children. The professionals who *must* report under state law generally include physicians, nurses, social workers, medical examiners or coroners, dentists, mental health professionals, school teachers, counselors, and administrators, law enforcement officers, and child care workers.

In addition, most state statutes permit any other person to report cases of suspected child abuse and neglect. Reports from neighbors, friends, and relatives make up a large proportion of the protective services caseload.

To Whom Are Reports Made?

A central social services agency in each locality is the receiver of suspected child maltreatment reports in nearly all states. Some states provide for twenty-four-hour, seven-day-per-week statewide telephone hotlines for reporting. Most experts in the social, legal, and medical fields agree that existing social welfare departments or more specialized offices of child protective services within such departments should be responsible for receiving reports. Implicit in this recommendation is the assumption that some sort of social service or treatment will be provided once the report is confirmed.[13]

Several states, however, provide that reports of suspected child abuse or neglect be sent to the police, the juvenile court, or the local prosecutor in addition to being sent to the child protection social agency. The Children's Bureau Model Child Protection Act expressly discourages the designation of police or law enforcement agencies as recipients of reports.[14]

How Are Reports to Be Made?

There is general agreement as to how reports should be made. Almost all states and all model laws instruct reporters to make oral reports by telephone to the appropriate agency as soon as possible, to be followed by a more complete written report within a short time.[15] Local child protection agencies provide a supply of the necessary reporting forms to hospitals, schools, law enforcement agencies, and others who need them.

Confidentiality of Reports

All states allow anonymous reporting, and some prohibit agency disclosure of the identity of the reporting person without his/her permission. The Children's Bureau Model Act permits but does not encourage anonymous reporting.[16]

Reports generated by child abuse and neglect reporting laws are confidential and may not be disclosed except as specifically allowed by law. A criminal misdemeanor penalty generally attaches to persons who disclose such information without proper authority. The material in a record may be unfounded and based on reports of malicious neighbors or family or be erroneous. Even if the material is true, there is a need to protect the rights and sensibilities of those who are named in these records, for they contain information about the most private aspects of personal and family life. Without adequate safeguards, these personal data are susceptible to improper disclosures and could stigmatize the future of those mentioned. The children and families involved in the process have a moral right, if not a constitutional right, to have the information in these records kept confidential.[17]

Abrogation of Privileged Communication

Communications between physicians and patients, husbands and wives, attorney and client, psychologist and client, and social worker and client among others are held to be privileged and confidential in nearly every state. Waivers of such privileges for purposes of reporting or giving evidence in a case of suspected child abuse or neglect are a standard part of reporting legislation among the states. Many cases of known or suspected child abuse or neglect would not be reported if the privileges remained intact. All but three states preserve the lawyer-client privilege, since confidence between attorney and client must be protected in order to secure a fair trial.[18]

Medical Examination, Photographs, and X-Rays

Many state laws require or permit physicians to make appropriate medical examination of a child suspected of being abused or neglected without parental consent including photographs, x-rays, and laboratory studies. Often immediate medical care is needed for the child, and preservation of the physical data is desirable either for future decision making within the hospital or social agencies or for use as evidence in legal proceedings.[19]

Immunity from Liability

State statutes generally provide immunity from liability for persons reporting or doing any other act under child abuse and neglect reporting laws. Immunity for reporting in good faith is essential to a child protection system which relies on third-party reports. Otherwise, fears of lawsuits for slander, libel, defamation, invasion of privacy, and breach of confidentiality may discourage reporting of known or suspected maltreated children. The immunity provisions are not absolute, however. States generally extend immunity only for good-faith reports, and state law cannot extend immunity against suits for deprivation of constitutional rights brought under federal statutes and the U.S. Constitution.

Central Registries

Central registries of some form are maintained in forty-seven jurisdictions. Thirty-three of these registries are mandated by law, while the remaining fourteen are maintained as a matter of administrative policy.[20] Reports of suspected child abuse or neglect are maintained in the central file unless the report is found to be unsubstantiated. The single repository of reports and findings of child abuse and neglect has several purposes: (1) professionals suspecting child abuse or neglect may consult the Central Registry and gain further family history which will assist in identification and diagnosis of the problem; (2)

hospital shopping by parents to avoid detection of child abuse may be avoided; (3) once a protective services worker, physician, or other professional determines that a child is abused or neglected, knowledge of prior reports and their outcome can help evaluate the seriousness of the family's situation and can be an important factor in determining whether the child should be removed immediately from his home or not, as well as determining what services the family as a whole may need;[21] (4) a unified system of record keeping provides statistics on the actual extent and seriousness of the child abuse phenomenon and can monitor and measure the child protection system's overall performance.

Certain dangers are inherent in the presence and use of a central data file. Persons using the Central Registry need to recall that it includes reports of suspected abuse, *not* verified findings that abuse has occurred. The information must be used with caution. Parents and children may be stigmatized as abusing parents or abused children. Prior reports may prejudice professionals dealing with a family. The principle dangers of prejudice and stigma must be guarded against to as great an extent as possible. The recording of cases with a Central Registry must not result in jumping to a conclusion of guilt in a subsequent situation of suspected child abuse. Nor should parents or children be unfairly or unduly stigmatized as a result of a report of suspected child abuse.

Penalties for Failure to Report or Act

Ultimately, the success of a reporting law must rely upon the willing cooperation of professionals and citizens concerned about the welfare of endangered children. However, the law must include sanctions for those few persons and officials who refuse to accept their legal and moral obligation.

Most states provide that any person required to report suspected child abuse or neglect or to perform some other act under child maltreatment reporting statutes who knowingly fails to do so is guilty of a criminal misdemeanor and shall be civilly liable for damages proximately caused by such failure.

Duties of the Child Protection Agency

Many state reporting statutes detail the duties of the child protection agency. Those duties typically include responding to a report of suspected or actual child abuse or neglect within a specified period of time, investigating the report, assessing the family situation, determining whether social services should be provided, and determining whether court action to protect the child should be initiated and, if so, gathering and organizing the evidence to support such protective action in court. In addition to these rather substantial case-based duties, the child protection agency may be expected to develop resources for prevention and treatment of child abuse and neglect, provide public education on the subject, and provide training to its own staff and the staffs of private social agencies, courts, hospitals, and other institutions.

Conclusion

Reporting laws provide for the finding of cases of suspected child abuse and neglect. Once suspected cases are identified, they must be investigated. Many reports turn out to be unfounded; others present only slight problems, and the parents are warned, perhaps given referrals to voluntary resources, and the cases are immediately closed. In other cases the protective services workers remain involved with a family to provide certain crisis-oriented services and to monitor the family situation. The great majority of child protection cases fall into this latter category, where services are offered and received on a voluntary basis.

Still other reports of suspected child abuse or neglect (about 10 to 15 percent) result in court action either to protect the child from immediate danger or to ensure the cooperation of reluctant parents in rehabilitative treatment efforts. Court action is necessary when parents refuse to cooperate voluntarily with the social agencies or when their cooperation, which is necessary for the protection of the child, cannot be relied upon. The court needs to be involved when the personal rights of parents or children stand to be infringed. The liberty of parents and children may be taken away only according to due process of law.

Emergency Protective Custody

In most child abuse and neglect situations the child need not be removed from his parents' custody in order to protect his well-being and future development. Indeed, in many situations removal may be harmful to the child and counterproductive to any treatment efforts. Removal may destroy the fragile family fabric and make it more difficult for the parents to cope with the child when he is returned to their care.[22]

However, in some crisis situations a child may face imminent danger of physical harm and need to be removed from that dangerous situation immediately, before there is time to obtain a court order. Legal authority to act quickly on behalf of such children is a necessary part of each state's child protection system.

Most states allow police officers to place children in protective custody on an emergency basis. Some states allow physicians to detain a child in a hospital until the next business day of the court, while others permit child protection social workers to detain children. Authority to place children without court order is generally limited to serious emergency situations subject to court review in a very short time.

Emergency removal methods are not favored by everyone. DeFrancis and Lucht favor obtaining court orders in all cases and argue:

> There is no question but that the highest of motives prompted the enactments which seek to deal with emergency situations. But we cannot afford to substitute good motives for effective skilled services. [Emergency removal measures] are, in our judgement, unnecessary and may even be antithetical to the development of truly skilled and effective protective service workers.[23]

In a commentary, the Children's Bureau Model Child Protection Act says:

> There is always the danger of careless or automatic—though well-meaning—exercise of the power to place a child in protective custody. In the past, in too many situations, the practice has been to remove a child from his home first—and to ask questions later. The Model Act seeks to reduce this possibility by preventing the indiscriminate use of protective custody.[24]

The Model Act clearly states that not only must the child be in imminent danger, but also there must be no time to apply for a court order. Only in grave and urgent situations, where the child's life or safety is in imminent danger and there is no time to apply for a court order, may a child be removed without prior court approval. At least one Federal District Court has held that our U.S. Constitution *limits* the states to such occasions for removing the child.[25]

The American Bar Association—Institute of Judicial Administration Standards on Abuse and Neglect reflect the need for some authority to protect a child in a true emergency while balancing the serious dangers of overuse or inappropriate use of the power. "The costs and risks of emergency custody, in terms of the child's psychological trauma, disruption of the family, and possible violation of due process with regard to parental rights, are formidable."[26]

The Danger of Overreaching

Social workers and other helping professionals involved in child protection activities intend no harm to client families, but aspire instead to stabilize the family as a unit, protect the child, and impart skills of childrearing where they are lacking. In spite of the benevolent motives of child protective services, however, significant intrusions by government into personal and family life are possible without the safeguards of due process of law.

Children's service workers and supervisors should recognize that their clients often attribute considerably more power and authority to them than they may actually possess. The threat of court action is present in every child welfare case, whether expressed or implied. Clients may agree "voluntarily" to protective services involvement out of fear that they will lose their children.

Add to the above the fact that child welfare clients are often poor and powerless. How shall personal freedoms of parents and children be preserved in child welfare? Basic fairness and good social work practice and ethics require that clients be fully advised of the protective services role and the limits of agency authority from the very first contact.

Because child abuse and neglect cause such great societal concern and because the child protection network has been seen as benevolently motivated, society has, up to now, been willing to run the risk of occasional coerced and perhaps unwarranted invasions of family privacy in exchange for swift identification of and response to child abuse and neglect and related ills. The law has not required that notice and hearing be provided before child protective services is allowed to become involved with the family. Child welfare professionals, however, ought to be aware of the personal liberty issue and be responsive to it in every dealing with potential clients.

The Court Process

Introduction

Hopefully the summary of the court process which follows will be useful to readers from many different states. Please remember that each state is free to establish its own procedures and your state procedure may vary somewhat from that described below. Nomenclature is likely to be the largest variant from state to state. What one state calls the "preliminary hearing" another state may call the "probable cause hearing" and yet another the "show-up hearing."

The name of the court in your state which has jurisdiction over cases of alleged child abuse or neglect may be juvenile court, family court, probate court, or dependency court, to mention only a few. Bust despite the differences in names, historical development, and breadth of jurisdiction and authority, the various child protection courts function quite similarly. In the essence of what occurs in each court at each stage, the legal process is quite similar from state to state. It is the essence of the legal process that the following attempts to describe for the nonlawyer.

The Role of the Court

The distinguishing feature of the court which sets it apart from all other elements of the child protection network is that the court acts as an *arbiter of personal rights*. When the society at large, through child protective services, attempts to intervene in the life of a family on behalf of a child, it is the court which must assure that the rights of the parents and the rights of the child as well as the rights of the society generally are properly protected and are abridged only after full and fair and objective legal process. It is only the court that can abridge these personal rights in other than emergency situations. It is only the court that can compel unwilling parents (or children) to submit to the authority of the state. The court, then, controls the coercive elements of our society and allows those coercive elements to be unleashed only after due process of law.

Although the family or juvenile court generally has social service resources at its disposal, and sometimes under its own roof, the court is not primarily a social treatment institution. Even though social treatment is one part of its function, the juvenile court is first of all a *judicial body*. It is true that once the court has completed its judicial function and taken jurisdiction over a child, our juvenile laws and the structure of our juvenile court allow broad latitude in devising a "disposition" which will best meet the needs of the child in question and his family. In the dispositional phase of the court process, juvenile court is a partner with physicians, social workers, and mental health professionals in devising and following through on an appropriate family treatment plan, i.e., a disposition. However, in the predispositional phases of the process the court's formal role is purely judicial.

After first assuring the safety and well-being of the child, the court procedures will allow the judge to thoughtfully and fairly balance and test the rights of the child, the parents, and society at large. This balancing and testing of rights is accomplished in a manner devised over centuries to protect against arbitrary and unwarranted intrusions upon personal rights and to ensure *fairness*—a method of proceeding that has come to be called "due process of law."

The Concept of Due Process of Law

In the context of child protection both parents and children face deprivation of their *liberty*. Parents may lose custody of their children or may have their constitutionally protected rights to raise their children as they see fit suspended. Children may be taken from their parents' home. Our U.S. Constitution and the constitutions of most states guarantee that the state shall deprive no person of life, liberty, or property except by due process of law. What is "due process of law," and how does that legal concept apply to child protection?

The U.S. Constitution does not fix the various elements of due process of law. Courts vary the requirements according to factual circumstances, the legal interest involved, and the necessities of the situation. But although the content of due process cannot be defined specifically, its purpose is clear: that is, to ensure fair and orderly administration of the laws. The effect of the due-process guarantee in child protection is to prohibit invasions of personal liberty (of both parents and children), except in emergency situations, without notice and opportunity for hearing. The orderly administration of child abuse and neglect laws in each state is spelled out in the child protection reporting law, the statute which gives the court its authority to act on behalf of maltreated children, and court procedural rules. Procedural due process requires that one subject to deprivation of liberty be given notice of the proceedings and the charges against him and be given an opportunity to defend himself, and the question of the appropriateness of the deprivation under circumstances presented must be resolved according to some settled course of judicial proceedings.

Legal Neglect: The Community's Minimum Standard of Child Care

The Statute

The law holds out a standard against which the performance of a parent or condition of a child is measured. The law seeks to identify a minimum standard of child care below which the parent must not fall lest the court assume the parental responsibilities, temporarily or permanently.

Children, then, are guaranteed a certain minimum level of food, clothing, shelter, parental care, freedom from physical harm, etc. How does one determine what the minimum standard of child care is in his or her community?

The first and most important way to determine what legal neglect is in a given community is to examine the statutory definition of child neglect, which states when the court may take over the parental responsibilities. The statutory definition of neglect is not likely to be very precise.

Keep in mind that the definition of suspected child abuse or neglect for purposes of reporting is different from and broader than the judicial definition of child abuse or neglect which empowers a court to order coercive governmental intervention in the family. In juvenile or family court the court may actually take away the parental rights and responsibilities for some period of time.

In many states, the abuse and neglect statutes use fairly general language such as the following: "The Court shall have jurisdiction over a child whose parent or other person legally responsible for the care . . . of the child neglects or refuses to provide proper or necessary support, education . . . medical, surgical or other care necessary for his health, morals, or . . . well-being; who is abandoned by his parents, . . . whose home or environment by reason of neglect, cruelty, drunkenness, criminality or depravity on the part of the parent . . . is unfit."[27]

Apart from the general language cited above, statutes generally do not provide more specific guidelines as to exactly what kind of care is proper or necessary. For example, how long may an eight-year-old be left alone without being considered abandonment? How long may a five-year-old be left alone? What kind of neglect, cruelty, or drunkenness is necessary to constitute an unfit home? Can a home be unfit merely by being dirty? How dirty?

A VALUE JUDGMENT IS REQUIRED

The question of whether or not legal neglect exists is also difficult in juvenile court because a two-step analysis is required. First, the judge must determine whether or not the facts of the case as alleged in court are true. Second, the judge must make a normative judgment that is a value judgment, as to whether or not the facts as proven violate the *community's minimum standard of child care* below which a parent shall not fall lest the state intervene on behalf of the child.

When the judge is convinced that the community's minimum standard of child care is breached given the facts of the particular case, then legal neglect exists. Legal neglect or abuse does not exist until the court so declares.

Unlike other areas of the law, therefore, a finding of legal neglect requires a "normative fact judgment." Not only must the facts be proven as true, but the facts as proven must violate community norms of childrearing. In criminal law, facts are alleged to be true—for instance, "Green struck Red on the head with a beer bottle." The allegations are then proven true or not true and the defendant is convicted (assuming other factual elements of the crime are also proven) or acquitted. In child neglect, on the other hand, facts again are alleged—"Brown left her eight-year-old child alone for four hours"—and the allegations are proven to be true or not true. But then the value judgment must be made. Does leaving an eight-year-old child alone for four hours under these circumstances constitute child neglect? Does such an act breach the community norms, i.e., the community minimum standard of child care? Similarly, a severe spanking with bruises on the bottom may be found to be abuse in one community but not another.

Because interpretation of the facts and the law in child abuse and neglect depends so much on normative judgments that are somewhat personal and idiosyncratic, the community minimum standard of child care varies from state to state, from community to community, and even from judge to judge within the same community. One can seek to ascertain the community's minimum standard of child care from three sources: (1) the statute, (2) the decisions of the local court, and (3) the cases opened by the local child protective services.

The Petition

Once the statutory standard of legal neglect has been identified, a petition must be drafted and filed with the proper court asking that the court exercise its power over a certain child or certain children. The petition must state what facts and what legal authority permit the court to take the action asked for by the petitioner. Who may petition the court is established by state law. The most common petitioner is a child-protective services worker.

Due process requires that a person subject to deprivation of liberty be apprised of charges against him with enough clarity and specificity that he may prepare a proper defense. The petition also limits the scope of the court's inquiry into the family's affairs. The parents are entitled to notice of what the charges are against them so that they may prepare a defense. The petitioner may generally not raise at trial matters which are not contained in the petition, since the parents have not had an opportunity to prepare a defense. As a general rule, additional elements may be raised at trial only if the petition is amended.

Negotiation and Mediation

NEGOTIATED SETTLEMENTS ARE VERY DESIRABLE

Just as the social worker has negotiated with the family prior to invoking the power of the court, the negotiating process should continue through all the formal phases of the court proceedings. The social worker recognizes that contested court proceedings are costly to the child and his family. The relationship between agency and parents becomes, at least for a time, adversarial. Resolution of contested cases is time-consuming for all concerned. The treatment goals for the child and his family are not usually furthered while the court action is pending. In many cases, the negative effects of adversarial court action may be reduced by a negotiated resolution.

Professionals regularly involved in the court process can generally predict with some accuracy what the court is likely to do given the strength of each side's legal case and the reasonableness of each side's position. In the process of negotiation, information is shared in a persuasive fashion so as to convince the other side of the strength and reasonableness of one's position. Likewise, one assesses the case of the opponent and in light of that assessment modifies one's position if one's case is found to be weak or not reasonable. By the process of mutual give-and-take some prediction is made by each side as to what the court is likely to do after full hearing. Negotiation is an opportunity to agree to a resolution of the problem which is pretty close to what the court would order if a contested and adversarial trial were to take place.

If the assessments of the strengths and weaknesses of the cases differ, no negotiated settlement will result. In addition, certain elements of each case, e.g., the safety of the child, will be nonnegotiable always. The process of give-and-take, of assessing one's own case and the case of an opponent, is quite complicated.

FLUIDITY OF POSITIONS PROMOTES NEGOTIATED RESOLUTIONS

Even the most intractable parent may change his position once court action is begun. The prospect of appearing in court and the advice of a lawyer may temper a formerly uncompromising attitude. On the other hand, information not previously available to the social worker may surface which tends to alter his evaluation of the case. The social worker may have been mistaken as to the true facts or may have misjudged important elements of the case. Therefore, positions of both the social worker and the parents may become fluid as the court process starts. A negotiated resolution may become possible.

In some cases, nothing short of court wardship and a period of foster care will adequately safeguard the child and the legal case is also quite strong. Then, unless the parents are willing to admit the petition or not contest the petition, there may be no basis for negotiation. Similarly, the attorney for a set of parents may disagree with the allegations of the petition and the worker's assessment of the petition's strength, and his clients may be unwilling to consent to any form of state intervention and may have instructed him to contest all allegations. Here again, negotiations will not be successful. A contested hearing (trial) will likely result.

In many cases, however, new information as to the reasonableness of each side's position and the strength of its legal case can be discovered. New information or new understanding creates some degree of fluidity and fosters voluntary or negotiated resolutions.

Negotiating Options

To effectively negotiate in the legal contest, one must be keenly aware of the various *options* available. On the issue of whether or not the court should take *jurisdiction* of a child, independent of consideration of where the child should be placed, consider several options in escalating degrees of court involvement.

Agree *not* to petition the court.
File petition.
Agree to withdraw a petition already filed or to recommend dismissal by the court.
Amend the petition to add or delete allegations.
Adjourn.
Parents plea no contest.
Parents admit allegations of petition.
Parents deny allegations of petition, trial date set.

Custody of the child(ren) is generally paramount to the parents. In that regard consider the following negotiating options:

Return the child home forthwith.
Return the child home soon (on the condition that . . .).
Return the child on a date certain (on the condition that . . .).
Visitation arranged daily, weekly, overnight, weekends, supervised or unsupervised, depending on the child's needs; visita-

tion arrangements may be conditioned on parents' actions of one sort or another.

Place child in a home requested by parents, e.g., home of relative or licensable friend of family.

Certain elements of a treatment plan that the social worker considers desirable may be particularly onerous to the parents. Identify them. Attempt to fashion a treatment plan most likely to be accepted by the family. You may wish to bargain away an element of a plan that is particularly distasteful to the family in exchange for their agreement to accept court jurisdiction and a dispositional order that will meet the family needs.

Consider negotiated resolutions like the following:

Withdraw petition.	Parents agree to accept services plan.
Adjourn.	Parents agree to use time to improve conditions and correct deficiencies.
Return child. Child placed in parent-requested home. Generous visitation allowed.	Parents admit petition or plead no contest and agree to needed services contained in dispositional order.

CHILD'S ATTORNEY AS MEDIATOR

The child protection statutes in all states now allow for the court appointment of an attorney for the child if the case is to go to court. The child's attorney may play a significant role as mediator once he has been appointed. He is neither the petitioner's attorney nor the defense attorney. He need not take an adversarial position on either side. The interest of his client is often served by voluntary resolution of the legal dispute, thus avoiding contested trial. A contested hearing will not only delay adoption of a treatment plan but put additional stresses on a family. A child's return home may be delayed by contested hearings. The child's counsel therefore may be a useful mediator and may assume responsibility for finding terms of settlement which all parties find acceptable.

The Preliminary Hearing Phase

NOMENCLATURE

The hearing or hearings held by the court between initiation of court action and the adjudicatory hearing (the trial) are variously named among the states. Despite the variation of nomenclature, the functions of this initial stage of the court process are largely the same.

Advising Parents of Rights

At their initial appearance in court the respondents, usually the parents, are advised of the allegations in the petition and of their legal rights including their right to counsel. In many states the court will appoint a lawyer for them if they cannot afford one. Generally, the child's attorney is appointed and is present for this hearing. The judge or referee (a court official subordinate to the judge) explains the nature of the proceedings to the parents. Often lawyers for both parent and child are present at the very first court appearance. In other cases the matter is adjourned for a day or two so that the parents may confer with a lawyer.

Preliminary Finding

Following a general orientation to what the legal process is all about, during which the parents may obtain legal counsel to advise them, the court will move to a preliminary finding of the merits of the case. In nearly every jurisdiction, when a child has been removed from his home, the petitioner must prove that probable cause exists to believe the facts alleged in the petition are true and that those facts constitute legal neglect. That is, the court must find probable cause to believe that the court has power and authority to act on behalf of the child.

Following the preliminary finding that the court has authority to act, the court must decide where the child should be placed pending a full trial.

The petitioner need not prove his entire case in the preliminary hearing phase, but only present enough proof to justify continuing the matter over for a full trial at a later time. In many states sworn affidavits from medical professionals and other hearsay evidence are admissible at this hearing. In other states the evidence presented must be "competent," that is, meet the usual evidentiary standards, so that hearsay testimony is not admitted. The social worker on the case nearly always testifies at the preliminary hearing.

Placement of the Child Pending Trial

Following the preliminary finding that the court has power and authority to act, the court must decide where the child should be placed pending a full trial. Placement pending trial is a complex yet important decision for the child and his family. Many factors must be balanced, including the risks to the child at home, the age of the child and the trauma of separation, the available services to the family, etc. Most state laws and practice presume that the child should stay with his family unless his health or safety would be in serious jeopardy.

Preliminary Orders

The court may also enter several kinds of preliminary orders, which may include orders of placement and of visitation, orders for medical care, and orders for further investigation, including perhaps mental and physical examination of a child and/or, in some jurisdictions, his parents before trial. Medical follow-up for the child may also be ordered.

The Pretrial Conference

A pretrial conference may be arranged by the parties involved in the case. It is an informal meeting among the attorneys, social workers, and sometimes other professionals at which the goals and objectives of the petitioner are discussed and the facts of the case are clarified. Assessments are made as to what issues remain in controversy, and the issues are narrowed for trial. For example, issues of privileged communication and confidentiality may be dealt with in advance of trial. Other evidentiary issues may be settled in advance of trial.

The pretrial conference is also a structured way to seek settlement short of contested trial. The matter could be dismissed, or the respondent could enter a plea to the petition as it stands, or some other negotiated settlement could be reached with possibilities limited only by the facts of the case and the imagination of the participants. Generally the parties are present, i.e., the parents and the child, if old enough, although they do not participate directly in the conference. Their presence allows the attorneys to confer with them and negotiate settlements or stipulations with full information from the clients and with their consultation and approval. Sometimes the judge or referee is present at parts of the conference to discuss procedural points and to clarify issues still in controversy.

The Trial

At trial the petitioner attorney for protective services must prove his allegations that the parents are legally neglectful of their child(ren). Most of the procedural steps up to this point have been in preparation for a full and fair presentation of the case to the judge (or the jury) with the respondent parents given a chance at trial to counter the allegations against them.

The question before the court is whether or not the child is an abused or neglected child under the state's statute. Does the state have a right to interfere in the privacy and freedom of these parents and this child? The state has such authority only if the petitioner proves that the facts alleged in the petition are true and that those facts constitute legal neglect according to that state's laws.

The following is not a comprehensive description of a trial but is presented as a broad outline of the basic elements.

Outline of a trial:

1. *Ascertain presence of proper parties.* Appearances are entered on the record by all counsel; all persons present in the courtroom are identified.

2. *Service.* The judge determines that notice of the proceedings has been properly served on all interested parties or that notice has been properly waived.

3. *Issues before the court are identified.* The allegations of the petition are read.

4. *Proceedings and legal rights are explained.* The nature of the proceedings is explained. Parties are asked if they understand the proceedings. If respondents do not have counsel, they are told of their right to counsel. Respondents are told of their right to have the matter heard by the judge or by a jury. Respondents and children are told of their right to remain silent and that any statement they make may be used against them.

5. *Opening statements.* All parties may present an opening statement to the court outlining the case that they will present and the witnesses they will call. This is an opportunity to familiarize the judge with the case so that he may better follow the testimony and see how it all relates together. Opening statement may be waived.

6. *Testimony.* Witnesses are sworn, their testimony is taken, and all other evidence is introduced. The order of examining all witnesses is generally as follows:

   a. *Direct examination.* In a question and answer format the witness's testimony is elicited by the attorney who called him.

b. *Cross-examination*. Other counsel has an opportunity to cross-examine the opposing witness.

c. *Redirect examination*. At the conclusion of cross-examination the attorney whose witness is on the stand has an opportunity to ask some additional questions on redirect.

d. *Recross-examination*. Other counsel has an opportunity to ask additional questions of the witness on recross.

e. *Questions by the judge*. Finally the judge may ask questions of the witness.

f. The witness is then excused by the judge.

7. *Objections*. During examination of witnesses and presentation of other evidence, opposing attorneys may object on a variety of legal grounds generally based on a failure to comply with the rules of evidence. The judge will allow the objecting attorney to state his objection and the grounds for it, will then hear arguments from the counsel objected against, and will rule on the objection. The trial will then proceed. Unless an evidentiary objection is made at trial, it generally cannot be raised again on appeal.

8. *Petitioner's case*. The petitioner, through his attorney, calls the first witnesses and presents all his evidence first.

9. *Respondent's case*. The respondents, through their attorney, present their case next. They need not present a defense, nor need they take the witness stand. Often the respondent's attorney will make a motion to dismiss or a motion for directed verdict asking the court to dismiss the petition on the grounds that the petitioner did not prove a prima facie case in support of the petition. After presenting their case, the respondents rest.

10. *Findings and order*. The court decides whether it has jurisdiction. Are the facts as alleged true? If so, do they bring the child within the statute?

Disposition

At disposition the court formally addresses the question "What shall we do to protect and help this child and his family?" If the court decides that it has the power to act on behalf of a certain child, the court then considers what orders shall be entered to deal with the unfitness of the child's home environment.

The court will ordinarily not hear testimony on disposition of a case until after jurisdiction is formally taken, i.e., until the court decides it has the power to act. In most jurisdictions the proofs at disposition need not meet the standards of the formal rules of evidence, meaning that written reports and other hearsay evidence may be admitted as long as the evidence is reliable. Sometimes the court considers disposition immediately following adjudication (the trial), and sometimes the court adjourns the proceedings to another date for dispositional hearing.

The dispositional orders should be reasonably specific as to where the child is to be placed, what treatment plan is to be in place, the expectations of the parents, and the expectations of the various agencies and professionals involved with the family. The dispositional orders generally set time for future court review.

If settlement and agreement are reached among the parties, a dispositional order might be negotiated and entered by the court with all parties consenting to it. Negotiation can short-cut the formal requirements of trial if the respondents either admit the allegations of the petition or consent to court authority by not contesting the petition.

The dispositional orders provide the parents with notice of what is expected of them before their child may be returned or before in-home court supervision of their childrearing will cease. The parents are given an opportunity to cure and correct the problems that prompted state intervention in the first place.

In subsequent review hearings the court will demand to know not only what the parents have done for themselves to reestablish a home for their child but also what the social agency has done. In anticipation of the court holding the agencies and other professionals accountable, the social worker generally should document the social treatment plan and share written copies with the parents, the attorneys, and all treating and helping professionals involved in the case. The plan should specify what the parents are to do and when, and what others will do and when.

Termination of Parental Rights

The Critical Social Work Decision

The ideal for every child placed in foster care is a return to live permanently with his natural parents. Unfortunately, that ideal is not met for about 15 percent of children placed in foster care. Of every 100 foster children past experience tells us that 15 will remain permanently outside their natural parents' home. The social worker responsible for a case should continuously assess the potential of the family, and after six months of case work should attempt to decide whether to pursue termination of parental rights or some other out-of-home plan or to press for return of the child home. That decision point for the social worker is critical. Shall he become an advocate for terminating the parental rights of the parents? Shall he become an advocate for return of the child home? The easy position is to wait, to temporize. However, because of the instability of foster care placements, to temporize or wait and see may be the worst thing for the child. Since permanency is generally critical to a child's development, often it is more important for the child that a decision be made than what the decision actually is. At this critical point considerable information must be brought to bear.

It is essential that a structured treatment program (case plan) for the family be established early and that the foster care worker and other professionals do everything possible to accomplish the goals of that program. It is essential that the case plan provide the parents with clear notice, preferably in writing, of (1) what they should accomplish, (2) how they should accomplish it, and (3) who will assist them in accomplishing the goals. It is important that the duties of the various treatment professionals be reasonably clear and that a division of responsibility among them have taken place. The parents should be provided ample opportunity to participate in the structured treatment plan and to achieve the goals set forth and should understand the consequences of their failure. Expert evaluations may be done in anticipation of the critical decision whether to ask the court for termination of parental rights or not. The decision making should best be shared among all the professionals working with the family, even though the court-authorized social agency supervising the case has the final responsibility. It is assumed that a careful record has been kept of the implementation of the treatment plan.

THE TERMINATION OF PARENTAL RIGHTS PETITION

In most states, termination of parental rights may be sought at the initial court proceedings regarding a child as long as prior notice of possible termination is given. Apart from abandonment cases and cases where the parents are clearly abusive and unworkable, the more common occurrence is for the child to be made a temporary court ward and for some efforts to be made to correct the problems in the home environment. Following a period of working with the family, either the child should be returned home or termination of parental rights should be sought.

The states' standards for termination of parental rights vary somewhat. The standard is generally more restrictive than the standard for temporary court jurisdiction, just as the temporary court jurisdiction standard is tougher, more restrictive, than the standard for what cases need be reported.

Typically a new petition requesting termination of parental rights and stating the factual and legal basis for it is filed by the social worker. The procedures outlined above apply to termination proceedings except that the parents are given clear notice that permanent termination of their parental rights is being sought.

If a termination case is successful, a child is typically placed for adoption or sometimes in a permanent arrangement such as guardianship or foster care.

Appeals

If any party, including parent, child, or state, feels that he has not been treated fairly by the court or feels that some error of fact or law was made by the judge, he may appeal. In an appeal one presents reasons to a higher court to show that the lower court made an error on the law or on the evaluation of facts. The appellate courts generally defer to the lower court on evaluations of what facts were true or not but are more likely to consider and overturn a lower court on errors of law.

The right to appeal and thereby hold the lower court accountable for its actions is an important due-process right. That right, however, often extracts a cost from the child involved and his parents. Appeals often take one to two years or longer to complete. Children otherwise available for adoption have to wait, often in temporary foster homes, until the appeal has finally been decided. Parents, who may eventually regain custody of the child, may be deprived of that custody for long periods of time. At the end of the appeal children may be returned to their natural families. However, it is more likely that after appeals the child will remain under the court jurisdiction or be placed for adoption after all.

Social workers and others may reduce the negative effects of appeals on children by planning foster placements which may mature into adoptive homes or permanent homes once the appeals have run their course. The worker must be perfectly candid to the foster parents about the legal unavailability of a child for adoption and the uncertainties of the appeal process. Such placement planning, however, makes it less likely that a young child will have to be separated repeatedly from his psychological parents.

Notes

1. Caffey, "Multiple Fractures in the Long Bones of Children Suffering from Chronic Subdural Hematoma."
2. Kempe, Silverman, Steele, Droegemueller, and Silver, "The Battered Child Syndrome."
3. Shepard, "The Abused Child and the Law," pp. 182–184.
4. U.S. Dept. of Health, Education, and Welfare, Children's Bureau, *Model Child Protection Act with Commentary.*
5. Ibid.
6. DHEW, Children's Bureau, *op. cit.* Sussman, "Reporting Child Abuse: A Review of the Literature."
7. Sussman, *Ibid.*, p. 249.
8. National Directory of Child Abuse Services and Information, 1974.
9. Katz et al., "Child Neglect Laws in America."
10. 45 Code of Federal Regulations Part 231.1. See also Michigan Compiled Laws, 722.622.
11. Institute of Judicial Administration-American Bar Association, Juvenile Justice Standards Project, *Abuse and Neglect* [Cited below as IJA-ABA Standards], p. 65. DHEW, Children's Bureau, *op. cit.*
12. Besharov, *Juvenile Justice Advocacy, Practicing Law Institute*, p. 120. Sussman, *op. cit., supra* note 6, p. 285. DHEW, Children's Bureau, *op. cit.*
13. Sussman, *Ibid.*
14. DHEW, Children's Bureau, *op. cit.*, p. 40.
15. Sussman, *op. cit., supra* note 6, p. 279.
16. DHEW, Children's Bureau, *op. cit.*, p. 19.
17. DHEW, Children's Bureau, *op. cit.*, p. 89.
18. IJA-ABA Standards, *op. cit.*, p. 68; the attorney-client privilege is generally preserved except in the reporting statutes of Alabama, Massachusetts, and Nevada.
19. DHEW, Children's Bureau, *op. cit.*, p. 21; Michigan Compiled Laws, 722.626(2).
20. IJA-ABA Standards, *op. cit.*, p. 77.
21. DHEW, Children's Bureau, *op. cit.*, p. 74.
22. *Ibid.*, p. 23.
23. DeFrancis and Lucht, *Child Abuse Legislation in the 1970's*, p. 15.
24. DHEW, Children's Bureau, *op. cit.*, p. 24.
25. *Roe v. Conn* 417 F. Supp 769 (M.D. Ala, 1976).
26. IJA-ABA Standards, *op. cit.*, pp. 78–81.
27. Excerpts from Michigan Compiled Laws Annotated 712A.2.

PART V

Special Issues

11

Sexual Abuse

Kathleen Coulborn Faller

Introduction

Social workers are likely to encounter sexual abuse in a variety of contexts. A worker may discover that in a family referred for other problems there has been sexual abuse. For instance, the family might be referred for alcoholism, a prevalent condition in families where there is sexual abuse, or for marital discord, usually present where there has been incest. Children presenting with unusual sexual behavior, emotional problems, and school failure may be having these difficulties because of a sexual encounter or encounters. Adolescent acting-out behavior, such as promiscuity, drug abuse, and prostitution, may occur as a consequence of sexual abuse. Or adolescent suicide may be related to sexual abuse. Finally, adults who present with sexual dysfunction, homosexuality, or other problems in functioning may have been sexually abused as children.

In other instances children may seek the help of a professional, alleging sexual abuse. In such cases children should be believed, even though the perpetrator denies the abuse. Alternatively, protective services may refer a sexually abusive family to a social worker for treatment, or the referral may come from the court. Thus it is important to be aware from the diagnostic viewpoint that sexual abuse may present itself in many forms, and social workers will benefit from knowledge about the problem because they may need to provide treatment.

Scope of the Problem

What Is Sexual Abuse?

It is physical contact between persons at different stages of development (usually an adult and a child) for the purpose of the sexual gratification of the more mature person. While the encounter may have other functions aside from sexual, as an exercise of power of one person over another or an interaction which is humiliating to both parties involved, it is first of all a sexual act.

Within the general definition, there are several subcategories of behavior one needs to be aware of. The first is *sexual contact or fondling* of one or both participants' intimate parts. Intimate parts include the penis, vagina, pelvic area, buttocks, anus, and breasts. Fondling may be fondling of the victim by the perpetrator, or the perpetrator may induce the victim to fondle him/her (the perpetrator).

Second, there is *oral-genital* contact (fellatio, cunnilingus). Again the perpetrator may stimulate the victim's genitals by sucking or licking or may persuade or force the victim to so stimulate the perpetrator, or both.

The third category is *sexual intercourse.*

The fourth category includes *any other intrusion*, however slight, into the child's body. Anal intercourse falls within this category. So do the use of the child's armpit for sexual gratification and interfemoral intercourse (placing the penis between the child's legs).

How Extensive Is the Problem of Sexual Abuse?

The problem of sexual abuse is probably not increasing. We are becoming aware of greater numbers of cases because of new reporting laws for abuse and neglect, which include sexual abuse, and because of an increased emphasis upon the importance of reporting. Yet we still can only estimate the prevalence of the problem. One figure we have comes from the *National Analysis of Official Child Abuse and Neglect Reporting*, (compiled by the American Humane Association), which had 6,087 cases reported to it in 1978.[1] We can be well assured that this is only the "tip of the iceberg" and that the real incidence is much higher. This assertion is supported by a recent study of students at six New England colleges and universities. Students were asked about their sexual experiences with adults while they were children; 19.2 percent of women and 8.2 percent of men reported having been sexually victimized as children.[2] In 75 to 85 percent of reports of sexual abuse the victim is female the abuser is male.[3] Mother–son incest is the least common type of sexual abuse reported. Therefore one of the limitations of our discussion of sexual abuse is that most of the information available is about situations between adult men and girls, and more specifically about father-daughter incest.

Where the victim is female, the encounters are likely to be heterosexual and the two parties are likely to be related. In contrast, when the victim is male, the relationship is more likely to be homosexual and to involve nonrelatives. The average age of female victims is around ten; males are slightly older, around eleven.[4]

Configurations of Sexual Abuse

There are many ways to categorize sexual abuse. It is important for our purposes to use a classification system which includes the range of configurations a social worker is likely to see in practice.

Sexual assault is the term used when the perpetrator is not related by blood to the victim. It includes situations of rape as well as ones where force is not used and actual intercourse does not occur. The perpetrator may be a complete stranger, someone the child recognized but does not know well, a friend of the family, or someone actually living in the household but not related to the child (such as mother's boyfriend).

Incest is the term used when the victim and perpetrator are related by blood. The perpetrator may come from within the nuclear family or be a member of the extended family.

The technical distinctions between incest and assault are useful guidelines for the beginning of the diagnostic process. However, the more essential diagnostic issue is the closeness, or intimacy, of the relationship between the perpetrator and the victim. Determining this will be much more important in social work intervention. This intimacy has implications for the psychological impact of the encounter, the way in which the relationship develops, how long it persists and how frequently sexual contact occurs, whether force is used, and the response of the victim and of the family to it. One might think of configurations of sexual abuse as representing a continuum of relationships based upon the degree of intimacy between victim and perpetrator.

At one end is what one customarily thinks of as assault. That is a single encounter with a stranger, where there is no forewarning, and force may well be used. The child is likely to tell her parents right after it happens, and they in turn will respond appropriately, taking the child to the hospital, reporting the incident to the police, and seeking mental health treatment for the child if this is seen as necessary.

At the other end of the continuum is the *classical* incestuous relationship. These are sexual encounters involving natural fathers and daughters. In contrast with assault, the relationship evolves gradually, beginning with appropriate affectionate interaction which becomes sexualized. The behavior is likely to progress from the adult fondling the child, to mutual masturbation, perhaps then to oral-genital contact or interfemoral intercourse, and may never involve full genital intercourse. Force is usually not used, although the father may bribe the child or use other inducements. Sometimes these relationships begin in early childhood and continue until adolescence. Sexual contact may occur as often as once or twice a week. The child may be persuaded by the father not to tell. If she does tell her mother, the mother's response may not be appropriate. That is, the mother may fail to support the child and may blame the child, sometimes will refuse to believe the child, or may not seek treatment for the child or report the relationship to professionals. It is not uncommon for the relationship to come to light only during adolescence when the child refuses to continue involvement because she wishes to establish relationships with peers, and often as an older child rebels, a younger child or children are socialized by the father into sexual activity.

Between typical assault and classical incest there is a wide range of configurations of sexual abuse. In general, one finds that the relationships evolve more gradually and are of longer duration than in assault but less so than in incest. Force is less likely to be used than in assault but is a factor more often than in incest. Families will be less appropriate in their response to discovery than in assault but more appropriate than in incest. An important characteristic of these relationships is that the incest taboo either does not exist or is attenuated. Further, as a rule, the perpetrators are less deviant in their functioning than in either classical incest or rape. It also appears that the encounters tend to be less damaging to the victim than those at the two ends of the continuum. The reason for this is that incest and assault are characterized by different factors associated with pyschological damage. In cases of incest, damage results because the adult in normal circumstances would be a trusted person whose responsibility is to protect the child, not to exploit her. Force, a second factor associated with trauma,[5] is likely to be used in assault.

There are a number of commonly identified configurations falling between the incest and assault ends of the continuum to which professionals should be alert. One is a situation in which the perpetrator is a stepfather or mother's boyfriend. It appears that such unrelated individuals are at higher risk for sexual abuse than are natural fathers. However, it is not uncommon to find in situations where stepfathers or boyfriends abuse that the natural father was quite deviant and may also have been sexually abusive. Mothers in such families tend ot be stronger than mothers in cases of classical incest. This is demonstrated by the fact that they have been able to put the first husband out of the home or divorce him. However, frequently they choose subsequent partners similar to their first. Nevertheless, one may be able to see mothers in these circumstances over time seeking more appropriate partners and learning from earlier mistakes.

In cases where daughters were initially socialized into sexual relationships by their fathers, the sexual molestation by later partners of the mother is initiated quite quickly. One may find that the mother's new partner appears to be consort to both mother and daughter, and there may be a great deal of jealousy and competition for his attention between mother and daughter.[6]

Another common configuration is one where there is an ineffectual young man, either in adolescence or early twenties, and a fairly young victim. The perpetrator may be related or not, a cousin or uncle or a babysitter or family friend. Typically the abuser experiences heightened sexual drive, characteristic of this developmental stage for men. Yet he feels too inadequate to attempt a relationship with someone his own age. Thus he initiates sexual encounters with young children, usually heterosexual but sometimes homosexual.

Finally, a fairly frequent type of sexual abuse is one involving an older abuser, a grandfather or aged uncle or occasionally someone unrelated to the victim or victims. The old man usually engages in behaviors other than intercourse, such as fondling or oral-genital contact. He may well be physiologically impotent, and his wife or partner may be deceased or may have long since ceased having sexual relations with the abuser. Victims can be of either sex. Sometimes these old men have past histories of sexual aberration, sometimes not. Families attempt to control this deviant behavior in a number of ways. They may instruct children never to be alone with the abuser or never to let him touch them. Adults in the family may also take the responsibility of seeing to it that the perpetrator is never alone with young children. In addition, occasionally the family will place the old man in a nursing home or sheltered living situation even though he does not need institutional placement.[7]

Child–child sexual behavior deserves separate consideration. What will be said applies both to incestuous relationships between children and encounters between children who are not related. For the most part, this behavior should be classified as sexual experimentation and is developmentally normal. While we can accept four-year-olds playing "doctor" and "I'll show you mine if you'll show me yours," we have greater difficulty with ten- or twelve-year-olds attempting intercourse. While such experimentation should not be encouraged, it is important not to overreact. Rather, the meaning of such intimacy should be communicated to the children involved. If sexual experimentation is harshly punished, the participants may have difficulty with sexual performance later.

There are some guidelines that can help the professional and the parent determine when child-child sexual behavior is problematic. If there is a large age or large developmental differential between the two participants, there is cause for concern. If, for example, a thirteen-year-old boy attempts intercourse with a five-year-old girl, then the boy has a considerable power advantage over the girl and this is deviant behavior. Second, one should be concerned if force is used. Finally, if the relationship is so consuming that the participants do not engage in developmentally normal relationships, particularly peer relationships, then it should be regarded as problematic. Even so, such encounters should not be handled as other sexual abuse cases.

Further Differential Diagnosis for the Purposes of Case Planning

In addition to determining where a case falls upon the incest-assault continuum, it is possible to categorize cases in a way which will further refine intervention strategy. While these categories will be mainly applicable to incest cases, they will also have utility with some assault cases. Decisions which need to be made are whether the behavior can be stopped; whether the child can remain in the home or must be removed; whether the perpetrator should be allowed to stay at home or should leave, through criminal prosecution or in another way; what the prognosis for successful treatment is; and what combinations of people should be seen in treatment.

1. First, a small percentage of cases fall into three fairly easily recognizable categories. One is what we shall call the *polymorphous family*. This is a family where many or even all of the family relationships are sexualized. That is, there is likely to be father-daughter incest involving all daughters; there is usually mother-son incest; sometimes sexual relationships between siblings; there may be homosexual as well as heterosexual liaisons; and the encounters may extend beyond the nuclear family to other relatives. Relationships may be transitory and shifting, there may be sexual encounters involving several people, or dyads may be fixed, with unstated rules about who may and may not be involved. The polymorphous family is fairly rare, but needless to say, it makes a rather striking impact upon the professional community where it is discovered. These families may justify their in-

cestuous behavior with some sort of ideological underpinning. They are also extremely difficult to treat because there are so many relationships to be broken up and because there is pervasive, often overt support of the appropriateness of the sexual behavior within the family. That treatment can be successful is very unlikely. Therefore, probably the most efficacious intervention is to remove young children who have been molested and find permanent substitute homes for them.

2. A second type of case is one where either the victim or the perpetrator is *mentally retarded*. In such cases the degree of retardation and other functioning will need to be assessed by a psychologist and a plan made accordingly. However, as a general rule, the behavior is likely to continue if the opportunity is there. Consequently, if one wants to stop the sexual abuse, the retarded person will need fairly constant supervision or to be placed in a sheltered setting. Thus separation of the family may be necessary.

3. A third category is the family with a *perpetrator who is psychotic* and has some delusions which support sexual involvement with the victim. Two factors must be assessed: whether the psychosis is chronic or acute and whether the condition will respond to medication (including whether the perpetrator will take the medication). If the psychosis is acute and responds to medication, it will usually be possible to keep the family together and provide treatment. If this is not the case, the psychotic must be hospitalized and treated. If his response is not good, then the family should probably be encouraged to separate the child from him.[8]

These three categories of sexual abuse probably represent a minority of cases. Most of the remainder of incest cases have some general dynamics in common. I shall describe these and then discuss how to differentiate workable from unworkable cases.

4. It is well known that incest is a family affair, not merely a situation of a father who molests his daughter. (Again I should emphasize that the relationship we have a fair knowledge of is father-daughter incest.) We find particular role relationships among mother, father, and daughter, which have led to the sexual behavior between father and daughter.

With respect to *mother*, we find that she usually has abdicated her sexual role responsibilities. The sexual relationship between her and the father is either nonexistent or devoid of any emotional quality. This may be because mother does not enjoy sex, is overwhelmed by many children, and/or fears conceiving subsequent ones, or was herself sexually abused as a child and thus is "programmed" to facilitate the same interrelationships in her own family.

In addition, however, she has usually abdicted some or all of her maternal role responsibilities. That is, she may no longer do such household tasks as fixing the meals, doing the dishes, and cleaning the house. Further, child care responsibilities such as getting children up for school, feeding the children, and supervising them may not be fulfilled by her.

Sometimes mothers in incestuous families are very immature and role reversal takes place between them and the victims. Others lack any real interest in what goes on in the family, including an interest in its affective and sexual activity. Still other mothers are physically or mentally incapacitated, so that they may be there in body but are functionally absent. Finally, in some cases of father-daughter incest mothers have deserted the family or died, or there is a divorce with the father awarded custody. In this kind of case the family is usually geographically or socially isolated so that there is no one outside the family who comes in and takes over maternal duties.

What are the characteristics of *daughters* in incestuous families? Typically as mother abandons responsibilities, daughters take them on. Thus not only is the daughter the sexual partner of the father, but also she does the household and child care tasks in the family. She is often called a "parental child." Such daughters often appear very sexual and seductive. It is important to bear in mind that they have been socialized to relate in a sexual way, and are often unaware of the image they present.

Finally, what are the characteristics unique to the *father* in the incestuous family? He tends to be a man with low self-esteem. Often he does not function very well in the world outside his family and expects to get all of his needs satisfied within the family. He looks to the family as the arena in which to exert dominance and control as well as to receive nurturance. Thus often he is a tyrant at home, exerting his authority in sexual and other areas. When his relationship with his wife does not satisfy his need for nurturance, he turns to his daughter. Because of his feelings of low self-esteem, he does not pursue a relationship with another adult woman outside the family.[9]

Within these general dynamics there is considerable variability in how pathological the family is. One of the consequences of increased concern and new reporting legislation for child abuse and neglect, including sexual abuse in most states, is that we are becoming aware of a much broader range of sexual abuse cases. Previously only grossly pathological families came to professional attention. A good number of cases uncovered more recently look to the outside world like model families. Others seem to have considerable strengths as well as difficulties.

There are dimensions of both mother's functioning and father's functioning which are key factors in diagnosing the degree of family pathology and determining prognosis for treatment. For mother, they are the extent of her dependence upon father, how collusive she was in the sexual abuse, and her affective relationship with the victim and other children. For father, dimensions to be assessed are how much guilt he feels regarding the sexual abuse and how he functions in other areas of life.

The importance of dependence in perpetrating incest is borne out by a study conducted by the American Humane Association comparing families of victims of incest to those of victims of rape. It found mothers of incest victims to have married earlier, to have larger families, and to be less likely to have worked outside the home. The more dependent the mother is on the father, the less likely she will be able (and willing) to change the incestuous family system. Independence in the economic sphere is suggested by working outside the home, having worked in the past, having a marketable skill, or being the grantee for public assistance. Economic independence has a key practical role to play because when the dust settles, the mother may well have to support herself and her family. Other indicators of independence are mother's capacity to confront the father, to disagree with him, to do things despite his objection, and to support the children against his wishes.

The issue of collusion of the mother is one which must be assessed, but it is also one which is commonly misunderstood. As a rule mothers do not actively connive in the seduction of their daughters. Most of the collusion that occurs is on an *unconscious* level. Thus when mothers state at the time of discovery that they did not know about the sexual abuse, they are quite often telling the truth. What must be examined is their response to clear indications of the incest. The more collusive they are at this point, the less good the prognosis is for treating the family intact. This list is of some possible maternal responses to discovery, beginning with most collusive and ending in least collusive:

1. Mother observes the sexual behavior and actively encourages it.
2. Mother observes the behavior and acts as though she has not, perhaps walks out of the room.
3. Victim reports the abuse; mother accuses her of being a liar, having a dirty mind, etc.
4. Victim reports; mother tells her to avoid the perpetrator but not to tell anyone.
5. Victim reports; mother confronts perpetrator; he denies; and mother believes perpetrator.

6. After confrontation, mother initially sides with daughter, believing her and supporting her, but subsequently sides with the father.
7. Upon discovery (seeing or report) mother supports daughter; mother calls protective services or police and throws father out, insists that he get treatment or gets a divorce; she sticks to her decision once it is made.

The final area of maternal functioning to be assessed is the extent to which she loves her children. If a mother is cold and rejecting of the victim, views the victim as responsible and culpable, and/or is jealous of and in competition with the victim, then chances are not good that the mother will be protective. Frequently, if at the time of discovery the victim is an adolescent, the relationship between the mother and daughter has deteriorated to a considerable degree. Often, however, the discovery of the incest will evoke maternal protective feelings which can be capitalized upon, and the mother will be useful in protecting the child.

The two dimensions in the father's coping which must be examined are his functioning in other areas than sexual and the extent to which he feels guilty about the sexual behavior. Questions to be asked are as follows: Is he employed or unemployed? Does he support his family or spend his income without regard for their need? Does he appear to genuinely care about his family, or is he a wife abuser and a child abuser as well as a molester? Is he regarded by the community as an upstanding citizen, or does he get into difficulties outside the home, and has he been in trouble with the law? Does he have a substance abuse problem? The better his general functioning, the more likely intervention is to be successful.

In terms of guilt, the prognosis for the family is improved if the father feels guilty. Suicidal fathers and those who describe the sexual behavior as an act of self-humiliation are likely to respond to treatment. In contrast, if the father rationalizes the behavior or discounts its importance, the situation is less promising. Thus if he makes a statement that his daughter seduced him or that it was only for sex education or that it was not really sexual abuse because no penetration took place, he is not accepting responsibility for his own behavior.

Fathers who experience no guilt (and they also usually malfunction in many other areas) are psychopaths or sociopaths. There is very little hope that they will respond to intervention. Therefore they should be removed from the home. If the mother appears to have a good relationship with the children, responded appropriately to discovery of the behavior, and has the capability to function independently, then the mother-children grouping should be offered treatment. However, if there is a psychopathic father and a cold, collusive, dependent mother, the victim (and probably other children) should be removed permanently.

If the father is appropriate, that is, feels guilty and functions reasonably well, but the mother is hostile toward the victim, collusive, and dependent, an attempt should be made initially to work with the mother to see if she will protect the victim. Concurrent work should be done with the couple. If mother will not change to protect the child, then at least temporary removal of the child is indicated and perhaps permanent removal, depending upon response to treatment. When both parents are appropriate, treatment should be provided. Usually it is not necessary to remove the victim from the home.

	Father	
Mother	*Psychopath*	*Not a Psychopath*
Dependent, cold, collusive	Remove children, terminate parental contact	Work with mother, treatment to parents
Independent, loves kids, reacts appropriately	Remove father, treatment for mother and children	Treatment of the family, children in home

This formula looks clear-cut and straightforward. Unfortunately it is not so easy to categorize a real family, particularly if one is making a decision on an emergency basis. Many fathers feel only somewhat guilty and have some areas of life where they malfunction. Further, guilt may be difficult to assess because the father denies having done the sexual abuse. Mothers may appear ambivalent about the victim, or they may assert they are not dependent when the spouse is absent but behave differently when he is there. Or mothers may love their children but nevertheless be dependent, or they may be cold toward the children but independent.

In these mixed and uncertain cases, the worker should first be sure the child is protected and then try treatment and carefully assess its impact. Time limitations should be placed on how long therapy should be tried, and court intervention should be used as necessary to facilitate treatment goals.

Intervention Techniques

We are just learning about the treatment of sexual abuse, and there is some controversy about what the best approach is. Again, we need to differentiate among types of sexual abuse.

Sexual Assault

As a rule, sexual assault is much easier to treat than incest, and in many cases the intervention may be provided by the parents. The need for professional help is indicated if there have been several incidents, if the encounter(s) involved force and physical trauma, if the child shows some emotional disturbance subsequently, or if the parents seem unusually upset about what has transpired.

The basic approach is a supportive case-work one. The child is encouraged to ventilate feelings about what has occurred and to express any fears or worries she may have. Frequently the child may feel ruined or damaged, or that she is responsible for the incident(s). The encounter(s) may raise some concerns about sexuality which ordinarily would not surface until a later time in the child's development. In general, the child needs to be reassured that she is not damaged, and needs to be helped to understand that what happened was not her fault so as to counter guilt feelings. Some sex education may be indicated, but within the child's capacity to understand. It is important to avoid equating the sexual assault with ordinary sexual behavior.

Obviously the child also needs to be protected. Therefore if the perpetrator is known, the child should not be exposed unsupervised to that person again. The perpetrator should also be gotten into treatment if he is known. Many people are presently advocating the use of or threat of criminal court prosecution to get the perpetrator into treatment. (Because the perpetrator is not the child's parent or caretaker in situations of sexual assault, as a rule he cannot be brought into juvenile court under the child protection law and juvenile code. Rather, if court intervention against him is sought, it must be in the adult court alleging criminal sexual conduct or sexual assault.)

The final step in treating the victim of sexual assault is to have the child gradually resume her ordinary daily activities—which are usually curtailed after a sexual abuse incident. The treatment of the victim shortly after the incident is extremely important in forestalling later sexual problems. Parents may also need supportive counseling because of the incident.

Incest

The treatment of incest is more difficult than that of sexual assault.

SAFEGUARDING THE CHILD

With incest, the first task is generally to ensure that the sexual behavior stops. (There is still some controversy about the priority of absolute, immediate cessation, but in general it is seen as important.) This can be achieved in a variety of ways. The method which provides greatest certainty is removal of either the victim or the perpetrator. Both of these solutions dramatically disrupt the family and therefore should be carefully considered and weighed against less radical alternatives.

Removal of the child is legally the simplest, requiring only a court order in the juvenile court at an emergency or preliminary hearing. If the child wants to be placed, this should be done. However, removal may in many cases be quite traumatic for the child; it may be perceived as punishment; the child may miss her family; and she may have difficulty adjusting to foster placement. Further, the family may close ranks against the victim in her absence.

It is less traumatic for the father to be out of the home than for the child. However, this is more problematic to achieve legally. It can be done at the adjudicatory stage only in the juvenile court, that is, after the case has been proven. If there is enough evidence, the criminal court might be used and the father arrested and detained at least temporarily prior to trial. Sometimes a voluntary agreement can be obtained that the father will temporarily reside elsewhere. However, such an arrangement is likely to be unstable because of the mother's potentially ambivalent feelings about choosing the children over the father. The mother may allow the father to return because she is financially and emotionally dependent upon him.

A third strategy for protecting the child is to have someone else move into the household. This is especially feasible when the incest developed because the mother was incapacitated or there was no mother present. This person might be a relative or a homemaker.

Fourth, a strategy which holds promise is improving the mother–daughter relationship so that the mother accepts the responsibility of protecting the child. Although this may be difficult to do because of the hostility and ambivalence in the relationship, it is the only strategy which is likely to have long-term effects (more specific discussion is provided later in the chapter in the section "Treatment Techniques").

Lastly, there may be some purely logistical maneuvers that will ensure the child's safety. For example, if the victim is sleeping somewhere which is particularly accessible to the father, she might be moved somewhere inaccessible. Frequently in evaluating these families, one finds parents do not sleep together, or mother goes to bed many hours earlier or later than the father. A goal in such a situation would be to get them sleeping together or in bed at the same time.

The Issue of Court Involvement

In the treatment of incest, one of the controversies is whether and how the court should be involved. Some professionals believe that incestuous fathers need to be prosecuted criminally in order to force them into treatment. Others believe that criminal or even juvenile court prosecution serves only to alienate and, in many cases, dissolve the family and should be avoided.

The courts should be used when safeguarding of the child and treatment cannot be brought about without court intervention. The categorization of families done earlier should offer further guidelines concerning the need for coercion. The course of action is fairly straightforward with polymorphous families and those where there is a mentally retarded individual or a psychotic perpetrator. As a rule, children should be removed permanently in polymorphous families, and the court can be used to institutionalize both retarded and psychotic persons as needed. With cases where the father is clearly psychopathic and the mother is unworkable, the court should be involved to remove the children and terminate parental rights, and where the father is psychopathic but the mother fairly appropriate, the best course may be criminal prosecution of the father. On the other hand, if the family is willing to engage in treatment, the court should not be involved (unless it is necessary to go into the juvenile court to temporarily remove the child).

With cases where the family is denying the incest or resisting treatment or there is a question about how deviant the father and mother are, a useful strategy is to escalate coercive intervention gradually. Thus if urging does not get the family into treatment, juvenile court action might be threatened. If the threat is not successful, one can then petition in the juvenile court. One might ask the judge to order the father out of the home until the family is meaningfully engaged in treatment. Criminal court procedures can be used similarly, first as a threat, to be carried out if needed. Some criminal court judges will order treatment rather than a jail sentence. Throughout the process, the professionals involved should assess the family's response to the court pressure and whether any progress is made in therapy if they become involved. Clearly in situations that do not improve, permanent separation will need to be sought. In the juvenile court this would involve seeking termination of parental rights. In the criminal court it might involve allowing the perpetrator to be sentenced to prison.

TREATMENT TECHNIQUES

Professionals do not agree about what kind of treatment is indicated in cases of incest. Some people think that family therapy is the appropriate intervention, working on the other problems in family functioning as well as the incest.[10] Others[11] feel that members of the incestuous family must be treated individually and in dyads before they are ready for family treatment. Still other programs for the treatment of incest have available to them a range of possible treatments and prescribe what seems appropriate to the individual family.[12] For example, a program would have available individual therapy, marital treatment, family therapy, group therapy, perhaps separate groups for perpetrator's, victims, and mothers, sex education, parenting training, and substance abuse treatment. A recent innovation is the development of self-help Alcoholics Anonymous-type groups, called Parents United, for sexual abusers, as well as groups for other family members.[13]

These specialized programs for the treatment of sexual abuse are the exceptions rather than the rule in most American communities. Workers usually have to rely on local voluntary and public agencies to provide treatment for these families. For practitioners placed in this situation, there are some guidelines for treating incest cases.

First, with cases except those where the father is psychopathic, discovery is likely to lead to at least a temporary cessation of the sexual behavior. Therefore the therapist has some breathing space. However, unless some basic changes occur in family structure, the problem is likely to recur.

Second, the perpetrator should not be the only person who receives treatment. Incest is a family problem and cannot be safely treated merely with therapy for the perpetrator. With such an approach, a distressfully common scenario is as follows: The father insists to the therapist (who may never have met the family) that the sexual abuse did not occur. Sessions pass with much frustration for the therapist because of the father's denial. Eventually the therapist moves on to other problem areas the father will address, which are likely to be numerous enough, and the incest is never really dealt with. During or shortly after the termination of the course of therapy, the incest resumes. Therefore, even in cases where the father gets individual treatment, other family members need help also so that they have a lifeline and someone to report to if the sexual abuse resumes.

A question often asked is whether sexual abuse can be treated without an admission. An admission is hoped for sometime in the course of therapy, and treatment is much more likely to be successful if all family members mutually acknowledge the incest behavior. Structural changes can be made in the family which will prevent future sexual abuse and resolve many family problems without a confession. Nevertheless, it is probably true that this treatment is incomplete, since a major issue is unresolved.

Another important question is, What type of treatment? My position is that progress can be made using many types of treatment and often using more than one approach concurrently or consecutively with a single family. Individuals who are part of a sexually abusive family can benefit from individual treatment. Dyads composed of husband and wife, mother and victim, or father and victim can profit from intervention. It is often useful to treat the children as a group, as well as to involve individuals in the family in group therapy. Further, family therapy can be of some considerable benefit.

The general goals of individual therapy in incest are to enhance the client's self-esteem, to allow for ventilation of feelings, and to help the person differentiate him/herself from the family. The first goal is pursued by being supportive, assuaging guilt feelings where appropriate, and helping the client engage in activities where he/she can gain a sense of competence. It is important for all members of the incestuous family to develop interests and lives separate from the family, as these families tend to be enmeshed. With adolescent girls, the fathers often do not allow them to date, to engage in extracurricular activities, or even to have girlfriends. Parents also often have no interests outside the family.

Working with the mother-daughter dyad may well be the most useful intervention which can be made. This is true regardless of whether the father remains in the home or is out. The mother-daughter relationship is frequently the most volatile relationship in the family. Victims often state they have greater animosity toward their mothers for not protecting them than toward their fathers for having abused them.

The first task of the therapist attempting to improve the mother-daughter relationship is to support the mother and encourage her to be the protector of the daughter. Aside from merely exhorting the mother to do this and appealing to her maternal sympathies for the victim, a useful strategy may be to emphasize that they both are victims; not only has the daughter been exploited, but often the father has physically harmed the mother and certainly he has emotionally harmed her. Emphasizing the strengths of mother and daughter to one another can also be a part of this strategy. Such an approach is most useful when the father has been excluded from the home.

Another strategy which can change the quality of this relationship is programming mother-daughter interactions so that the mother and daughter engage in activities together which are mutually enjoyable. Often by the time the sexual abuse surfaces, the mother and daughter are doing nothing together except fighting, and a series of positive encounters can have a dramatic impact. The worker may also have to mediate some of the conflicts between mother and daughter and see that solutions are arrived at.

Finally, it is appropriate to redistribute role responsibilities between mother and daughter, so that the daughter is no longer the "parental child." Often there is resistance to this, particularly by the daughter, because she enjoys having this control. Therefore, a good strategy may be to first take away from her those responsibilities she is most willing to give up, then to move into the ones she values more.

A second dyadic relationship where intervention can have a substantial impact is that of the husband and wife. If this relationship can be improved, the husband will no longer have the need for a quasi-adult interaction with the daughter. One of the goals of the therapist will be to make the bond between husband and wife more cohesive and create a generational boundary between this dyad and the children. This can be done by improving the parents' sexual relationship, by helping them to decide as a couple how to handle family problems and to resolve conflicts, and by facilitating their capability to spend time together without always having the children with them.

Third, aside from stopping the incestuous sexual interaction, there may be other changes which need to be made in the father-daughter relationship. Often prior to the discovery of the sexual abuse, the father has been overinvolved with and overcontrolling of the daughter. After discovery, they may well have no contact for a period of time. The task of the therapist is at least twofold: to assure that the daughter has age-appropriate privileges and autonomy and to program activities so that the father and daughter do things together that can rectify their relationship.

Further, it may be productive to have the daughter express her anger at having been abused to her father and to have him admit his guilt and accept responsibility for the sexual encounters.

Working with the children as a group is especially useful if several children in the family have been victims. In fact, often one of the things which comes out in such a group is that there is more than one victim. It can be helpful to have the support of other children in working through a victim's guilt feelings. Or nonvictims can become more empathic because they have witnessed the statements of victims. Nonvictims also absorb the therapist's assertion that children are not to blame. Further, a group approach can reidentify the "parental child" as a child and change that child's role. Other issues such as child-child disputes or child behavior problems can also be addressed in such a group.

Family therapy has considerable utility in sexual abuse but is especially crucial in families which remain intact or will be reunited. Often it is appropriate after smaller groupings within the family have already been engaged in treatment, or the issues mentioned for focus in smaller groupings can be dealt with in the family context. Some advantages of family therapy are as follows: First, it facilitates and improves communication in the family. Often in incestuous families there are many secrets never discussed openly. Second, treatment frequently moves more quickly in family therapy as opposed to other types of treatment. Against these advantages have to be weighed the problem of control and manageability. If the father is the tyrannical type of incestuous father, the therapist may get locked in an unproductive pitched battle with the father for control of the family. Such an encounter may usefully be avoided by first establishing alliances with individual family members. Further, if the family is a large one or the relationships are very volatile or both, the therapist may have difficulty making an impact upon the family if all members are initially together in therapy.

TRAINING

For communities trying to set up treatment programs for sexual abuse, training programs are now beginning to appear. A community might choose to send one or two people to such a program. Two such training programs are the Program in Human Sexuality, University of Minnesota, Minneapolis, Minnesota, and the Child Sexual Abuse Treatment Program in Santa Clara County, California. Skills and knowledge can also be acquired by reading, by attending less formal training, and by working on cases.

Notes

1. American Humane Association, *National Analysis of Child Abuse and Neglect Reporting*.
2. Finkelhor, *Sexual Victimization of Children*.
3. Schultz, *The Sexual Victimology of Youth*.
4. Finkelhor, *op cit*.
5. *Ibid*.
6. The author has assessed or treated over a dozen such cases in the last four years.
7. Again, the author has seen a number of such cases and had discussions with other professionals with similar experiences.
8. See Summit and Kryso, "Sexual Abuse of Children: A Clinical Spectrum," p. 237, and Bagley, "Incest Behavior—the Incest Taboo," pp. 505–19, for further discussion of categories of sexual abuse.
9. DeFrancis, *Child Victims of Incest*.
10. Garrietto, "Humanistic Treatment of Father-Daughter Incest."

11. For example, the Sexual Abuse Treatment unit at Children's Aid Society in Wayne County, Detroit, Michigan.
12. Zaphiris, *Incest: The Family with Two Known Victims*.
13. For example, the University of Minnesota's Program in Human Sexuality, Minneapolis, Minn.
14. Garrietto, "Sexual Victimization of Children; Trauma, Trial, and Treatment."

12

Abuse and Neglect: The Adolescent as Hidden Victim

Marjorie Ziefert

Introduction

The abused and neglected adolescent has been overlooked both in the child abuse and neglect literature and in the development of appropriate treatment services. Although the past decade has witnessed a growing literature in the area of abuse and neglect (Helfer and Kempe, 1976; Martin, 1976), there has been little if any reference to the plight of teenagers who are the victims of familial violence and neglect. Adolescents in need have historically fallen between the service "cracks" in most of our human service agencies. Not yet adults and no longer children, adolescents have the needs of both and the status of neither. And many communities, social service agencies, and juvenile authorities clearly have failed to define necessary and appropriate programming for this population. Their responses, instead, range from denying the existence of the problem altogether to acknowledging complete frustration with service delivery attempts.

Reasons for these failures are many, and will be discussed in the first section of this chapter. Following that, we will explore the clinical dynamics of the phenomenon and implications for treatment and intervention. Generally, this chapter will seek to establish the need for the development of both theory and practice specifically concerned with the particular needs of abused and neglected adolescents.

Identification Issues

The fact is that close to 30 percent of all reported "child" abuse and neglect cases have involved children over twelve years of age (American Humane Association, 1978). But because they are no longer regarded as children, abused adolescents do not generally evoke the same sympathy as younger victims. While emotional trauma can be at least as intense, the physical signs of abuse are usually not as severe. Violence often resides in the eyes of the beholder, and adolescents are sometimes seen as being big enough to protect themselves, or even "deserving" of the beating. Violence-prone families also tend to create patterns of family abuse in which the adolescent may physically abuse his/her parents. In such situations the adolescent is not likely to evoke support, and is more likely to be labeled a perpetrator, rather than the victim he/she is.

The natural course of human development also creates many difficulties. The adolescent's transition to adulthood is normally turbulent and, at times, intolerable to many adults. It is often difficult to find a human services worker who enjoys involvement with this population. Perhaps painfully identified with the conflicts of the adolescent's developmental tasks, or threatened by the youthful contrasts to their own waning youth, workers steer clear of the adolescent client.

In this context of intergenerational conflict, the particular problems and behaviors of abused adolescents compound the resistance. The anger and mistrust felt by these young people make it most difficult to develop a close working alliance, and tend to complicate both the identification of adolescent abuse and its treatment. Often abused adolescents come to our attention only through conflict with teachers, the police, and other authoritarian institutions in the community. Once they are labeled for delinquent behavior or status offenses, the issue of abuse or neglect is overlooked. The relevance of the personal history of maltreatment is often ignored in both assessment of antisocial behaviors and ongoing treatment planning and intervention.

As with younger children, the behavior of abused or neglected adolescents ranges from extreme withdrawal to violent acting out. Their behavior, however, has more significant societal consequences and is often more visible and "bothersome" in the wider community than that of younger children. Teenagers who have been lifelong scapegoats or who have lived with a continual sense of futility and neglect are, during adolescence, at much greater risk for depressions, drug dependence, anorexia, and withdrawal. Many, fulfilling parental expectations, become involved in an array of antisocial behaviors—the function being to reaffirm those expectations. Deflected anger at violent and withholding parents often manifests itself in behaviors destructive both to self and to others. Arson, theft, belligerence, recklessness, substance abuse, and running away all are common strategies for acting out a deeply rooted and deeply felt sense of hurt. Similarly, many adolescents who have experienced sexual abuse emerge in statistics, not as victims of assault, but as sexually promiscuous teenagers, prostitutes, adolescent mothers, and teenagers who act out in other ways.

Abused and neglected adolescents are often the most ambivalent youth to work with. With them the normal developmental conflicts relating to dependence and independence are exacerbated by their long-standing unmet needs and desire to escape painful situations and personal confrontation. This tendency itself creates frequent frustration, even for the most dedicated service provider. It is not uncommon for a worker to engage in an exhaustive search for alternative living arrangements for an obviously battered teenager, only to be thwarted by the adolescent's demand to return home. Running away, both literally and figuratively, is often a cry for help. Unfortunately this cry is either ignored, or, inappropriately, dealt with only as a "status offense." Where cases are not appropriately identified and the underlying issues are not addressed, there are predictable outcomes for the adolescent victim of abuse and neglect. Where human services fail to create needed alternatives, the adolescent develops a lifelong pattern of pursuit of gratification, denial of unmet needs, and acting-out behavior.

Clinical Issues

While maltreatment may first be recognized in adolescence, it either can be a long-standing familial pattern or one which emerges only in adolescence. We have been able to identify three somewhat distinct forms of adolescent maltreatment: (1) chronic maltreatment which continues during adolescence, (2) maltreatment which begins in adolescence, and (3) maltreatment which intensifies during adolescence.

Whether the abuse and neglect are historical or new phenomena during adolescence, they occur in a context of radical changes for the adolescent, for the parent, and for the family in a new stage of development.[1] The themes of separation, individuation, and control—

major issues for the normal adolescent and his/her family—emerge as problematic areas in families where both parents and children are having difficulty evolving new parent-child relationships. Often developmental conflicts concerning autonomy which first arise at the two-year-old stage are repeated at a new level during adolescence.

For some chronically maltreated youths the task of separation and individuation is nearly impossible to achieve. Their low self-esteem makes it difficult for them to see their parents from a critical perspective. Hence they blame themselves for their plight, and their acting out merely serves to reinforce both their poor self-image and the abuse and neglect they receive. These young people are generally identified not because of abuse and neglect, but because of severe delinquent behavior or mental health problems.

Other maltreated youth are actively engaged in a radical redefinition of self and others. They are busy establishing identities of their own, exploring different lifestyles, developing intimate relationships outside the family, and building a more critical perspective on the whole—including their relationships with their families. As a consequence they may begin to resist, protest, and act out against long-standing victimization in the family. Their choices, however, are limited. The adolescent may refuse to submit to parents, confide in another adult or peer, or choose to leave the situation. *All* of these new behaviors heighten conflict in the isolated, stress-ridden family as it protects itself from public revelation of private family weaknesses or secrets.

The battles around control and separation which are characteristic of this period in the family's development sometimes are manifested in abusive behaviors directed toward the adolescent. Parents who have a great need for control or who are fearful of impending loss and separation easily become embroiled in anxious battles which may precipitate abuse for the first time or turn what historically was physical discipline into less controlled violence. Violent responses to threatened loss of control or separation are not atypical at this stage of the family's history. Often one hears these parents describe the perfect child who within a six-month period began lying and failing in school and changed his/her peer group, this radical shift resulting in an extreme response from the parent. For both parent and child in this situation, the evolution from childhood to adulthood can occur only through violent revolution, with the child pushing the issue to extremes and the parent responding in a desperate attempt to stay in control. When this does not work, these families may abrogate their responsibilities toward their teenagers completely, thereby creating a rapidly increasing group of neglected adolescents currently referred to as "throwaways."

Abuse and neglect are phenomena most frequently occurring in families already laden with psychic and social stress. The coinciding "crisis" of adolescence and the midlife "crisis" of the parents of adolescents creates still another dynamic toward increased family conflict. For the adolescent, the end of childhood and the beginning of adulthood are both frightening prospects, difficult to confront and seemingly uncontrollable in consequence. For the parent, letting go of a child is threatening in its demand for redefinition of self as well. Watching, and participating in, all of these intensely emotional developmental changes—concerning identity, sexuality, intimacy, career, lifestyle, etc.—confronts the parent both with his/her own changing status and with the inevitable passage of time. Fighting to hold on to a growing child then becomes a way of holding on to one's own identity and sense of meaning. In families where such parental "need" is strong, the adolescent's developmental struggle is apt to be stormy and painful for all.

Treatment Considerations

Understanding the individual and family dynamics as well as the social context within which abuse and/or neglect occurs is crucial to the creation of a meaningful intervention plan. As with all cases of family dysfunction, the family must become the primary focus of intervention. With the adolescent's involvement, however, there are a variety of special considerations which successful intervention must take into account.

Of particular importance is the nature of the adolescent's status and how that affects possibilities for treatment. Because adolescents are legally defined still as children, agencies are not permitted to evaluate or to treat teenagers without prior parental approval. This technicality creates a complex problem in reinforcing the youth's role as "child" in the family and in prohibiting him/her from asserting positive independent action toward problem resolution. It also reinforces the counterproductive concern of the already mistrustful adolescent that the agency, representing the adult world, must be "taking the side" of the parents.

In the same vein, it is important to recognize that behavioral symptoms such as running away, delinquency, sexual acting out, and dropping out of school are usually impossible to treat in structured, time-limited, weekly sessions. We have evidence from analysis of programs nationally that "outreach" programs are the most successful. Such programs exist in an array of formal and informal agencies often referred to as "alternative services"—crisis centers, runaway houses, and hot line services. Persons working in the programs are viewed by most adolescents as friends and allies who understand and respect their problems, and these services have demonstrated a strong commitment, idealism, and impact over the past fifteen years. Although in the past the idealism and ideology of the alternative services have fostered hostility and antagonism between them and more traditional agencies, there has emerged in the recent past a growing mutuality of awareness of potential for more positive interaction. This increasing respect and recognition has found consequence in some exciting and creative attempts at more comprehensive service delivery for abused and neglected teenagers. In several communities, traditional agencies are now offering family therapists for a combination of training, supervision, and direct service tasks within the runaway or crisis centers.[2]

In other communities, relationships between child-protective service agencies and runaway houses have led to a more functional and effective sharing of protective services staff trained to work specifically with adolescents.[3] Traditional social services agencies are now widely expressing relief that alternative agencies exist to help deal with a population thay have historically been unsuccessful in confronting.

The development of a service delivery network geared toward families with adolescent members provides opportunities for reduction of tension and conflict in the home. Helping identify alternative educational arrangements, part-time employment, appropriate recreational activities, and adolescent-oriented counseling all contributes to a reduction of pressures and strains at home. These services also work toward increasing self-esteem in abused and neglected youth with poor self-images. Relationships and activities which enhance self-esteem help the maltreated adolescent see his/her parents more objectively and help reduce self-blame by the youth. Once the youth sees him/herself as more worthwhile, it becomes easier for him/her to constructively handle separation and individuation.

At the same time that the adolescent is developing this new sense of self, the other family members too should be involved in a process which helps them cope with feelings of loss of control and separation anxiety. Helping the parents come to terms with their own developmental crisis frees the whole family to redefine their relationships.

Often an abused or neglected youth is the scapegoat in a marital conflict. Removing the adolescent from the center of the conflict forces the parents to confront their own relationship. The adolescent's role in the marital conflict is both an inappropriate burden and a total misappropriation of power. Separation is far easier without this responsibility. Marital counseling often helps to remove the adolescent from his/her pivotal position. Ongoing family therapy and outreach, oriented toward reduction of external sources of family stress, also are invaluable; network interventions, in which attempts are made at involving friends and relatives in planning and problem solving, are yet another set of useful options.

There are times when the removal of an adolescent from his/her home is the most appropriate intervention. The family may have divested itself of emotional involvement with the troubled, acting-out teenager and refuse involvement. The living situation may continue to be so mutually destructive to adolescent and parent that temporary or permanent separation is needed to reduce the pain. In some instances the parents may be resistant to confronting their own problems and continue to scapegoat the adolescent.

If foster care proves to be a necessary step, it is crucial that serious attention be given to the various issues that impinge on the potential effect of this strategy. Providing care for adolescents outside their homes is highly demanding and creates additional strain on many agency workers. Foster homes for adolescents are most difficult to recruit, and the young person is likely either to run away or to re-create the dynamics which led to abuse at home. The use of group foster homes for teenage placements can be a successful alternative in many instances.[4] The use of any foster care setting should be assessed on the basis of the individual youth and family's needs; a setting should not simply be exploited on the basis of easy access or availability. Generally, younger adolescents seem to do better in nuclear family settings where they are the only or youngest child, while older adolescents tend to do better in a group setting. Other critical variables include the youth's own wishes for independence, self-sufficiency, and more intimate peer relationships, evolving relationships within the family, planned length of residence, and the need for and ability to tolerate provision of nurturance and warmth.

Understanding symptomatic behavior in relation to its underlying causes provides a much clearer perspective from which to plan and implement intervention strategies. With the mistreated adolescent, symptomatic behavior is often dealt with as the problem, with little attempt at confronting the underlying issues. Abused and neglected adolescents are often found among delinquent populations, status offenders, and severely withdrawn, depressed teenagers. A good social history, which covers the maltreatment, developmental struggles, and conficts of all family members, as well as other stresses, helps us to understand, assess, and plan appropriately for the family. Remembering that the adolescent is neither just a "big" child nor a "little" adult also helps us to better shape services to meet the adolescent's needs.

Notes

1. I. Lourie, "Family Dynamics and the Abuse of Adolescents."
2. In Ann Arbor, Michigan, for example, the Catholic Social Services Agency has such a relationship with Ozone House, a local runaway program developed in the late sixties.
3. For example, the National Institute of Mental Health has funded several innovative programs for abused adolescents that attempt to enhance the relationship between child-protective services and alternative service agencies.
4. J. S. Gordon, "Alternative Group Foster Homes: A New Place for Young People," unpublished paper, National Institute of Mental Health, Rockville, Md., 1974.

PART VI

Interdisciplinary Roles and Collaboration

13

The Interdisciplinary Team and the Community

Marjorie Ziefert and Kathleen Coulborn Faller

A range of disciplines now acknowledge their need for collaboration in working with child abuse and neglect issues. We have an understanding that unless we regard child abuse and neglect as a social, legal, psychological, and medical problem, we will arrive at only partial solutions that will resolve little for families or the community. This understanding has lead to the evolution of a "team approach" for cases of child abuse and neglect.

The two major purposes of interdisciplinary teams in child abuse and neglect are (1) to understand the problem from a comprehensive perspective, and (2) to implement solutions which address all aspects of the problem. Beyond these purposes there is an overriding principle in child abuse and neglect work which is that nobody should be working or making decisions in isolation. Each professional and indeed each nonprofessional is in need of continued support and consultation. Struggling with personal feelings, the community's response, and the difficulty of the decisions which must be made is very stressful and often creates frustration, anger, and anxiety. With lack of support, these feelings are not addressed and may find targets in colleagues, the families, and/or oneself.

Having a team of people examine the situation and respond to it increases the chances that knowledgeable and effective decisions will be made and implemented. Success of a program or treatment plan often is a reflection of agencies' and staffs' coordination and communication. However, it is important to keep in mind that we are working with truly difficult families who, sadly, may not have the capacity to respond to any intervention. Sharing and collaborating with colleagues increases the chances of differentiating between the failure of professionals and failure of the family to respond to appropriately planned services.

Interdisciplinary teams can have four different functions: (1) coordination and evaluation of services, (2) community and continuing education, (3) case assessment and consultation, and (4) treatment. Having all of these functions fulfilled by one team may entail full-time jobs for several professionals. By involving many community members in problem solving in all of these areas, the work can be divided so that each function is carried out by a persons representing a cross section of agencies and professionals. Thus each agency will have a part to play in each area and staff involved will include both line workers in child abuse and neglect and persons performing other agency functions.

In larger communities, coordination and education may be done by one team, case evaluation by a second group, and treatment by a third and ever-changing group, depending on the complexity of a specific case. In small communities, all four functions may be served by the same team or several communities can come together to share resources. Creativity, flexibility, and optimal use of resources are the keys to a comprehensive approach to working with child abuse and neglect families.

Organizing child abuse and neglect teams must be done through the collective effort of the professional community. It may be difficult to develop all team functions at once, and energies must be put where the greatest assessed need exists. For some communities initial energy may best be spent in coordination of agency efforts; others may need to focus on treatment; in still others more information about child abuse and neglect may be the priority issue. Out of positive joint efforts will come the energy for increased cooperation and collaboration. Major responsibility for organization can come from a variety of sources. Because of its extensive involvement with child abuse and neglect cases in the community and its knowledge of existing resources, child-protective services needs to be in a pivotal role in the structure, perhaps in a coordinating position.

Many communities have established "children-at-risk committees" made up of a wide range of service agencies and organizations that come together to discuss problems, share resources, and begin to analyze service gaps and strengths. These committees might become responsible for establishing and facilitating the implementation of a variety of community-wide agendas. Functions for these committees may be community education, specialized professional education in child abuse and neglect, fundraising for a needed service, and ongoing evaluation of service delivery. These children-at-risk committees form the beginning of a service network whose members are linked to each other and back to their own agencies, where they can encourage increased participation and commitment.

The case evaluation team may have membership from the same agencies as children-at-risk committees. It may be either hospital- or community-based but must be composed of the disciplines with technical expertise relevant to determining if abuse and/or neglect has occurred and how to help alleviate the problem. This team minimally includes a social worker, a pediatrician, and an attorney. Often a psychiatrist's evaluation or psychologist's testing is an essential resource; ideally people from both professions should be members of this team. This case evaluation team may have personal contact with the families or may act in a consultation role to individuals, professionals or the treatment team.

The treatment team has an open-ended membership of primary service providers working with the given family. Its role is to share information, vent frustrations, and find solutions. Whenever three or more treatment people are involved with the same family, there is generally need for structured communication and meetings to occur. Meetings may be regularly scheduled or held as needed. In either case, who convenes the meetings must be clear. It is sometimes helpful to include the family members in treatment team meetings. Clients can often tell us what they need, and their participation in planning can be a motivating force in their cooperation with the plan. Client involvement should be balanced against the need of team members to work out ongoing or transitory difficulties with each other or frustrations with the case. Flexibility is again the key.

For the team process to work effectively, it is crucial for team members to know each other and have ongoing relationships that foster trust and mutual respect. Since members are working together to make difficult decisions, it is important that they understand each other's personal and professional perspectives. They must together develop a common language and understand each other's jargon. Members must also be able to define and articulate their professional role on the team.

Beyond the commitment of the individual members to the concepts of coordination and collaboration is the need for the community to give active support to this process. Engaging all of the relevant agencies in ongoing work for the "team" ensures its relevance to the total service community. Agencies must see the benefits of a multidisciplinary approach to donate staff time for meetings and administrative tasks. Some administrative support, often in the form of a coordinator, is necessary to oversee and implement team functions. Outside funding for a coordinator from a local service club or organization may be sought, or a key agency or consortium of agencies may donate administrative support. State and federal funding sources can also be pursued. However, with or without funding, it is naive to think that multidisciplinary teams can do an adequate job without some administrative support.

14

The Role of Physicians

H. Mark Hildebrandt

Reporting and Medical Management

All state child abuse and neglect reporting statutes require that physicians report suspected child abuse and neglect and sexual abuse of children. Physicians usually readily report those children who have severe injuries and who would be at substantial risk if returned home. On the other hand, children with milder nonaccidental injuries are less likely to be reported, since many physicians feel that reporting the child may be damaging to the physician–parent rapport or that the available intervention may be disruptive to the family; or a physician may simply prefer to avoid becoming involved in court proceedings.

The physician has an essential role in the evaluation and medical documentation of injuries which are suspected of being nonaccidental. A careful medical evaluation will include documentation of a child's skin injuries or scars by marking them on a skin map with measurements and descriptions of each injury or scar, and a careful physical examination for other sites of injury or evidence of neglect. (See Appendix C(2), "Skin Maps.") Most children who are seen with bruises will have blood drawn to determine whether there is a bleeding or clotting disorder. Infants who are seen with skin injuries will usually have x-rays of the entire skeleton to determine whether the child has sustained any fractures during the previous six months. A complete evaluation will usually include photographs of all skin injuries, although this is sometimes difficult to obtain at night or in a busy emergency room. Some emergency rooms have a Polaroid camera for this purpose. Photographs as part of the medical evaluation are authorized by the reporting act in many states without necessarily having the consent of the parents.

In cases involving obviously severe injuries, hospitalization and treatment of injuries may involve specialists who have extra training and experience in the care of burns, head injuries, or internal injuries. Some children are hospitalized because of the character of the injuries and the risk of further injuries should the child be returned home. In many hospitals, the hospital social worker will be in touch with the family and the protective services worker to plan the discharge so that appropriate arrangements can be made for the child to be discharged to a safe home situation.

Sometimes a child with a medical illness may resemble a child with neglect or a nonaccidental injury. Among the many children I have evaluated for abuse, some were referred with apparent bruising over the buttocks who in fact had normal pigment patches over the buttocks commonly found in children with Asian or African backgrounds (Mongolian spots). Some children who were seen with possible burns turned out to have skin infection due to impetigo, unrelated to nonaccidental injury. Some infants who were thought to have nonaccidental fractures had Osteogensis imperfecta (fragile bone disease).

If neglect is suspected as a cause of growth or developmental delay, hospitalization may be necessary to determine whether defective functioning of any system is responsible for the child's condition. A child who is hospitalized with suspected neglect may have to stay in the hospital for several weeks for evaluation of the child's progress with a standard nutritional program. If the child thrives in the hospital, this is substantial evidence that there was neglect.

The examination and evaluation of the child who has been sexually exploited should be done with the greatest sensitivity and gentleness, preferably by someone who is experienced in working with children. Since the genital tissues are rather elastic, it may be difficult for a physician to state unequivocally whether a child has sustained sexual penetration in the absence of tissue injury. However, specimens can be collected to determine whether semen can be recovered from the vagina or whether venereal infection has occurred.

Health care maintenance of abused children should be arranged as part of the follow-up so that adequate immunizations and comprehensive medical services can be available regardless of whether the child is in the family home or a foster home. Where there has been a problem of failure to thrive, follow-up visits are essential to determine the progress of the child and should be planned as part of the intervention program. Communication with the health services provider should be maintained to determine compliance.

Working with a Community Child Protection Team

Physicians who have evaluated abused or neglected children are frequently called as expert witnesses in legal proceedings. The physician's role in cases of abuse will usually be to describe in detail the evidence of physical injuries, and to present an opinion as to the likely cause of the injuries, usually based on his understanding of the force necessary to produce injury, the studies done to exclude nonaccidental causes, and the distribution of injury sites. In cases of children with neglect, the physician's role would be to interpret the medical information which excludes medical illness as a cause of the child's condition, behavior, or problems in parent–infant interactions. A physician who has had experience in evaluating abuse cases and has had court experience is much more likely to be comfortable providing testimony.

Children's hospitals and many major teaching hospitals have established child protection teams, sometimes known as SCAN teams (suspected child abuse and neglect) consisting of pediatricians, nurses, social workers, psychologists, and others concerned with the evaluation and management of children with abuse and neglect. These have usually developed out of the need for interdisciplinary coordination and cooperation between hospital staff and community services in handling the difficult problems that abuse and neglect present. In most hospitals, the team will provide consultation on all cases of abuse and neglect admitted or seen at the hospital, and will review the cases at a formal conference or at a working meeting with the persons directly involved in the care of the patient. In addition, team members will make themselves available for assistance to community agencies that must handle the home evaluations and legal aspects of the case. If you are working in an area where there is a regional children's hospital, it would be well worth your time to contact the children's hospital and inquire about the meetings of the child protection team and arrange to attend one of the meetings and get to know some of the staff, who have special experience in the area of child abuse and neglect. They can be exceedingly useful in obtaining consultation for difficult cases, which may be seen in any community.

In those larger communities that do not have a children's hospital, there is usually a pediatric department in the general community hospital. If this is a teaching hospital with a pediatric training program, there may be a child protection team. Private hospitals may still not have a protocol for handling children who are seen with abuse and neglect which requires a consultation with one of the staff pediatricians and communication with the hospital social worker. However, some private hospitals will have a child protection or SCAN team meeting regularly.

Certain communities with several hospitals will have a community SCAN team or child protection team consisting of representatives of the different hospitals and the community agencies who meet together regularly to discuss problem cases which may have been seen in the community and to improve on the services provided by the hospitals or the community agencies. Some states require such interdisciplinary teams in the large communities in the state.

In those communities where there is neither a hospital nor a community child protection team, it may be necessary to contact each pediatrician or emergency-room physician to find one who is interested and willing to become involved in the evaluation of children who may be identified with abuse or neglect. Many physicians find it difficult to participate in the evaluation and management of children with these problems because of the unusual time required for the evaluation and the occasional necessity to arrange time to appear in court. However, in most communities it should be possible to find at least one physician who is interested enough in the plight of the abused and neglected child to be able to find time to commit him/herself to this important area. Once a local physician has identified him/herself as being willing to be available for evaluation of children with abuse or neglect, other physicians in the community may refer cases from their practice. This arrangement has been especially helpful for certain physicians, such as psychiatrists, whose treatment role with the family or the patient requires maintaining rapport.

15

Legal Roles

Donald N. Duquette

Attorneys may be involved at various stages in the management of cases of child abuse and neglect. However, typically they become important only on those cases which go to court. There are in fact three separate attorney roles, with requirements which vary according to whom the attorney represents. These roles are the child's attorney, the agency attorney, and the parents' attorney.

The Child's Attorney

Statutes in nearly all states require or permit the appointment of an attorney for the child in child protection cases.[1] That lawyer is generally charged with representing the "best interests" of the child and with making an independent judgment of what the "best interests" might be. The statute in Michigan is illustrative:

> The court, in every case filed under this act in which judicial proceedings are necessary, shall appoint legal counsel, who in general, shall be charged with the representation of the child's best interest. To that end, the attorney shall make further investigation as he deems necessary to ascertain the facts, interview witnesses, examine witnesses in both the adjudicatory and dispositional hearings, make recommendations to the court, and participate in the proceedings to competently represent the child. [Michigan Compiled Laws Annotated 722.630.]

In most settings the lawyer has a client to articulate what he or she wants, and this determines the position the lawyer will take. In a criminal case the client wants off as lightly as possible; in a civil action the client wants as large a recovery in dollars as possible. In child protection, however, the position to be taken by the lawyer is often quite unclear. The child is often too young to express a view. Even when the child is old enough, the attorney, charged with representing the child's "best interests," may be compelled to disagree with the youthful client and advocate for a different position.

The anomaly deepens when one recognizes that there are two other attorneys participating in the proceedings. Child protective services and its attorney often perceive their goal as achieving the best interests of the child. The parents' attorney will argue for what his clients see as the best interests of the child, which is usually to be at home with the parents. And, of course, the judge makes the final and ultimate decision of what is in the best interests of the child. Many judges act as advocates in terms of assuring proper social services to the child and his family. Describing the role of the child's attorney as advocate for the best interests of the child does little, then, to distinguish his role from that of the other actors in child protection. Nor does this description give the attorney guidance as to what he or she should *do* in pursuit of the nebulous "best interests of the child."

If the lawyer for the child is to decide what is in the child's best interests, nothing in his training as lawyer has equipped him or her to assess parental conduct, to appraise the harms to a child presented by his environment, to recognize strengths in the parent-child relationship, or to evaluate the soundness of an intervention strategy proposed by the social agency. The role of the child's counsel is complex. He must synthesize the results of the protective services investigation, the child's psychological, developmental, and physical needs, the child's articulated wishes, his own assessment of the facts, and the treatment resources available. The ultimate decision as to the course of action to be taken by the child's attorney in any given case is basically *nonlegal* in character. The role of the child's counsel imposes heavy responsibility and requires independent social judgments.

In coming to a position for the child, the attorney must ascertain the facts of the case. Many commentators have suggested that the child's attorney do a completely independent investigation including interviews with all relevant witnesses before arriving at an independent position.[2] While such zeal on behalf of a child is commendable and probably necessary in some cases, it is also an expensive duplication of effort between the protective services worker and the lawyer. The lawyer could rely on the protective services investigation in most cases—interviewing family members, neighbors, and other witnesses only if warranted by the case. The lawyer should interview, or at least see, his child client in every case—even if only for the purpose of getting a "feel" for the child as a real person facing a serious personal dilemma. The child should be personalized—known to his lawyer beyond the paper work of court petitions and social work reports.

The emphasis of protective services and its attorney in the court is generally on proving the facts alleged in the petition and gaining court jurisdiction. The child's attorney's role goes beyond that. He must look at the entire proceeding—both the legal and social aspects—from the perspective of the child. He must come to an independent judgment as to what course of action will be best for the child based on his personal appraisal of the totality of the circumstances affecting the child.

Having come to a position on behalf of the child, the attorney should advocate vigorously for that position both in the courtroom and within the social service bureaucracy. The traditional role of a guardian ad litem, still the name given to the child's attorney in some jurisdictions, is not that of advocate but rather that of technical watchdog. Traditionally, the guardian ad litem would examine pleadings and other material in the file and ascertain that the proceedings which affect the child are legally correct.[3] In child protection proceedings the child needs more than a technician to ensure legal precision; he needs more than a passive observer and adviser to the court; he needs an *advocate*.[4]

The attorney's advocacy should begin with the social agency that has filed the petition. Questions about the child's separation from his parents should be raised. How long ago did the separation occur? What is the likely harm to the child of prolonged separation? Are regular visits, supervised if necessary, being arranged for the child? *What is the agency treatment plan for this child and this family*? The agency must be pressed to come to an intervention strategy quickly for the child and family so that the intervention by the agency and the court does not just drift aimlessly without guidance or direction.

The child's lawyer must not agree with social work recommendations without question. He should question closely and extract the underlying basis for the social work position and recommendations. The child's counsel may or may not defer to the social work judgment and may or may not agree with the recommendations. The lawyer's conclusions should be reached by independent thought processes even though the protective services worker may be the person most often relied upon to supply fact.

Despite disclaimers to the contrary, child protection proceedings normally reflect most of the essential elements of an adversary proceeding. The attorney for the child, however, unlike lawyers in most other litigations, is not required to take an adversary position. He is not called upon to either prosecute or defend, but rather to ensure that all relevant facts necessary to adjudication and disposition are presented to the court, and to exert his efforts to secure an ultimate resolution of the case which, in his judgment, best serves the interests of the child.

The child's attorney may play a significant role in facilitating negotiation and mediation. Swift resolution of the legal dispute is nearly always in the child's interest. A cooperative and nonadversarial resolution which provides the needed protection and services to the child is also nearly always in the child's interest. The child's attorney should encourage negotiation and could even play the role of mediator between agency and parents in the interests of a swift and nonadversarial resolution of the dispute.

The role of the child's attorney after adjudication should remain vigorous and active. He should press and persuade the responsible social agencies for services and attention which the child client (and perhaps his family) needs. Case workers are often overextended with caseloads that are too large. Advocacy within the bureaucracy may ensure that the lawyer's client gets the services and attention he needs. Preferably such nudging of the social agencies can be done in a collegial, nonaccusatory manner. If, however, a social worker or agency is not behaving responsibly toward a particular child (or the parents), the child's attorney should insist on a higher standard of service either by a direct request to the agency or by formally raising the issues before the court.

Methods of appointment and payment of lawyers for children must encourage vigorous advocacy, in and out of court, over the long term. Often attorneys are appointed or paid only for a single court action without a mandate to advocate before trial or to follow up after the court has entered its orders. Vigorous advocacy over time is discouraged by short-term lawyer appointments for children. The term guardian ad litem implies a temporary appointment for the litigation only. Some fee schedules pay a lawyer in such a way that court preparation, mediation, and independent case assessment are not encouraged. For example, a lawyer may be paid per court hearing attended or per case handled rather than by the hour spent. The fee schedule may be so low that the economics of law practice do not allow the experienced lawyer to spend the necessary time and energy to perform the lawyer role as he or she might like. Vigorous, competent, and long-term child advocacy has a price tag. Economics significantly affects the quality of legal representation provided children.

Considering that much of the child's attorney role is nonlegal in nature and that traditional law school education does not prepare a lawyer for this role, should lawyers be the ones representing children in such cases? Lawyers are well equipped to handle the procedural aspects of child protection cases, but the judgments as to what is in the best interests of the child and the critical surveillance of the social service agencies may be done as well or better by nonlawyers. Perhaps paraprofessionals or volunteers trained in the legal and social aspects of child protection cases can perform this function economically and with lawyer consultation and service as needed. Communities experimenting with nonlawyer representatives for the child, as complement to the child's attorney, include Seattle, Washington and Kalamazoo, Michigan.[5]

Protective Services Attorney

Traditionally in child protection cases no attorney appeared in most court actions on behalf of the social agency or individual who filed the petition alleging child abuse or neglect. In the recent past, if an attorney did appear, he was likely to be a young assistant prosecutor or assistant county corporation counsel with little preparation time, limited experience in such cases, and little familiarity with juvenile court and child protection law. The child neglect attorney was often the one most recently arrived in the office. Attorneys complained about the lack of specificity with which their social worker clients presented their cases and about the "murkiness" and lack of legal standards in the juvenile court generally. Juvenile court, and especially child abuse and neglect cases, often received low priority among members of the bar.

In recent years, concurrent with the due-process revolution in juvenile court, the role and functioning of all attorneys in juvenile court have acquired important and greater definition. The need for competent legal advice for petitioning agencies in child protection is increasingly recognized. Proving child abuse or neglect in child protection cases is very difficult. The parents are generally represented. The child may be independently represented. A petitioning protective services worker is at a distinct disadvantage if he is charged with the burden of proof in an adversarial court without legal counsel to back him up.

The role requirements of the petitioner's attorney in child protection cases include conventional attorney duties but differ from the traditional lawyer tasks in several respects. Some of the special problems faced in child protection are addressed below.

Lawyers who represent banks learn the banking business very well. Lawyers who represent labor learn labor unions and organizing from top to bottom. Lawyers who represent child welfare agencies should likewise know and understand social work as a profession and the child welfare system. The child welfare lawyer must understand and appreciate the emphasis on nonjudicial (yet fair) handling of child protection cases. In addition to traditional legal skills, understanding juvenile court and family law and philosophy is essential. The child welfare lawyer should know and respect the functions, the capabilities, and even the limitations of social workers and other behavioral scientists. The foster care system—its limitations and its strengths, its advantages and its disadvantages, the benefits and risks to children—also must be appreciated.

What is the nature of the attorney-client relationship between the child protection agency and its lawyer? The legal agency which assumes responsibility for legal representation of the child protection petitioners in the juvenile or family court varies from state to state and sometimes even from county to county. The duties are variously assumed by the local prosecuting attorney, the state attorney general's office, the county corporation (civil) counsel, and sometimes lawyers who are actually employees of the child protection agency. Some legal agencies representing protective services assume a quasi-judicial role, so that they will initiate legal action as requested by the social agency only if in their judgment such action is warranted. The lawyer exercises a sort of prosecutorial discretion about what child protection cases are brought to court.

In contrast, a recommended position is that the legal representatives of the agency see themselves in a traditional attorney-client relationship. The child protection agency, in fulfilling its responsibilities to children and to families, needs assistance and authority from the court from time to time. In invoking the court system, the agency should have access to a lawyer whom it can trust and who will act as its advocate as necessary.

Points of view and judgments about strategy may differ between the lawyer and the agency personnel, but such differences are not unusual between lawyer and client; they are rather common in both personal and corporate practice. When such disagreements occur, the lawyer should assume the traditional counselor function of the lawyer in which the matters are discussed in-house and recommendations for actions arrived at. If differences cannot be resolved in this manner, the lawyer should defer to his social agency clients in matters within the scope of their expertise, i.e., in social judgments and assessments as to what the needs of the child and family are, while the agency should defer to the lawyer in matters of trial strategy and legal judgment. Unfortunately, the legal and social spheres of expertise are often not clear and distinct in this context. Almost every judgment in child abuse and neglect cases reflects a value judgment that certain parental behavior constitutes legal neglect. Normative fact judgments are made at every step of the child protection process—by the reporting person, by the social worker, by the social work supervisor, by the lawyers, and finally, and most importantly, by the judge. What is the minimum community standard of child care to which every child is entitled? What is the threshold of child care below which the state may and should intervene, even coercively, on behalf of the child (and for the good of the family unit, or so goes the theory)? These questions, addressed in every child protection case either consciously or not, blur the distinction between legal and social spheres of expertise.

With the understanding that the spheres of competence are not always clear and distinct, the attorney and his client agency ought to arrive at in-house positions, each deferring to the other's expertise where appropriate, with the lawyer acting as advocate for the position jointly arrived at between the child protection agency and legal counsel.

The interface between the child protection agency and the court system must be explored and understood by the attorney representing the agency. The role of the court must be placed in context for the agency by its lawyer. The court acts as arbiter between the individual citizens and the social agency as to the agency's right to intervene in the privacy of the family. When the family does not voluntarily agree to the agency intervention, the court must decide whether or not the circumstances justify coercive and authoritative state intervention on behalf of the child.

Delivery of services to the dysfunctional family remains the duty of the child protection agency whether or not court action is taken. The social workers have the charge and the skills and the expertise to actually provide assistance to the children and their families. The court's role is to authorize the agency to act in cases in which parents will not voluntarily accept services. The court's authorization facilitates the agency intervention. The court itself, however, has no treatment expertise, nor should it be relied upon to develop a treatment plan. The social worker may not recognize the limited role of the court as judicial body and that the social agency bears the responsibility to develop and implement a treatment plan for the children and family. The agency lawyer must make clear to his social worker clients that the court itself can do no treatment or social planning for a family. The court's role is to prevent unwarranted interferences with their private lives.

The agency lawyer must understand the role and functioning of protective services enough that he can identify the social objectives of the agency as separate and distinct from the generally shorter-term, more immediate legal objectives. If the lawyer understands the agency goals, he can be more creative in the use of the court process. The agency lawyer should not define his client's goals only in terms of legal objectives—for instance, to acquire temporary jurisdiction, to prove probable cause, or to obtain emergency detention. With the help of the social worker, he must identify the *social goals* of the agency with as much particularity as is possible. Thereafter, by creative use of the court process, the lawyer may be able to accomplish the social goals, whether or not the most apparent legal goals are attainable.

The legal process itself may contribute to the family dysfunction to which the agency is trying to respond. Sometimes the trauma of adversary litigation cannot be avoided. But often, when the social objectives of the agency are clearly in mind, an attorney can accomplish the goals of the agency without trial through strategies of negotiation, mediation, and pacing the litigation.

The attorney should work closely with the protective services agency. In the initial interview with the agency social worker the lawyer must ask, "What do you want to result from the legal action? What are your professional (i.e., social work) goals for the client family?" The lawyer should test the social work strategy in a collegial but "devil's advocate" way. Will court action facilitate the social work intervention strategy? How will it do so? Can each of the elements of the intervention plan be justified by facts presentable to the court?

The social worker, with his experts and team members, must be able to articulate the social objectives of court action. The lawyer may wish to attend treatment team meetings (SCAN meetings) regarding cases on which he is or may be active. The lawyer needs to know the behavioral science reasoning behind a particular intervention strategy and may also be able to contribute knowledge to the team as to the legal process available to facilitate the strategy. Knowing the plan and its bases, the lawyer is better able to support it in court through expert and material witnesses.

The further challenge for the lawyer is to achieve the social results in an efficient, effective, and direct way which avoids or minimizes the negative effects of the adversary process. A process of mediation or negotiation may avoid the adversary system, in which family members must testify against family members and helpers such as social workers and physicians must testify against the parents they are trying to help. Skills and tactics in negotiation and mediation are especially important to the child protection attorney.

We have identified two separate aspects of the attorney role for the protective services agency—first, to prove and present his client's case in the most persuasive fashion possible; second, to understand and embrace the social goals of the client agency and to further those goals by nonadversarial means if possible.

We now come to a third aspect of the agency attorney role, that of preparing his client agency for ongoing court review of a treatment plan ordered by the court. Certainly preparation of the treatment plan remains the sphere of the social worker. However, the lawyer understands the degree of specificity and prompt action required by the court for such plans, and well serves his client when the client is prompted to efficiently and clearly state what the goals of a plan are, and what the specifics of a plan are. The lawyer understands the legal importance of the treatment plan and ramifications that noncompliance by the agency or the parents may have in subsequent court proceedings.

The court retains ultimate responsibility for the well-being of children under its jurisdiction. It cannot abrogate that responsibility. New legislation and several recommended model statutes contain procedures for formalizing the legal standards for review of continued intervention in a family under court authority.[6]

At a review hearing the child protection agency is in a position of giving account of its stewardship. The court earlier took jurisdiction over a child and ordered certain interventions, which may have included placement of the child and counseling or other treatment for the family. At a review the agency must give account to the court of what services have been provided and what progress has been made by the family. The agency attorney can aid his client by not letting matters drift. Correlatively, the parents must give account of themselves and show what progress they have made in correcting problems that brought their child to the attention of the court.

The agency, in essence, is asking that the court continue authorization for the agency to intervene in the family, including perhaps continued placement of the child. The agency must show that a treatment plan has been in place and that the legal and social intervention is justified by correlative benefits, either realized or nearing realization, to the child and his family.

If the agency cannot justify its continued involvement in the family by demonstrating good-faith efforts to rehabilitate the family, the court may revoke the agency authority to act, i.e., end the court jurisdiction, or return a child in placement home in spite of agency requests to the contrary. Admittedly, a return home against the agency recommendation is a rare and probably risky thing for a judge to allow without some expert opinion to counter the agency recommendation or without additional resources to deal with a particular family.

The agency attorney role demands well-developed traditional lawyering skills. However, the role also requires that the attorney know the procedures of the child protection agency very well. Ultimately, a successful intervention in a family requires close collegial cooperation between the lawyer, the child protection agency, and the psychiatric, psychological, and medical consultants to the agency.

Attorney for the Parents

The attorney for the parents is charged with representing the interests of his clients zealously within the bounds of the law. Advocacy for the parent usually takes the form of minimizing the effects of state intervention on the family. Advocacy for parents may include diplomatic attempts to get petitions dismissed, in-court advocacy for dismissal, insistence that the charges brought by the state be legally proven in court, and negotiation for dispositions that are most acceptable to the parents.

Representation of parents in cases of alleged child abuse and neglect requires unique skills and resources in addition to traditional lawyer advocacy. Lawyers must first deal with their negative feelings toward the client parent accused of child abuse or neglect. The feelings toward a client parent, unless dealt with properly, can sabotage a lawyer's advocacy either at a conscious or unconscious level. These feelings must be dealt with from the beginning. One means of dealing with personal feelings toward allegedly abusive or neglectful parents is to understand the dynamics of child abuse and neglect. Read the rest of this book for that. Parents accused of child abuse and neglect often have difficulty trusting others, forming relationships (including relationships with their lawyers), and deferring gratification. (See Chapter 3.) The lawyer must understand and cope with these and other characteristics of many parents.

Lawyers are counselors at law as well as advocates. In the agency attorney role, the lawyer may advise a client social worker to pursue nonlegal avenues in a case before taking legal action or to consult other professionals about treatment strategy before initiating court action. Similar advice may be given to parents.

The lawyer as counselor to parents must feel comfortable engaging the parents as persons. He must evaluate the parents' difficulties and their legal and social situation, and then provide legal counsel as to how to accomplish their goals. The lawyer may well explore with parents whether or not personal and family problems exist with which the social agencies may assist. He may counsel parents to accept certain services, seeking postponement of the court process in the interim. As a result the parents may be willing to accept some limited assistance from an agency voluntarily. The parents may even be well advised to forgo immediate legal advantage in order to benefit from a social intervention that is calculated to prevent recurrence of abuse or neglect.

The parents' attorney can sometimes perform valuable functions for the parents by encouraging nonjudicial resolutions of the case. A voluntary plan of treatment may avoid formal court jurisdiction and still protect the child and address the problems which may have been identified by protective services. Nonjudicial resolutions with legal representation of the parents avoid the danger of improper invasion of personal liberties without due process. A lawyer representing parents should provide an assurance that whatever agreement the parents enter into is done voluntarily and knowingly, i.e., with full awareness of possible consequences.

Where the parents are willing to accept some services under the shadow of court action, the parents' lawyer should obtain from the social worker a detailed treatment plan for the family. The social worker should also make a contract with the parents defining in concrete terms the problems that are to be worked on, the obligations of the parents and of the agency, and what is expected to be achieved by the parents prior to return of the child or termination of intervention by the agency.

The counselor role is quite consistent with traditional lawyer functioning. It is based on trust and dealing with the client parents as important individuals. However, these nonadversarial tasks of the lawyer may be even more important in child protection than in other areas of the law. In exercising his counselor function, the lawyer must be careful to establish whatever trust he can with the clients. When recommendations of cooperation with social agencies are made, they should be made carefully so that the clients understand that if the suggestions of the lawyer are not accepted, the lawyer will still stand by them as advocate of their position in subsequent proceedings.

After exercising his counselor function, the lawyer may decide that vigorous advocacy to accomplish his clients' goals is necessary. This decision may be based on an appraisal that the case against the parents is weak or unfounded, or the agency response may seem unduly harsh or drastic in light of the problems identified by the agency or the parent. The decision may also be based on the clients' firm denial of the allegations in the petition and their instructions to contest the case. If counseling parents does not lead them to a position the lawyer thinks is more appropriate, he must nevertheless zealously advocate his client's position. While others may believe that a child may be at grave risk, the lawyer's duty is to advocate for his client regardless of the opinion of others and regardless of his personal beliefs in the matter.

The lawyer's advocacy should start in the agency itself. Some discussion and negotiation may lead to a resolution of the conflict between parents and agency. Lawyers must learn the important art of persuading a large bureaucracy, convinced of the inherent rightness of its position, to modify it. In spite of the desirability of nonjudicial resolutions of disputes between the parent and the social agency, it is often necessary to proceed to trial. Lawyers must first possess traditional skills of trial advocacy and be ready to go to trial when necessary.

Responsibility of the parent for injuries to or possible neglect of a child may be a contested issue. The lawyer has a duty to defend this client with the utmost vigor and resourcefulness. The lawyer in juvenile court, no less than in any other court, must stand as the ardent protector of his client's constitutional and personal rights. He must bring to the task the usual tools of the advocate—familiarity with the applicable law, the ability to logically present the pertinent facts, and the facility for forceful and persuasive exposition of his client's cause.

Other professionals often find the lawyer's role as zealous advocate for the parent in serious child abuse cases disquieting and difficult to understand. This issue is one raised regularly in interdisciplinary groups concerned with child abuse and neglect.

In the dispositional phase of a case, the parents' lawyer may serve several different functions: (1) He can ensure impartiality by acting as a counterbalance to pressures exerted on the court by the very nature of the issues. (2) He can assure that the basic elements of due process are preserved, such as the right to be heard and the right to test the facts upon which the disposition is to be made. (3) He can make certain that the disposition is based upon complete and accurate facts and that all the circumstances which shed light upon the conduct of his client are fully developed. (4) He can test expert opinion to make certain that it is not based on mistakes arising either from erroneous factual premises or from limited expertise. (5) He can give the frequently inarticulate parents a voice in the proceeding by acting as their spokesman. (6) His relationship with the parents may even enable him to give the protective services or court staff new and meaningful insights into the family situation. (7) Finally, the parents' attorney can interpret the court and its processes to his clients and thus assist the parents in genuinely accepting the actions of the court.[7]

Attorneys in child protection, whether representing the child, the parents, or the state, face unique challenges for which traditional law school education has probably not prepared them. To function effectively in any of the lawyer roles, the attorney needs advice and consultation of social work and mental health professionals. Nonlawyers in child protection need to have some idea of what to expect of the lawyers they meet in the court system. Interdisciplinary knowledge is as important to effective legal proceedings as it is in other aspects of state intervention on behalf of children.

Notes

1. U.S. Dept. of Health, Education, and Welfare, National Center on Child Abuse and Neglect, *Excerpts from Child Abuse and Neglect State Reporting Laws.*
2. Fraser and Martin, *The Abused Child.*
3. Delaney, "New Concepts of the Family Court," p. 350.
4. *Ibid.*
5. Downs," Guardian ad Litem Program in Seattle." Personal cummunication, Hon. James S. Casey, Kalamazoo Juvenile Court, June 1979.
6. Institute of Judicial Administration-American Bar Association, (IJA-ABA) Juvenile Justice Standards Project, *Abuse and Neglect.*
7. Isaacs, "The Role of the Lawyer in Child Abuse Cases."

16

The Role of the Psychologist

Janet Stubbs

The psychologist may be involved in the assessment or the treatment phase of abuse and neglect. However, by the nature of the referral system used by the psychologist, she/he is usually not the first person to become aware of a case of suspected child abuse or neglect. The psychologist is generally requested by a social worker, physician, teacher, lawyer, or other professional to assist in the assessment of suspected cases of child abuse and neglect, or to provide treatment in a substantiated case. The treatment provided, which is fairly generic to mental health professionals, is discussed in the treatment section of the manual. (See Chapter 5.)

Purpose of a Psychological Assessment of the Child

The major role of the psychologist in the assessment of cases of child abuse and neglect is to provide a psychological evaluation of the child, with the major purpose being to gain a general understanding of how the child functions. The purpose is *not* to assess the effects of the suspected abuse or neglect on the child's development. Knowledge of the effects of abuse on a child's development is presently limited. There are a number of characteristics, such as low self-esteem, cognitive deficits (Martin, 1976), pseudo-mature behavior (Morris and Gould, 1963), aimlessness (Galdston, 1971), hyperactivity (Green, 1978), and aggressiveness (Kinard, 1978), which seem to be overrepresented in a population of abused children. Further, children who have experienced emotional deprivation, unlike organically impaired children, often exhibit uneven patterns of functioning on developmental tests. Despite some developmental trends among abused children, it is not yet altogether clear whether the developmental problems antedate abuse, or are attributable to factors other than abuse, such as poverty (Elmer, 1977; Gil, 1970). In addition, individual differences among children in their patterns of adaptation to the environment (Chess and Thomas, 1977; Murphy, 1976) will result in differential responses of children to the stresses of the abusive environment. Thus the psychologist can, at best, provide an overall description of the child and *speculate* on possible factors which might contribute to the child's level of functioning.

While a number of professionals can provide some of the assessment information which the psychologist generally provides, there are at least two reasons why a psychologist may be the most advantageous professional to call upon for the psychological appraisal of the child. First, the psychologist is viewed as a developmental specialist, with specific training in principles of development. Should later legal involvement become necessary, the psychologist will be viewed by the court as an "expert" in testifying about child development. Second, the psychologist, unlike the psychiatrist, has specialized training in the administration of developmental tests. While the psychiatrist can accurately document development by less standardized assessment techniques, the psychologist's use of tests which have substantial validity and reliability enable him to provide more standardized measures of the child's developmental level.

Area of Assessment

The psychological evaluation of a child's development includes assessment of three areas:

1. The child's cognitive developmental level
2. The child's personality characteristics, including social and emotional development
3. The quality of parent-child interaction

Based on the data obtained from the assessment of the child's cognitive and personality development, the psychologist will be able to form hunches about explanations of the obtained data, including speculations about the quality of the parent-child interactions.

Being cognizant of the inherent limitations of observing parent-child interactions, the psychologist will attempt to "test out" the possible explanations of the developmental data by observing the parents and child together and assessing the quality of the interaction.

The Process of Psychological Evaluations

The specific nature of the psychological evaluation will vary considerably depending on the individual style and theoretical orientation of different clinicians. It is therefore helpful to "know" the psychologist and his orientation prior to requesting evaluations.

Ideally, a comprehensive psychological evaluation should include at least three tasks:

1. An interview with the parents
2. A test of the child's cognitive development and an evaluation of his personality characteristics
3. Observation of parent-child interaction

Interview with the Parent

Except for cases of very young children, the parent interview is generally carried out in the absence of the child. The primary purpose of this phase of the evaluation is to obtain data about the child, and to begin to form hypotheses which may or may not be borne out during the evaluation. The data obtained during the interview with the parents include a history of the child's development and an assessment of the extent of the parent's knowledge about the child. The latter provides information about the physical and emotional availability of the parent to the child. Specific questions which the psychologist attempts to answer at this stage in discerning how well the parents "know" their child include:

1. Are the parents informative about the child's fears, worries, strengths, concerns, daily routine, developmental milestones, behaviors when he is happy, sad, angry?
2. Is the quality of the description the parents give of the child negative, positive, realistic, unrealistically glorified?
3. Are parental expectations of the child realistic and developmentally appropriate?

Evaluation of the Child

Evaluation of the child involves both formal testing and observations of the child. There are a number and variety of objective and projective tests which can be used appropriately with children for assessment purposes. The specific test used by the psychologist is not the important factor unless the test is totally inappropriate, such as use of an infant test with a pre-school-aged child. The important factor is *how* the test is used to elicit the needed data about the child's developmental level and response pattern. For a complete discussion on specific tests and their uses see A. Anastasi, *Psychological Testing* (Anastasi, 1968).

Both quantitative and qualitative information is sought in the evaluation of the child. The quantitative information is derived from the test pattern and score. This provides an estimate of the child's present level of functioning as well as specific strengths and weaknesses. The qualitative information is derived from responses to the projective test, which provides indirect means of eliciting children's concerns, worries, and conflicts. Qualitative information about a child's personality can also be derived from observation and interpretation of a child's approaches to the test tasks and responses to direct questions.

Observations of Parent–Child Relationships

Aspects which are important in the assessment of parent-child relationships include a child's attachment to parents, degree of ability to separate from parents, amount of trust, quality of object relationships, nature of identifications with parents, style of coping, and handling of anxiety. Obtaining information about these aspects requires the psychologist to focus on both parent and the child, and to attend to the process of interaction between them. Since there are limited direct empirical data on which to base interpretation of observational data of parent-child relationships, such interpretations rely heavily on the psychologist's experience with children and clinical training related to family interactions.

The specific questions the psychologist attempts to answer while observing the parent-child interactions include:

1. How and to what extent is the child's behavior different in the presence and absence of the parents?
2. How do the parents respond to the child and his needs and demands?

In some situations the psychologist will share the results of the assessment with the parents at the time of the evaluation. When this occurs, the interest shown and the specific questions asked by the parents can provide additional information about the quality of the parent-child relationship.

Evaluation of Parents

Formal psychological evaluation of parents, beyond observation of their interactive and nurturant abilities with the child and their responses during interviews with various professionals, is not necessary unless there are indications of bizarre and extremely inappropriate behaviors. In such cases formal diagnostic assessment, including projective personality tests, can be helpful in clarifying the nature and extent of parental personality difficulties.

Conclusion

Taken together, the quantitative and qualitative information derived from parent interviews, formal testing, and observations of children and parents can provide a general understanding of the psychological development and needs of a child. To the extent that the data from psychological evaluations are integrated with data obtained from the assessments of other professionals involved in the case of child abuse and neglect, knowledge of the child's development will be enhanced.

17

The Role of the Psychiatrist on an Interdisciplinary Team

Ann E. Thompson

Who is this "shrink person" and how does she/he function on an interdisciplinary team? A psychiatrist has completed training to be a medical doctor and has three years additional training in the specialty of adult psychiatry. In this training, she/he learns how to diagnose and treat the milder disorders of emotional functioning as well as the more disruptive illnesses of the psychotic individual and those with both organic and emotional illness. The psychiatrist may have an additional two years training in working with children and their families. This qualifies one as a child psychiatrist. Training in this latter area focuses on developing the capacity to evaluate and understand the emotional strengths and weaknesses of the child and his family. A variety of ways to facilitate the child's and family's functioning are learned as well. At the end of this "residence training" the psychiatrist has "board-qualified" status. After passing written and oral examinations given by the American Psychiatric Association, she/he is "board-certified." The psychiatrist is unique among mental health professionals. Medical training allows a psychiatrist to assess organic components of overall functioning and to prescribe medications and other organic treatments. In contrast with psychologists, the psychiatrist is not generally trained to administer or interpret psychological tests and she/he frequently lacks a knowledge of social systems and social intervention in which the social worker is "expert."

As a member of an interdisciplinary team the psychiatrist will have many functions within the team and as a team member in contact with the community. These functions will include those of educator (and hopefully of pupil too!), consultant, liaison person, evaluator, child advocate, and expert witness.

Education or sharing of the psychiatrist's knowledge can occur in the formal setting of seminars or a variety of informal settings including case conferences. Aspects of child and family development, of parents' individual psychological functioning, of parenting, and of treatment can be shared as decisions are made on behalf of the child.

Another way in which the psychiatrist's experience is shared is in the role of expert witness. Especially if the psychiatrist works in an area where the court does not yet acknowledge the "expertness" of those with other training, she/he may be the best person to convey the team's data and recommendation to the court. In the course of evaluation and decision making there is the opportunity to educate attorneys and judges involved in the cases. There is also an opportunity to facilitate negotiation and move the legal process away from the usual adversarial stance, which is frequently destructive to both child and family. What is often not understood by those in the legal setting is that family relationships are characterized by both love and hate and to make decisions based on only one side of these ambivalent feelings is to do a disservice to the client.

The psychiatrist of such a team may also serve as a consultant in the evaluation of extremely difficult cases. A clearer idea of underlying problems and treatment recommendations may be needed. In addition, a time of evaluation can be one way members of the team have for sharing concerns and gaining new perspective on a case. The psychiatrist on such a team will have the same need for someone with whom to discuss cases.

As a physician, the psychiatrist has a role as liaison person for the team in medical settings. She/he will understand the language and systems governing hospitals and medical clinics. As an M.D. she/he will also be able to communicate to those in medical settings in a unique and helpful way.

The psychiatrist as an individual member of the team may be "child advocate" in a variety of ways. In this role she/he may educate and lobby on behalf of the child's developmental needs with foster care or adoption agencies. Another example of intervention on behalf of a child might be in the legal context, where the child is being assaulted by unthinking procedures such as a lie detector test.

On some teams the psychiatrist may serve as a person who can help the team understand its own functioning and process. It is important that this particular role be "given" to the psychiatrist by other team members, as otherwise it will be experienced as "put-down" analyzing or an assault on other team members' humanity.

The sometimes affectionate, sometimes derogatory term "shrink" implies something magical about how psychiatrists function. The magicalness may derive from an atunement to the vital importance of feelings and other aspects of being human which are not the usual focus of our "scientific," technological culture. In fact, psychiatrists' work involves a process of collecting data and then organizing and integrating them into a body of knowledge. Data are derived from written and photographed records (hospital records, school records, baby books, home movies) and from an interview with the identified patient and family. As the interview proceeds, a great deal of important live data will also be available. This is particularly so if the family are seen together in their home. The patient's capacity to be aware of feelings and to be sensitive to reactions to questions and comments can be assessed. The patient's feelings and interactions toward the psychiatrist will represent a characteristic way of relating to those in authority. Another source of data is the psychiatrist's feelings and reactions toward the patient. These are useful to the degree that the psychiatrist is aware of them and able to differentiate those parts of the reactions originating with this patient and those parts which evoke reactions from the psychiatrist's own past. In this regard, those psychiatrists who have had therapy are probably at an advantage. In those instances where intelligence or organic impairment is in question, additional data may be gained by psychological testing.

At the end of an evaluation, the psychiatrist should have some idea about the patient's health, capacity to think, characteristic ways of interacting with people and managing anxious, sexual, angry, and loving feelings and an understanding of the conflicts of this particular person. In summary, there should be a clear idea of the patient's weaknesses and strengths along with an understanding of how the patient has arrived at this point in his/her life. Based on this "diagnosis" some idea of what areas are accessible to change and what areas are not should be formulated. Recommendations for changes in environment, for education, or for one of the many therapeutic approaches to change can then be made.

18

Psychiatric Evaluations

Judith Kleinman

Psychiatric evaluations of families in which child abuse and neglect are a major problem are challenging evaluations for mental health professionals. Although doing them requires the same skill and expertise as any other evaluation, they frequently present dilemmas and requirements which are unique to these cases and are worthy of special attention. All such cases come to mental health personnel because of a specific family symptom, whether it is abuse, neglect, or sexual abuse. It is necessary to start with that particular symptom, to evaluate a multitude of individuals as well as a family system, and to refocus on the initial symptom and recommended interventions in reference to that symptom.

Not all child protective services cases come to a mental health facility or psychiatrist for an evaluation. In general, the cases that come to most such clinics have already been screened by protective services personnel. There are several categories of cases which often require more mental health input: cases which are seen as hopeless and for which added data to serve in court are required; cases in which parental psychopathology is felt to be a major factor in the abuse and neglect; and cases in which there is concern for the child's mental health. Before the psychiatric evaluation is begun, it is important for the evaluator to have a clear understanding of the nature of the case from the viewpoint of protective services or the court and the reason for the request. This usually requires some preliminary conversation between the protective services or court worker and the mental health professional around the issues just described.

All evaluations of abusive and neglectful families must be based on a focus on the involved child or children. The mental health professional must know the concerns of protective services: the alleged abuse or neglect to the child in detail, and its impact on the psychological functioning of the child. The mental health professional should then broaden his/her assessment of the child to include the child's general functioning and general psychological health. As in any other mental health evaluation, one must look at the child's functioning in school, with peers, in learning, in relationship to other people outside the family, and in such daily functions as sleeping and eating; one must also assess through play the level of the child's fantasy play and freedom and flexibility in approaching a play situation. One can obtain needed data by talking with other people who have contact with the child, such as school personnel, relatives, foster parents, and parents, as well as by interviewing the child and sometimes administering psychological tests.

There are two frequent pitfalls in assessing children in this situation. The first is the confusion of reactive disorder and fixation in the child. Frequently, early in assessments of child abuse and neglect cases a child may appear quite immature and regressed, but often this is a regression that is reactive to the current trauma and turmoil rather than a fixation. The assessment of which of these is more likely is an important indicator of the child's strengths and an important indicator of how affected the child has been by the difficulties within the family. Confusion over this issue arises frequently with hospitalized children who on admission are whiny, clingy, withdrawn, and apathetic. If after a few days of hospitalization such a child has become perky, alert, and happy, the judgment is often that the child was so affected by "bad" parents that she/he was depressed, withdrawn, and isolated. Then the fact that after a few days in a "good" environment the child appears so different is seen as a confirmation of the deleterious effect the family has had upon the child. The truth usually is that the initial picture was a reaction to separation from parents to whom the child is attached.

The other major pitfall in assessing abuse and neglect is the temptation to focus on the actual abusive events and the pathology. The psychological effect of abuse and neglect is as much or more a function of the balance of positive and negative factors in the relationships of the child with the parents as it is of the actual abusive event. Thus if a child has bruises as a result of a whipping by a belt, it makes a tremendous difference whether that child is loved and was whipped as part of culturally accepted discipline or is neglected, scapegoated, and not loved by the rest of his family. It is very important to look beyond the initial event and to see the strengths and attachments and other good parts of the relationship as well as the negative parts of it.

Using all the skills that are standardly available for assessing children, the evaluator of a child in an abusing or neglecting family should focus on the child's general level of maturity, both current and the highest level previously achieved; sense of self and self-confidence; relationship with others; cognitive functioning; specific conflicts or environmental difficulties; general affective tone; and general adaptation outside of home in such places as school or a foster home, or with peers.

Assessing the Parent–Child Relationship

Through actual interactions in an interview as well as through taking a careful history, an assessment of both the strengths and the difficulties between each parent and each child must be made. Particular attention should be paid to any special focal conflicts either with one child or around one area of the child(ren)'s functioning or developmental stage. For example, some parents become abusive with their children at a particular developmental stage, such as toddlerhood, when the normal developmental behavior is stubborn, self-willed, and belligerent. Because of their own psychodynamics these parents find this stage very difficult. Another frequent example of focal conflicts is the scapegoating of one child either because of actual characteristics of that child or because of the parents' projection of undesirable characteristics onto that child. In such cases the evaluation must include a careful assessment of which specific characteristics are included.

Assessment of the Parents as Individuals

As with the children, evaluations of the parents must include assessment of their individual psychodynamics and strengths and difficulties, not only within the family but in all other areas of their lives. For example, if a parent is isolated, the evaluator needs to discover whether this is a primary difficulty, such as the inability to trust other people and tolerate intimacy in any relationships in his or her life, or is a symptom of reactive disorder. A careful psychological history which focuses on both strengths and difficulties is necessary to understand how the present problems fit within the person's life history. Again, with the parents as with the children, it is very important whether the current level of functioning has recently changed, as frequently happens in response to specific external stresses, or is chronic.

Family Assessment

In a more general sense it is often helpful to assess the family in terms of its structure and functioning. This is done most usefully with a family interview. Particular family structural problems tend to come up in abusing and neglectful families, such as poor generational boundaries or triangulation involving a child with the parents.

Summary

When all of these data have been obtained through whatever combination of interviews is necessary, the psychiatrist needs to resynthesize in more general terms all the data that he/she has collected. The summary should include:

1. *Diagnosis, or, more commonly, several diagnoses.* These should focus on the presenting symptoms of abuse and neglect and present hypotheses of the dynamics which have led to these presenting symptoms. They should also include a description of the role each person in the family plays in the situation and a description of the strengths of individuals and of the family.

2. *Suggested interventions.* These interventions are based on a realistic assessment of the presenting difficulties of abuse and neglect, the underlying dynamics, the psychological strengths, and the community resources. Often the interventions considered do not include traditional psychotherapy. A psychiatrist, however, can be very useful in considering the likely success of other interventions based on his/her psychological data.

3. *Prognosis.* There should be a prediction for the likelihood that intervention will be successful.

4. *Suggested method of monitoring the child's position and suggested goals of therapy.* It is critical to successful case management to keep in mind the expectations for change. When professionals become involved with families, they can lose objectivity, either becoming global in expectations or denying the fact that a family hasn't changed significantly despite great therapeutic input. It is important to be as objective as possible first in setting reasonable goals. Then a plan must be stated for periodic reassessment by professionals who know the family.

To get the optimum benefit from psychological assessments in abuse and neglect requires that a psychiatrist carry the evaluation beyond usual psychological assessments and be willing to integrate his/her findings and data into a larger whole and larger community involvement. It is not enough, for example, to decide psychotherapy would be helpful, outlining both the therapy and the goals, or to conclude psychotherapy would not be useful, suggesting the reasons. On the basis of one's psychological knowledge of the family, one must help other professionals plan what might be useful involvement either in addition to or instead of psychotherapy.

Finally, it is important to note that in assessing these clinical situations there are unresolvable clinical dilemmas presented to any therapist or clinician involved in assessing such families. I list these and call attention to the fact that they exist and that they are unresolvable. They are (1) the need for promptness and quick resolution versus the need for careful and detailed consideration of the family and individuals; (2) the need for permanence for the child versus the need for continuing contact with an absent parent; (3) the child's need for an adequate home with consistent, predictable care versus the child's psychological attachment to abusive and neglectful parents.

19

The Role of Social Workers in Multidisciplinary Collaboration

Kathleen Coulborn Faller and Marjorie Ziefert

Thus far we have described the roles of the social worker by and large as she/he works independently on child abuse and neglect cases and the special roles of other professionals on cases. We need also to describe the social worker's special role in the multidisciplinary process and how she/he collaborates with each of the other disciplines likely to be involved with a child abuse and neglect case.

The Social Worker as Member of a Multidisciplinary Team

Teams are frequently composed of individuals with only a few hours of commitment for team activities, typically one to three hours per week. Social workers, as well as other professionals, come to the team from a diversity of settings. Some social workers will work for public agencies legally responsible for provision of services to these families, such as protective services, foster care, or the court. Others may be in voluntary agencies whose role it is to provide services to abusive and neglectful families. Social workers in educational settings may identify cases and also work with maltreated children. And still others may be hospital-based and become involved when a maltreated child is brought into the emergency room or is hospitalized for a condition related to abuse and neglect. Because social workers are found in so many settings in the community and their work is so diverse, they more often come into daily contact with child abuse and neglect than do other professionals whose roles have been described. The context from which the worker comes will influence considerably what her/his team functions are.

The precise role of the social worker on a multidisciplinary team will also depend upon the type of team. For example, some types of teams are case focused, "hands on" assessment teams; others are consultation teams, never actually seeing family members face to face, but advising others who have direct contact, and still other teams are treatment teams composed of primary service providers working with an individual family. The term "multidisciplinary team" is also employed to denote community-level coordinating and policy-setting bodies. These work out interagency conflicts and develop new programs.

The training of a social worker may have an individual-case or interpersonal focus, or it may concentrate on social policy and program development issues, and most social work programs provide each student some training at both levels. Persons with the first type of training will be most useful in case-based teams, while those with the second type will work best on community-wide teams. However, a clear-cut strength of the social work profession in child abuse and neglect is its commitment to acquaint its members with issues at a range of levels. To adequately address the service delivery needs in the evolving field of child abuse and neglect, an individual must critically consider national policies, state child protection systems, how communities provide services, and special problems of individual children and their families.

Social workers with expertise in interpersonal and individual functioning may have a range of team functions. In small communities, a social worker may be both a treatment person and a social work assessment person. In larger communities, the assessment and treatment may be performed by different workers.

The social worker on the assessment or treatment team may have had more direct experience with the family than others on the team and generally is responsible for gathering and presenting the facts of the case and psychosocial history. In many communities social workers are the only human service workers who are available regularly, and they may have more knowledge of child development and psychopathology than others involved. The social worker has been trained to look at a case from a perspective which includes the family in the community and the individual in the family. From this perspective and with knowledge of available community resources, the social worker can be crucial to making realistic and workable treatment plans.

Social workers with community organization and administrative skills will be catalysts for mobilizing the community's agencies and resources. Workers with such expertise are also needed to initiate innovative programs for high-risk and maltreating families. Seeking funding, recruiting staff, organizing training and supervision and establishing lines of communication with referring agencies all are appropriate uses of social work skill.

Perhaps the greatest difference between the social work role and the role of others on the team is that the social worker is likely to have both a history and a future with the family. At times other professional roles are limited to a specific phase of the case. The social worker usually has an experiential history with the family and the prospect of being immediately involved in the implementation of future plans. This sometimes creates tensions on the team, particularly if the trust level is not high or members are defensive about their work. The plans proposed by the team, which may be "easier said than done," must be put in a realistic perspective, and this is usually done by the social worker.

Physician–Social Worker Collaboration

Diagnosis

As a rule child abuse and neglect are detected by injury to or physical condition of the child, while the factors leading to harming the child are psychosocial. Thus in many situations it takes the collaboration of a physician and a social worker to determine whether the child's condition is a consequence of abuse or neglect. In some cases the physicians with expertise in child abuse and neglect will be able to tell by the presenting symptoms whether the injury is accidental or not. However, he/she may still be left with the question of who inflicted the injury and how disturbed the parent-child relationship is. Psychosocial information will be required to make that determination. For instance, parents may bring a child to the hospital with a broken arm and describe it as an accidental injury. The physician may ascertain the injury is inflicted and ask the social worker to assess family dynamics. On other cases, the medical data will not be definitive, and it will take the combination of medical and psychosocial information to make a diagnosis.

Similarly social workers involved with families in a variety of contexts will need a medical diagnosis to determine whether a child has been abused or neglected even though they perceive from a psychosocial perspective risk factors in the family. For example, a social worker may see an infant who is listless and small and parents who are overwhelmed. The worker would seek a medical evaluation of the infant—looking specifically for failure to thrive (FTT).

Follow-up

Collaborative follow-up of families by physicians and social workers is often important. The child's physical condition may require medical intervention beyond the initial diagnosis. This is the case when the injury is severe or when the child is suffering from a serious neglect condition, such as failure to thrive. Further, the physician can monitor for subsequent harm to the child. Social workers should always be a part of such follow-up because equally important is the family's psychosocial functioning. Data are usually gathered by the social worker on the child's functioning, on the parent-child interaction, and on the family's current social situation.

Court Testimony

Physicians and social workers should collaborate (with counsel) on preparation of cases which must go to court. Each is qualified to provide expert testimony in his/her own specialty. Thus the physician should testify regarding the medical data base. The social worker should talk about the psychosocial information and what services should be provided to the family based upon her/his knowledge of community resources. It is important for credibility that neither go beyond the sphere in which he/she is qualified as an expert. It is also necessary that both recognize that a physician's testimony is likely to have greater weight in court and plan accordingly. This is the case because physicians have a much longer tradition of being qualified as expert witnesses and because as a rule their data are more factual and concrete than a social worker's.

Thus at several different points in case management medical-social work collaboration is essential.

Collaboration Between Mental Health Professionals

Sometimes it is assumed that mental health professionals are interchangeable on a multidisciplinary team. That is, a social worker can do what a psychologist or psychiatrist can do and vice versa, and therefore one mental health professional is all that is needed. While it is true that there is some overlap in areas of knowledge, the range of mental health expertise required is so broad that it is unlikely that one person will possess all the necessary skills. Further, because working in the area of abuse and neglect can be very difficult, much benefit can be derived from collaboration by mental health professionals. We will discuss the need for collaboration in diagnosis and treatment planning, in treatment itself, and in providing court testimony.

Diagnosis

The range of information necessary for diagnostic work includes a knowledge of child development and abnormal behavior in children, an understanding of adult behavior and psychopathology, comprehension of the impact of environmental conditions such as poverty, unemployment, and racial discrimination on the capacity of a family to function, knowledge of family dynamics, knowledge of treatment modalities and their utility with various types of clients, and awareness of what resources are available in the community.

Typically, psychologists, unlike social workers and psychiatrists, are trained in administering developmental, cognitive, and projective tests. Such data are essential in diagnosing children's problems, for we know that children under stress, either from maltreatment or from other problems, are not likely to progress in line with developmental norms. In addition, certain common themes appear in projective tests of children who have been maltreated as well as in tests of parents who harm their children. Further, we know that it is important to understand parents' intellectual capability and ability to abstract in determining both their capacity to respond to treatment and the kind of treatment which might be appropriate.

A psychiatrist's expertise can be invaluable in diagnosing and forming a prognosis about the course of a psychiatric illness and its potential for response to psychotropic drugs. Psychiatric input is also useful when someone in the family is suspected of abusing medication or drugs. A psychiatrist is in a good position to make the determination of such abuse, when it needs to be assessed, and its impact on the person's capacity to care for children if the person is one of the parents.

Typically the area where social workers have greater knowledge than psychologists or psychiatrists is the area of environmental impact on functioning and community resources which might be available for intervention with the family.

Individual mental health professionals, regardless of their professions, will vary in their areas of knowledge. For example, some will understand and work primarily with children; others will focus mainly on adults. Or some will concentrate on intrapsychic functioning, while others will work more with interpersonal dynamics or manipulation of environmental contingencies to improve functioning. Therefore it is invaluable to have two or more mental health professionals involved in diagnosis. This will assure that the full range of knowledge is possessed by the multidisciplinary team. Beyond that it is important to emphasize that in diagnosis two or more heads are better than one. Diagnosis in cases like this is often difficult. The amount of data an individual typically is able to accumulate is limited; thus the more people involved in looking at the family and the data, the better. Moreover, most mental health professionals would agree that the information relied upon in making such decisions is "soft." Therefore it is very useful for persons to collaborate in evaluating it.

Treatment

More than one mental health professional may also be needed in treatment of an individual family. This need will vary according to the case. In cases where one parent is mentally ill, in situations where the child evidences emotional problems, and in cases of sexual abuse, more than one therapist may be essential. In cases like these, one person may be doing treatment with one part of the family, for example the mentally ill person or the child, and another therapist with the rest of the family or the family as a whole. Co-therapy may be necessary if the family is very large or fairly disturbed. If mental illness requires regulation by drug therapy, a psychiatrist needs to be involved in the treatment.

Court Testimony

Finally, when court testimony is required, a careful decision should be made about which mental health professionals should testify. If several professionals have been involved in diagnosis or evaluation of the family, it can be useful to have two or three testify, each highlighting a different part of the case. Such testimony is likely to have greater impact than that of a single expert. At other times, however, the number of witnesses will be limited. An important consideration will then be whose testimony will bear the greatest weight. That will depend upon the tradition in the particular court and the disposition of the judge and the jury, if there is one. However, a psychiatrist's testimony is likely to carry greater weight than that of a social worker. In addition, the quantifiability of some of the psychologist's data may impress the court more than less concrete information.

A difficult issue is how to handle a court appearance if one is a therapist involved with the family. The therapist may feel that providing damaging testimony will preclude any possibility of working with the family in the future. Here again, having access to multiple mental health professionals can have great utility. Sometimes an outside evaluation of the family can be done by someone other than the therapist, and that person (or team) can appear in court instead of the therapist. Alternatively, agencies that provide treatment to maltreating families often begin by doing an evaluation involving several mental health professionals and then one person becomes the primary therapist. In such a case, other persons on the evaluation team might provide testimony rather than the primary therapist. A comparable issue not necessarily centering on the therapist may be dealt with similarly. Frequently several persons in addition to mental health professionals, such as doctors, homemakers, nurses, and school personnel, will be part of a multidisciplinary team servicing a family. In choosing who should testify, the person whose relationship with the family is the best or the most intense might not be called as a witness so that he/she will be in a position to continue to work with the family after the court case is over.

In conclusion, it should be clear that in many cases more then one mental health professional needs to be involved. Further, there are a variety of ways mental health professionals can be utilized with families who abuse and neglect their children.

Social Worker and Lawyer Collaboration

About 15 percent of reported cases of child abuse and neglect eventually go to court. In such instances collaboration between social workers and lawyers on case management is essential. However, having a lawyer available for consultation prior to the courtroom stage can also be very useful.

Collaboration in Case Planning

In general, where the social worker thinks that reliance on voluntary cooperation by the parents may not be sufficient in a case of abuse or neglect, legal consultation should be sought at the early stages of involvement. A lawyer can provide legal information which will ensure the smooth handling of the case. In addition, he/she can help the social worker make a long-range plan which will pace potential legal involvement so it supports the casework goals.

For example, legal advice can facilitate getting medical, psychological, and psychiatric evaluations which may be important for case planning. Specifically, if families refuse to participate in evaluations voluntarily, the lawyer can assist in getting these court-ordered. Further, the social worker may feel that from the psychosocial standpoint coercive intervention seems indicated, and legal consultation may be necessary to establish whether there are legal grounds for intervention. For instance, the worker may sense a tremendous amount of tension between a parent and child; or the worker may have heard from an interested party who refuses to appear in court that a family has mistreated a child. In both examples, although the social worker may feel that court intervention is indicated, the lawyer might well advise that there are not sufficient data.

Collaboration Regarding Treatment

Assistance from a lawyer may also be helpful in implementing a treatment plan. There are some families who will not cooperate voluntarily but will if the court orders treatment. However, some families will become more resistant if intervention is ordered. A lawyer is also invaluable when a protective services worker or agency social worker foresees that a treatment plan which is in place may not work and court intervention may be needed to remove a child. The lawyer can make suggestions about how to collect data for court, how to document intervention attempts, how to keep case records which will support the case, and when and how to advise parents about possible court intervention.

Preparing a Case for Court

When a case goes to court, there are several ways a social worker may be involved. If the worker is employed in a community agency, he/she may be asked to do an evaluation. This request is most likely to come from the attorney for the state (protective services) or from the court. However, the guardian ad litem (attorney for the child) or the parent's attorney might also make such a request.

Similarly, if a worker has the family or some family members in treatment, he/she might be subpoenaed to testify by any of the three interested parties (state, guardian ad litem, or parent's attorney).

If the social worker is employed by protective services, the role is somewhat different. The worker would collaborate closely with the attorney for the state in preparing the case. They may work together on decisions about what witnesses should be called, what testimony should be elicited, what relief should be sought. Further the social worker may testify as a material or expert witness in a case. Or alternatively the worker may submit a written report with recommendations to be used at the dispositional phase.

While this amount of involvement is ordinarily accorded to the protective services social worker, it may not be to a worker in a community agency. The community agency worker should seek to play a role in courtroom planning compatible with his/her relationship with the family.

Court Testimony

Many social workers become anxious about providing testimony in court. A good way to reduce that anxiety is to be adequately prepared.

Thus the lawyer and social worker need to confer prior to the court appearance. In this process it is important that each accede to the other's expertise. The social worker understands the psychosocial data and is the appropriate person to make treatment recommendations. The lawyer understands what is legally feasible, what is legally admissible as evidence, and how to structure testimony so it will be persuasive. The lawyer will also know the legal ways to secure the desired treatment.

In the conference prior to the court appearance, the two parties need to agree generally upon what questions will be asked. The attorney should also tell his/her witness what to expect upon cross-examination.

An important problem for mutual resolution is the difference in perspectives ethically. A lawyer's duty is to present the best case possible for his client and to argue it vigorously. In contrast, a social worker would compromise his/her professional integrity by taking such a stance. Rather a social worker examines all available data and aspects of the social situation and makes an assessment and treatment recommendations based upon that material. What the social worker should be partisan toward is that assessment and those recommendations, and the worker should attempt to set forth in testimony the facts which led to these conclusions.

Such an approach may mean that the social worker will want to present some facts which might give support to the other side's case. This should be done for several reasons; however, the social worker may have to persuade the lawyer that providing a balanced view of the situation is appropriate. It is important to present such a view first to preserve the social worker's integrity and second to preserve his/her credibility as a witness. No situation is either all black or all white, and if the worker so portrays it, the judge or jury is likely to doubt the veracity of the testimony. In addition, the worker is ever mindful of the impact of testimony on the client, and biased testimony will make it even harder to help the parents in the future. Beyond these reasons, if the other side is adequately prepared, it is likely to bring out facts which support its side on cross-examination. Such testimony is likely to do less harm to one's case if revealed in direct examination.

Based upon the education and experience of the social worker, he/she may qualify either as an expert witness or as a material witness. The qualification is established at the beginning of court testimony. The distinction is an important one, for an expert may state an opinion and make recommendations and may rely upon hearsay evidence in arriving at that opinion. In the court context, hearsay will be the testimony of other witnesses who were directly involved in the events the expert lacks direct knowledge of. In contrast, a material witness may not express an opinion and may only testify to what he/she has experienced directly.

Importantly, these rules of evidence apply at the trial or in the adjudicatory phase and are not adhered to at the preliminary hearing or at the disposition. Thus a social worker may testify to some events at the preliminary hearing that he/she did not directly observe, and a social work report may be considered in deciding what to do about a case once the allegations have been proven. There are also exceptions to the hearsay rule which apply at the trial phase. The lawyer will know these and help the social worker construct testimony which takes these exceptions into account.

Another important strategy in providing testimony is to focus upon concrete observations rather than make conclusory statements (even when testifying as an expert). Thus, rather than state initially that "the mother has poor impulse control," the worker should say, "I watched her smack the toddler and knock him down when he started to turn on the TV set." Such concrete testimony is much more persuasive than conclusory statements.

A related point is that the social worker should be sure the judge or jury understands his/her language. Thus he/she should not rely upon professional terminology or jargon. When a term is used, it should be defined, and in general technical language should be avoided. If one makes the analogy that speaking in jargon is like speaking in French (to someone with rudimentary knowledge of that language), it is clear what an obstacle such language is to understanding. Because the listener must be engaged in translating the terminology, he/she is likely to lose track of the substance of what is being said.

Appendix A(1)

Normal Child Development

Ann E. Thompson

In what follows, I shall be talking about parents and their children. The parent and the child are partners in an ongoing process of growth and development, one which is both parallel and interactive. While each evolves as an individual, the individual growth processes modify and catalyze change in the other as they interact. It is like a river and its bank. The amount and force of water coming down the stream affects the shape of the bank. The characteristics of the bank, whether rock or soil, will channel the flow of the water. This course through life may also be usefully viewed as a series of unions and partings. Psychologically the mother, as pregnancy proceeds, must first accept the growing infant within her body and then, preceding birth, recognize the baby as a separate individual. Behaviorally as she recognizes the baby as a separate person, we see her buying clothes for the new infant and choosing a name. Birth allows the mother to accept the infant as physically separate, but if all is to go well, a psychological attachment begins and is the hammock in which the totally dependent infant begins to grow. The infant, because of immaturity, experiences the mother (or primary caretaker) as an extension of the self, but with maturing experience and the parent's encouragement, a progressive series of psychological separations occur within the framework of this bond.

For all children, regardless of ethnicity or socioeconomic status, psychological stages and developmental tasks are more or less the same. Each stage or step of psychological growth occurs in a roughly predictable form and can be described.[1] In the material that follows, the characteristics of the child and the necessary complementary and reciprocal characteristics of the parent will be described.

Of necessity the descriptions will be somewhat stereotyped, yet it is hoped they will represent features shared by most developing human beings. The description of normal parents may be such that you find yourself protesting,

"But wait, no parent can be or do all of those things," and you will be right. The reality is that the ideal does not exist, and in fact there needs to be only "good enough" parenting for a specific child to master a specific stage. In reading the description of the child you may think, "I recognize Johnny as being like that at age three, but Suzie was like that at age two," and again you will be right. What is possible to be more accurate about is that there is an order of development and there are predictable sequences. For example, caretakers talk with their children, leading to a child's capacity to understand language and then in turn to the child's own capacity to use language.

One part of development can be accelerated while another lags. For example: Suzie, a three-year-old, spoke in long charming sentences, knew her colors, and counted to ten. However, when her mother or father left the room, she stopped playing, became distressed, and sucked her thumb. Because she had been separated from them repeatedly as a younger child, she lacked the capacity to maintain her inner equilibrium without their presence. She had been unable to adjust at day care. Her intellectual skills were advanced. Her sense of independence and self-trust were delayed.

Another principle of development is that there appear to be critical periods when developmental tasks are best achieved. For example, this is true of the development of basic trust in others in the first six months to a year of life. It is for this reason that special effort should be made to meet the needs of infants and young children when they are developmentally ready.

Finally, development is measurable in the sense that one can compare a given child to his or her age mates. There are standards for *ranges* of physical and neurological normality. Neuropsychological development can be tested in a newborn by the Brazelton Test, in a child up to age three by the Bayley Test. These tests are not predictive of later IQ but do indicate intactness of neuropsychological mechanisms. For the child over three the Wexler Intelligence Scale for Children and the Stanford-Binet Test can be used.

As the child develops, it is important to remember that the parent's childhood will be "relived." As she/he interacts with the growing child, the first experiences of the parent, although "forgotten," will be relived and reenacted. The needs of the developing child will bring to life the met and unmet needs the parent had at that stage of development. Joys and pleasures, as well as old conflicts between love and hate, trust and mistrust, and self-reliance and dependence, will begin to be replayed in living color. This provides an opportunity for confirmation, fulfillment, and growth for some parents. Other parents, who cannot meet the challenge of reawakened conflicts and have few if any golden times to call on, will neglect or abuse their children at problematic developmental stages.

Attachment

Psychological development of the child proceeds in the context of interactions with psychologically important adults. As the child and intimate caretakers interact, an attachment bond forms over time. This bond can be defined as "a unique relationship between two people that is specific and endures through time."[2]

This life experience can be described on a feeling level and can also be observed in adult and child behavior. What the feeling is for the child no infant has been able to tell us! For the parent, in the ideal case, the experience is the overpowering, engrossing, pleasurable one of falling in love. As attachment occurs, this infant whose head is far too large for its body, whose legs and arms are spindly and poorly coordinated, becomes beautiful, unique, and marvelous. For those who don't participate in the process, the infant remains "just a baby." These feelings do not occur in a vacuum as if by magic, but occur when infant and caretaker interact over time with each other—touching, looking, listening, and even smelling and tasting each other. Behavioral indications of attachment can be found in the observation of the infant and the caretaker interacting together.

When mother and infant are close together, they gaze into each other's eyes, automatically adjusting their heads so the gaze is direct and prolonged. This is called the "en face" position. (The newborn infant is capable of focusing his eyes while in the quiet alert state. This state is present for a relatively prolonged period just after birth.) Using the modality of touch as a way to know and interact, we see the first approaches of a caregiver to the infant as tentative "pokings" at the baby's arms and legs with fingertips. This progresses to stroking the body of the infant with the whole palm and fingers. When held, the infant molds his/her body, cuddling and snuggling against the caretaker. Mother and infant also take each other in and are special to each other in the way they hear each other. Tests show that by six days of age baby responds differently to mother's, father's, and strangers' voices.[3] Some delivery-room nurses claim they see this response in the delivery room. Mother in turn becomes uniquely sensitive to her baby's cry, waking in the middle of the night to the soft cry no one else has heard. This caretaker's response to the infant is vital, as it is only by crying that the infant can signal, "I have too much tension to handle, come help." Gradually an infant develops a "vocabulary" of cries that the mother learns to differentiate. As the crying baby is picked up and soothed, she/he is able to move from distress into a state of quiet alertness where learning is possible.

The function of the attachment bond is to serve as a mutually rewarding feedback system so that the totally dependent infant and the caregiver are drawn together. The positive loving feelings help to neutralize the normal frustration and anger which occur in the course of looking after a baby.

Evidence of attachment in the child over six to eight months of age can also be confirmed by reactions to separations and reunions with nurturing adults. The specifics of these reactions will be detailed later as we look at the sequence of developmental stages.

The initiation of attachment appears optimal in a period of time immediately after birth. The biological mother, who has had months of experiencing the infant within her, appears immediately after delivery to be in a special state of hormonal readiness to attach. The normal infant has a period of prolonged alertness in the hour or two after birth which allows him/her to perceive and respond to caregivers in a way he/she will not be able to again for the next several days.[4] Attachment certainly occurs when early contact is not possible, but appears to take longer. As it occurs, the adult, whether biological mother, father, adoptive parent, foster parent, or other nurturer, becomes the vitally important "psychological parent" to the child.

Whether attachment proceeds smoothly or not will depend upon factors originating within the child, the caretaker and the environment. With regard to the child, it is important that he/she be capable of responding to the caretaker in predictable, gratifying ways. A child who can be soothed in a predictable way allows the parent to feel capable and successful. A premature or sick child may not be capable of rewarding the parent in this way. In addition, physical separation for medical reasons may interfere with the physical contact necessary for attachment to form. The caretaker's capability of nurturing will depend upon the nurturant care she/he received as a child. If adults did not receive sufficient love themselves as children, they will have great difficulty in giving it to their own children. An intellectual understanding of the child's needs, experience with previous children, and the events of the current pregnancy and delivery will also affect the adult's capacity to attach. There are a number of life events which can make for difficulties. For example, it is difficult to make an attachment while mourning the loss of another important relationship. This can occur with death, divorce, or a move. Mental or physical illness during the pregnancy or difficult labor and delivery may stress the mother so that the infant is born into an atmosphere of negative feelings and anxiety. Even with the most normal of pregnancies and deliveries, with a wanted healthy child, emotional and physical support for the mother (husband, friend, grandparents) is important to help this primary caregiver so she can go on giving to the dependent infant. In the recent past, in an effort to decrease infant deaths due to infection, the infant was physically separated from mother and other emotionally important adults. With a better understanding of the emotional price paid by everyone, some hospitals now consider having significant others in the labor and delivery rooms. Delivery of the infant with as little anaesthesia as possible allows the infant and mother both to be alert for the important hour or two after delivery. Parents are now encouraged to take care of their premature infants who are placed in incubators.

Difficulties in attachment appear to have an important relationship to the occurrence of later abuse and neglect. Margaret Lynch reported in Harold Martin's *The Abused Child*,[5] a study examining factors affecting attachment in twenty-five abused children. She compared them with their thirty-five nonabused brothers and sisters. In using brothers and sisters as controls, she demonstrated that these parents had been able to parent well when elements interfering with attachment were decreased. In the study she found that 76 percent of the abused infants had one or more factors interfering with attachment while their nonabused siblings were exceptionally healthy and robust, and in 71 percent of cases there were no interferences with attachment in siblings. The factors interfering with attachment included:

	ABUSED	SIBS
Abnormal pregnancy. Defined—medical and emotional illness, concealed pregnancy, or pregnancy where prenatal care was refused.	40%	8.6%

Abnormal labor and delivery. Defined —labor>24 hours, operative delivery, gestation<36 weeks.	48%	5.7%
Neonatal separation>48 hours.	40%	2.0%
Other separations>48 hours in first 6 months due to the mother or child's health.	36%	5.7%
Illness in child the first year—major or frequent minor.	60%	Sibs very healthy

Parenting

Being a parent is one of life's most complex and difficult tasks. It requires optimally the energy of a teenager and the wisdom of a grandparent! At the same time, it can be enormously joyful and rewarding. Certain aspects of parenting can be spoken about in general terms; other aspects will be much more specific to a particular developmental stage or age. Parenting will proceed more or less smoothly in those stages and areas where the parent was him or herself as a child able to master developmental tasks the child is faced with. Each developmental period will evoke demands peculiar to that stage of development. At those stages the parent was not parented well enough or where trauma occurred, there will be an increased challenge to the parent to meet the child's needs. For example, a mother whose first six months of life went smoothly may be very able to nurture an infant but have extreme difficulty in managing the toddler, who developmentally needs to say "no" in order to separate from her. Some parents will be so overwhelmed by tasks at particular stages of the child's development that abuse and neglect will occur.

In general, parenting requires the capacity to be psychologically available to the child and to perceive the child as separate, dependent, and immature, and then to provide the child with whatever is necessary to facilitate development at each stage.

Even when engaged in other tasks, the parent is attentive to the child's signals and communications. In the early months these communications will be quite ambiguous. The difficulty of these preverbal times can be heard in every parent's wish—"If only she would tell me what she wants!" The openness to perceive a child's cues is an empathic capacity which depends in large part on the parents' own early life and how their parents treated them. The frequency of interaction should be located somewhere along the spectrum that avoids either isolation or overstimulation. When either isolation or overstimulation occurs, it means the child's own rhythms and needs are being ignored. Although all parents will at times have feelings of and even act on anger, it is hoped that this will be in a healthy context for the child. It is an attitude of respect, liking, enjoyment, and appreciation for the child that gives the child good feelings about him- or herself and allows good self-esteem to develop. When this is the case, parents usually speak of themselves as adequate, though not perfect, parents. They have confidence in themselves in this role.

With an understanding of a child's needs and capacities, a parent can provide adequate physical caregiving including diet, basic cleanliness, physical safety, adequate sleep routines, and health care. The parent will give the child "room to grow," not only physically but psychologically. Much of the art of being a parent is involved in judging when to move in and when to stay out, when to follow the child's signals and when to lead. This requires an awareness of the child's separate being with separate age-appropriate needs. Part of being aware of the child's needs means not burdening the child with problems and stresses within the marital relationship or the extended family or problems from work.

A recognition of the child's immaturity and need for the parent is also seen in the area of social relationships. From the earliest months onward parents begin to prepare their children for future relationships as they touch, speak, and play with the child. Play is a source of pleasure, instruction, and mastery. Appropriate space and materials should be provided, but parents do not need to buy expensive toys for children. Preparation for living with other people also involves learning rules which help children interact appropriately with their physical world, their family, their neighborhood, their subculture, and the larger culture as children grow older. First, the parent will need to be there physically and consistently to set limits. The word "no" and firm, calm physical removal combined are usually sufficient. If the parent feels either frightened or angry, this feeling can honestly be expressed along with the "no" and physical removal. Afterward, a reaffirmation of the good feeling of the parent toward the child with reasonable speed is equally important. The most devastating experience for a young child involves the loss of the parent's love. As rules are learned and limits set, it's vital that the parent keep the positive relationship between the child and caretaker as a primary goal. Without this all else will go awry. To a certain extent this applies all throughout childhood and even into adolescence and adulthood. With regard to physical punishment, children do learn because of fear, but it is learning loaded with resentment and anxiety. Basically children want to learn for approval and take joy in mastery. As they mature and become more capable, they want to be "like grown-ups."

Consistency of response is important in order to avoid cognitive confusion in the young child, who cannot possibly be objective or understand the complexities of the adult world. If there is not a sufficiently consistent response, the child may withdraw or repeatedly test limits. Consistency requires that parents' responses be fairly predictable but not that they be rigid or inflexible.

Development

We will now look at the sequences of development which occur in the context of the attachment bond. The emphasis here will be on the psychological tasks of each stage.

Infancy to Twelve Months

The development of trust in others is of lifelong importance. The capacity for this develops in the first few months of life. It develops out of multiple repetitions of experience wherein a baby experiences tension and is then soothed before the tension becomes too painful or overwhelming. Typically, the tension is from hunger, cold, or wetness. If we watch a baby go through such a cycle, we see how she/he first stirs in discomfort. This proceeds to whimpering and then to crying with arms and legs moving. If the baby is not soothed, tension builds and major distress is then evident in full-fledged screaming and crying with a red face, arms and legs flailing. The younger the child, the more speedily she/he moves from the beginning stirring to total involvement. The longer the child is left in great distress, the more difficult it will be and the longer it will take for the infant to recover from the progressively severe disorganization. If picked up before this point, the baby will become quietly alert and relaxed as the tension resolves. Over the first few months as biological tensions become less demanding, if the infant has not been left too long earlier, she/he will develop the capacity to delay frustration and be able to wait until the bottle is warmed. Multiple repetitions of moving from feeling bad to feeling good create in the child a confidence that others will help and can be trusted. In these same interactions caretakers develop a confidence that they are good, capable caretakers as they observe their child move from being unhappy to being happy.

In addition to repetitive soothing experiences which build a sense of confidence, the infant is concurrently developing an awareness that the good experiences are connected with an "other" separated from the "self." No matter how vigilant and wanting to give, mother or father is not always present to soothe the child instantly. It is from these experiences that the child gradually becomes aware that the tension is with self and soothing comes from an other. Further learning about self occurs and can be observed as we see the infant beginning to inspect those people and things around him. The body self is also discovered. It's delightful to observe the infant in this process of discovery. Usually a hand comes up and then flies out of range of vision because of poor neuromuscular control. The infant's face is a picture of interest and surprise. Over the next few weeks control becomes better, and the hand is held up and explored with eyes and mouth. The child has found that the thumb is always available for soothing while mother is not! At about three or four months in age, hands can be brought together in the midline and the infant "plays" with them, leading to an integration of right and left, both sides of the body.

The learning during these preverbal times is a direct, immediate learning through the senses, a learning of how things look, how they feel, taste, smell, and sound. At this point people and things in the child's environment are there when they are there and gone when they cannot be heard, touched, felt, or tasted. When one observes, for example, the infant when there is a particularly interesting toy which then is covered up (e.g., a red ball being covered with a cup), the infant's attention turns elsewhere and no attempt is made to find it. A little later, peek-a-boo games become interesting as in this magical world mommy or daddy is "gone" when the face is covered and comes back by taking hands away! Gradually memory traces are laid down which allow the infant to distinguish familiar and known from unfamiliar and unknown. That most fascinating of all things, the caretaker's face, has been looked at, mouthed, smelled, and touched and is *known*. Some children by four months and almost all children by eight or nine months react and respond very differently to strangers. If these first few months have gone well, most children will not develop fearfulness of the stranger with mother present, but there will be a quieting and an inspection of this unknown face. Once mother signals that this person is all right by her own smiling and talking to the stranger, the child's curiosity will lead him also to begin to interact with the stranger.

The social bond which began with attachment enriches in detail over the next few months. From birth the newborn preference for looking at human faces proceeds to the point where by the second month (normal range of two weeks to four months) the infant smiles and gurgles. There may also be a waving of arms and legs like a puppy whose whole body wags. Many things are interesting, but people and especially primary caretakers are the most compelling.

It is in the context of human interaction that the beginnings of language develop. As mother picks up the infant, she speaks to him. "Hello, Johnny. Are you hungry? I'm going to feed you and you'll feel better." As she walks with him to the chair to sit down, if his crying continues she may say, "Now, now, in a minute you'll feel better. It's okay." As he feeds, she may continue to talk to him: "There, I told you so. When you're finished, we'll both go back to sleep." If you were to ask her, she'd probably say, "Of course he doesn't understand me." But what she is intuitively providing is a soothing stimulus to his ear and hers. A way to name the experience and to tie it together for both of them over time is provided by a word which the child begins to understand.

By about six weeks the infant will begin making sounds. By four and a half months she/he can clearly vocally indicate pleasure with squeals—for eagerness, "ah, ah"; for satisfaction, "mmm, mmm." Shortly after the time when "no" (seven months) and other familiar words begin to have clear meaning, the first word, such as "da-da," appears. This only happens when children have been spoken to and when their vocalizations have elicited a positive response and verbal feedback from those around them. As we observe caretaker and infant, this will take the form of games of babble between them. The caretaker will talk to the infant, and the infant will "talk" back. It is by such feedback from an important person in a pleasurable, fun context that language and other learning best progress.

The beginning of growth toward selfhood or separation is seen when at about four or five months the child's awareness is less connected with the inner tensions of the child and more focused on the world around him/her. There is an increased amount of time spent in the alert state. To the observer there is a new bright focused expression on the child's face. When offered a toy, the child is persistent and directed in exploring its characteristics. By six to seven months the baby, when held, arches away from the parent instead of molding against him/her. Exploration of the caretaker with eyes, hands, and mouth begins. Beware if you wear glasses! When mother is not present, some soft object associated with her love and nurturing can be used for comfort, such as a blanket or a diaper.

Most play at this age takes place at the caretaker's feet. At seven or eight months one can observe the child in the presence of others visually checking back to mother's face. Along with this visual scanning and comparing there is increased curiosity with regard to strangers plus an increased wariness. As part of increased awareness of mother's separateness and importance, when mother leaves between six and eight months of age, there is now an acute reaction. The child may become sad and cry. Play is interrupted. It is these kinds of responses to the primary caretaker's absence that have come to be called "separation anxiety." During this time also the child is learning on a concrete physical level about separateness.

Over this time of course there have also been enormous physical changes. Birth weight has doubled by four months and tripled by a year. Between five and eleven months creeping and crawling begin; by six months the baby can sit unsupported. Most children stand alone by eleven months (normal range nine to sixteen months) and walk at twelve months (normal range nine to seventeen months).

Control over small muscles improves, and coordination of eye and hand progresses. The infant has by about the third month the capacity to reach toward things. Between two and seven months he/she has the capacity to pick them up using the fingers to squeeze them against the palm. Between seven and twelve months something of interest can be picked up neatly between thumb and forefinger. Having the opportunity to practice the use of hands and of hands and eyes together can accelerate this part of development.

In summary, at one year of age we have a "waddler" (that's a "wad between the legs" toddler), who is curious, responsive, mobile, verbal, and trusting of caretakers. He/she has moments of intense pleasure, of playfulness, of intense interest in the environment as he/she explores. There are times of distress, of course, but these are minimal and quickly recovered from once the caretaker provides assistance.

One to Three Years

Between one and three years of age many tasks of lifelong importance will be initiated. The child will move from being a lap baby to being a very competent child ready to be away from parents regularly for several hours a day. By three years of age a child will have learned some basic rules of how to get along with other people and how to control anger and other feelings so that they are not totally overwhelming. The most primitive form of empathy will begin to develop. ("That would hurt me, and I wouldn't like it if it were me.") An early form of conscience develops, along with progressive control of and responsibility for the child's own body including toilet training. Having had a vocabulary of a few words at a year, at three the child will be able to talk in simple two- or three-word sentences. Thinking during this period will be an unsophisticated "primary" process, but a huge store of information about the physical, nonlogical properties of the world will be built. By eightteen months most children will have a solid sense of their gender identity, and by three will be practicing many of the behaviors associated with this identity. All these achievements are important and lay the groundwork for future development.

Psychologically there is an evolution of a sense of independence along with a capacity to perceive, remember, think, and test reality. The psychological separation of self from other (mother or the primary caretaker) is probably the most complex and difficult task of this period. Along with the sense of separateness comes an expansion of trust in others to include a trust of one's self. (We are able to get an idea of how difficult and yet how meaningful this psychological task is each time we as adults begin a new job or take new risks in any way.) At the beginning of this period, the child experiences people as an extension of the self, with their function being to fulfill the child's needs. By thirty-six months the primary caretakers have become people in their own right with their own likes and dislikes, with needs and personalities of their own separate from the child's. ("Father likes squash, yuck!") The primary caretaker (usually mother) is still of central importance, but a fascination with things and people pulls the toddler further and further away. However, when tired, stressed, or bored, the toddler returns to touch mother in order to refuel and be comforted and rested. In between, contact is maintained from a distance by voice, ear, and sight.

There is a great joy in the many new achievements and interests of this age. Children at twelve months seem relatively impervious to frustration and are willing to repeatedly try a new task. During this time a caretaker's emotional availability is essential, along with his/her approval to explore and his/her pleasure in new achievement. Without approval the child's own fearfulness about moving away may be reinforced by negative signals so that the child inhibits that part of himself which wishes to explore and expand his universe. If, however, the primary caretaker signals to the child that he/she too is getting great pleasure from newfound skills, the child moves forward with exuberance.

During this period of time, when the caretaker is not present, there is often a low-keyedness of activity. When he/she reappears, there is a return to high spirits. There is some evidence that under a year of age a separation of more than five days from primary caretakers may be too much for a child to handle emotionally. The development of a sense of self may be delayed if a separation extends beyond this time. Anecdotally, it was found in one day care center that children under two were able to involve themselves comfortably in play and that their mood was greatly enhanced if a picture of their mother was pinned to their clothing where they could see her face. It appears that children of this age simply lack the capacity to hold a clear memory of mother along with all the comfort that that implies within themselves in her absence. Without clear memory the child begins to feel out of sorts and miserable but is not able to understand why. A few months later, when memories are sustained, the child will advance to knowing who is missed.

This capacity to hold a clear memory is confirmed in the testing situation, where prior to eighteen months when a toy is covered, a child will not have a clear enough memory of it to seek it out. After eighteen months he/she will look underneath a covering for a toy. Games of hide-and-seek and retrieving become endlessly interesting as this discovery is tested and retested. When the child is completely sure that the object will still be there, the game will cease to be of such interest. At about nineteen months (fourteen to thirty months) he/she will have memory well enough established to seek two hidden objects even when the covers are reversed.

At about fifteen to twenty-four months, a new subphase begins. Mother or caretaker becomes important in a new and different way. The toddler brings toys to her in order to play with them *with her*. It is a most difficult time for everyone because along with this wish for more involvement there is also the need of the child to assert his/her own will, to define and redefine the boundary between self and other. "Do it my way," "no," and "mine" are frequently heard words. In rapid sequence a toddler of this age may cling and ask for help, and immediately push away and refuse the offered help. This ambivalence is at a peak sometime between fifteen and twenty-four months.

The pain of being left appears to peak at this time, so that there is crying and intense emotional anguish at being left. When caretakers are gone, there is restlessness and increased activity. On their return their importance may be expressed in the backhanded compliment of anger expressed by pouting, ignoring the returning parent, or rejecting a new gift.

Even the separation involved in going to sleep alone in one's own bedroom at night is difficult for children at this age. Under this stress the new grownup behaviors can dissolve entirely. During the night strong feelings and conflicts of the day may appear in dreams, so that an occasional night dream with wakening is not unusual at this time.

To everyone's relief, at about twenty-one months this crisis period seems to resolve. The child seems to find the place along a closeness-distance spectrum which fits best his/her particular needs. He/she appears to do this by taking the parent's rules, standards, and attitudes as his/her own. A child in this stage may be overheard talking to a doll in exactly the way the parent speaks, or may swagger up to a playmate with exactly the same gait as one of the parents has. Words also give a child a new control through naming objects and being able to express desires more specifically. Play helps the child too, as here the most grandiose of wishes can be achieved and tasks mastered. It is as if the child has come to the realization "I can't be grown up, but I can pretend I am."

By twenty-three to twenty-five months this new sense of independence and separateness is seen in the appearance of the words "me" and "I" and "mine" and "yours," recognition of self in the mirror, and the capacity to follow instructions such as "Show me a picture."

Learning of Social Rules

As the child moves away from the caretaker, he/she intrudes on the life space of others and is expected to learn how to get along with them. It is all right to bite a carrot, but not a nose. It is permissible to dig in the sand box, but not in the flower garden. It is all right to poop in the toilet, but not in the bed!

From the child's viewpoint, all of this not only is arbitrary but stands in the way of what he/she wants *right now*! Frustration of desires leads to anger—anger directed at the person doing the frustrating. At this age these feelings have tremendous force and can dominate all other parts of the personality, as seen most dramatically in a temper tantrum. Hitting and comments such as "I don't like you" are universally normal experiences in our culture. A child at this age lives so much in the present moment that at this time there is hate.

At the same time his/her uppermost fear is loss of love of this important caretaker. This requires adults to come in and assist with reassurances—"I know you are angry"—and with action or word or a calm reminder that the world is not ending for either of them. If a temper tantrum continues, sometimes a calm holding helps pull things back together for a child and says you don't want the child to hurt him/herself. It's a bit like the practice of training wild elephants where a wild elephant is tied to a tame elephant. Over time it learns how not to hurt itself with wild rammings and ragings simply by being calmly pulled along at the task. Gradually the adult who is like the tame elephant lends the child help at times when he/she isn't able to manage.

This will be especially important at transition times like waking up and going to sleep and times of fatigue or extra stress, as when the child is sick or in a strange place with too many new demands. Gradually over this time the child will develop enough control and maturity to begin to realize that one can both love and be angry at one and the same person. The learning of social rules is helped along also by the innate wish to imitate, to identify with those who are bigger and more powerful, and the wish for approval. When the child has been treated kindly, one will begin to see acts of concern and helpfulness toward others in distress.

Along with increased interest in social interaction with parents, other children have become interesting to the toddler. This is accompanied by the wish to have and do as other children. Play at this age is play at games of imitation, with one child doing the same as the other, in contrast to the cooperative or true sharing that will develop after age three.

LANGUAGE

The responses to the infinite askings of "whazzat?" give the child the name for the object. The name for the object is stored and used as another property along with its color, weight, hardness, taste, and use. If caretaker or older children respond to the child's questions and show interest in the child's desire to learn, the process of acquiring language is enhanced.

Thought is synonymous with action at this period. Up to four years of age actual demonstration is necessary in learning a task. For example, if a child is requested to squeeze a bulb when he sees a light go on and this is described only in words and models, he/she cannot do the task. The instructing words must be accompanied by actual demonstration so that the child can imitate the action and initiate it by saying "go" to him/herself. Another characteristic of early thinking is that it is egocentric; i.e., knowledge about the world is subjective knowledge pertaining personally to the child's needs, wishes, and experience. In addition, the reason for things happening in the child's mind is based on the goodness or badness of the child or someone very important to him/her. Fantasy has a powerful realness and thrust as strong as what we adults consider to be reality. Fantasy will fill in the gaps where knowledge is not provided or understood.

Sense of Time

Only the dimension of *now* without future and past is possible for a child at this age. The concepts of hours, days, and weeks will not be learned until age five or six. A very long time may be the five minutes the child has to wait to eat. If there is a need to help the child understand tomorrow, it may be understood if one says at about noon of the preceding day, "You will have a nap, and then play and then eat supper and then go to bed with Snoopy. When you wake up, that is tomorrow and we will be going to Johnny's to play."

Sexual Development

The infant at home will probably have been in the bathroom with family members of both sexes. He/she may get dressed and undressed in the same room with older children and adults or may have joined the parents at the community swimming pool and in the changing rooms.

Sexual development, much like thinking and language, is well elaborated by three years of age but not mature.

By the age of three and for the next few years children in our society get an open chance to observe the many and wondrous variations in the old and young, fat and thin, pregnant and not pregnant bodies. They will be learning as children of this age learn—by touching, by seeing, and primarily by doing. They will be touching themselves, and they will find very early that touching their penis or clitoris is pleasurable. The parents' reactions without words will have major impact on whether the child gets the message "That part of yourself is bad" or "That's nasty," which will have long-lasting effect. Hopefully, the child will instead learn manners in sexual areas as he/she has learned manners in other areas. Incidents demonstrating sexual interest and curiosity can provide the opportunity to teach concepts of privacy and also confirm the essential goodness, pleasure and importance of sexual behavior. The child should learn that the genitals should not be touched in public; at the same time, guilt-free acceptance of this part of the child's self lays the groundwork for acceptance of this part of the self as an adult. (Women who have masturbated to orgasm are much more likely to achieve orgasm with a partner.)

Children have a natural curiosity, a desire to continue to learn, which we want to encourage and foster. They will touch all parts of their parents' body, including breasts and penises. Once they begin to speak, they are going to say as well, "What's that?" just as they ask "What's that?" about a million other things. Parents are best advised to respond in an accepting way and by giving appropriate names for the private parts, but also to tell their children not to touch others' private parts.

By age three (for most children by about eighteen months) this child will have a firm sense of boyness or girlness. We call this the core gender identity, and it appears to be irreversible once formed. Over the next period of time from about age three to age six or seven, children will be imitating and practicing what it is to be a little boy and/or man or little girl and/or woman in the particular culture in which they are being raised. These roles will be practiced and played at just as will other roles. If you observe children at play in these ages there usually are differences in play. Little boys will be more involved in large motor play and in identifying with the heroes on television or in their lives otherwise. Little girls will be more involved in small muscle play and will be pretending at roles that they see their mothers and other women in their life involved in.

If children of this age have an opportunity to observe intercourse, they will imitate this behavior too. To interpret this behavior as mature genital sexuality is as much a mistake as to interpret their playing house as actually understanding and taking responsibility for running a household as an adult.

Some behaviors and roles will be kept and some behaviors will be dropped according to approving and disapproving reactions of parents. If you think, for example, about a little girl who puts on lipstick, comments are usually a smiling approval of her cuteness and sexuality. If a little boy uses the same bright, interesting paint stick to adorn his body, he's told to "go clean up." It is by multiple repetitions of similar incidents that the child's behavior is shaped.

Meanwhile the groundwork is being laid for other aspects of successful mature sexuality. Some developmental issues which, when resolved appropriately, will enhance later sexual functioning are:

I am a separate whole person.
I can trust myself.
I can say no and protect myself.
I am likeable.
I can wait for what I want.
If I can't have it this way, I can have it another.
I can make choices.
I can share responsibility and live within family rules.
I can love or consider the feelings of others and communicate with them about my own feelings.
I possess the capacity for intellectual growth and learning.

Three to Five Years

By age four, most children's language is mature in structure and syntax. Children who must learn more than one language, for example that of their immediate environment and that of the dominant culture, will be somewhat delayed. However, the child of four will usually speak in sentences and have a rich vocabulary that far exceeds his thinking capacity. Pseudo-maturity of language and knowledge confuses unsophisticated observers, convincing them that children might be appropriate witnesses in court proceedings.[6] A vast storehouse of facts about the world is accumulating. The capacity for more mature thinking is based on the differentiation of function between cerebral hemispheres of the brain. At about age four or five the development of the corpus callosum, which connects the right and left hemispheres, allows communication between them so that functions can become differentiated. In the usual right-handed person, the right hemisphere stores single words, musical information, and visual imagery of dreams and daydreams. The left hemisphere is the site of logical and abstract thought, mathematical thinking, and complex language. The ability to reason is still very limited at four. Cause and effect are not understood. If an identical quantity of liquid is poured into a short, wide glass and a tall, thin glass, the child at this age will be convinced that the tall, thin glass has more in it. The capacity for differentiation is just beginning at age four or five, however, and will continue through adolescence. The thinking of the preschooler remains magical, egocentric, and moralistic and lacks the dominance of reality over fantasy.[7]

Social skills also advance. In the context of family and neighborhood day care and perhaps nursery school, play with others takes on new characteristics. In addition to imitation, elaborate fantasy play appears. The more or less independent, parallel play of the younger child now extends to cooperative play and more ease in sharing. Together children act out rich elaborate fantasies of what it is like to be a baby, a policeman, Superfly, Batman, or Wonder Woman. The things which men and women in these children's lives do is "played at."

In the context of the family, little girls at this age have a special "love affair" with daddy and make some resolutions. The little girl accepts that mommy and daddy belong together in a way she and daddy cannot ever, while to some degree she realizes that by being like mommy she can be big and have someone like daddy of her own someday. Little boys go through a similar process in regard to mommy (the Oedipal conflict). They have fantasies about replacing or even doing away with daddy in order to have an exclusive relationship with mommy. For most children the fantasies are translated into some type of behavior. For instance, little Suzie may crawl down between her parents in bed and then attempt to push mother out. Or Johnny may inform his father that mommy and Johnny have a lovely time when he (daddy) is gone, and they want him to leave for good.

The intensity and the duration of these "love affairs" with parents will vary with different children, but they are ordinarily resolved (in large part) by the time the child enters school. The resolution will be facilitated if the parent handles the child's attempts to usurp the adult role in a firm, calm, matter-of-fact way.

Considerable psychological trauma may result if the same sexed parent dies or there is a separation or divorce just prior to or during the oedipal period. This is because the child interprets the event as being a consequence of his/her murderous or competitive wishes.

The formation of conscience which began earlier with the fear of disapproval or punishment and a wish to imitate is now followed by the idea that "I do this and I don't do that because that's what my mommy or daddy does or doesn't do, and I want to be like him or her." Children at this age know the rules and will enforce them in regard to one another very fiercely. This may mislead adults into thinking that they truly have the capacity to withstand strong impulses when in fact they do not. Without an adult there and sometimes even with an adult there, the available candy will disappear and little sister will get hit! By age five these rules will be more truly a part of children and their own sense of guilt will help keep them from breaking rules.

Six to Ten Years (Latency)

The elementary school years are concurrent with further shifts in development on several levels. This is typically called the period of *latency*. It refers to the turning away of energies from the sexualized relationships with mother and father to an identification with the same-sex peers in the larger school and neighborhood culture. In this light it can be seen as a time of consolidation of sexual identity and roles. During this time the child's individual version of male or femaleness is integrated into the personality. This is done in the context of brothers and sisters and friends. During this time there is much normal discussion and investigation of sexual matters. Sexual behavior among brothers and sisters or playmates has no detrimental effect on development if the children are approximately the same age, if no force is involved, and if it remains at the exploratory level and does not become a fixed habit.

Members of the family on balance become less important and seemingly less perfect; in fact this is a time of disillusionment in regard to their perfection! Teachers and others in the child's social experience are now quoted and looked up to. The parent who when his son was four heard himself quoted as the ultimate authority now, at age six, hears the child's teacher quoted to *him* as the ultimate authority!

Learning in the classroom setting is possible because of improved impulse control and an increase in intellectual capacity. By age eight or nine logical "secondary thought" enables the understanding of cause and effect. Instead of the cause of an event being related by the child to his/her badness or goodness, by age eight or nine the idea that there may even be intermediate steps in the process of cause and effect and that things can be relative and arbitrary begins to be understood. Verbal explanations and symbolic drawings become understandable. The capacity to be objective appears with a shift away from magical thinking. One reflective nine-year-old was able to verbalize this shift with one foot in the past and the other in the present. He stood flicking water drops into a hot pan on the stove. The drops jumped and hissed and evaporated into steam. Reflecting on the phenomenon and his own capacities, he said, "I like to be magic, and I like to be logical." The more primitive forms of thinking remain, while the more sophisticated have increasing dominance. Under stress this higher level of control may be disrupted so that earlier modes of thinking will reappear. (Remember ghost stories around the campfire?)

The capacity to learn in the school setting will depend partly upon how responsive the school is to needs of children, be they very bright, average, or children with special problems. It will also depend upon how school and learning are regarded by the child's family. If parents value the child's school achievement, help the child when he has difficulty, and intervene on the child's behalf when he has trouble, he is more likely to realize his potential. If this kind of family support is not available and individuals at school are not supportive, the child may not do well.

Time will also at this period become less subjective. Past and future can be comprehended, although not on an adult level until midadolescence.

A child's conscience is well established by now. He/she will be able to abide by the rules of the game even when losing (unless there are rules about when it's okay to cheat). Play at this age is play of games, more frequently with peers of the same sex. Most of us can remember the exclusive cliques and clubs of those times and the disdain of the opposite sex. Boys, yeck! Girls, ugh!

Adolescence

Adolescence begins with an upsurge of sex hormones, beginning with girls at about eleven and boys a year or two later. Hormones catapult the child into puberty. The words "upsurge" and "catapult" are used as attempts to convey the rapid and major changes that occur and the resulting struggle to maintain a sense of balance. Hang on for the ride! There are changes in body shape and size and sexual functioning, in the sense of self, in one's relationships to family and friends, in intellectual capacities, and in the capacity to manage new and powerful feelings. As difficult a time as it is for all adolescents, those who have mastered previous developmental tasks will probably manage very successfully at this time.

The adolescent's process of clarifying a sense of individuality for him/herself involves a new separation from the family. The adolescent initially seems clear about who he/she is not, i.e., "I am *not* like my parents" or their standards, rules, or values. The criticism which accompanies this phase—"What horrible music" or "This food is terrible"—is an indicator that all is proceeding normally. In minority families, children may criticize how their parents relate to the majority culture. Parents may be belittled for not becoming assimilated or for becoming too assimilated.

Along with stating "who I am not," the adolescent explores and struggles with "who I am." In moving away from family, he/she derives support from and accepts the values and standards of the peer group. Fads and hair style and hair length, "in" language, clothing styles, and dancing serve not only to define the boundaries between parents and adolescents but also to provide a clear, mutually approved way to think and act.

If the adults involved are uncomfortable with "letting go" and react with increasingly harsh restrictions or disapproval, the adolescent may escalate into actual rebellion in order to break away. Part of separating from old values may include antisocial acts in the company of friends, such as stealing and other "crimes" against property. This may occur at about eleven or twelve years of age. Where development has been normal up to this point, it is likely that once this stage is over, the child's functioning will proceed well again. Minority and poor children are more likely to exhibit such reactions of alienation they feel toward society beyond the feelings of adolescence.

Overreaction, with criminal prosecution of such acts, can have a seriously damaging effect on the child's future functioning. In general, however, if standards are not too strict, supervision not lax, and punishment not too severe, true delinquency does not occur. If such antisocial acts appear later in development, however, at about thirteen to fifteen, there is much more cause for concern about the child.

The necessary mastery over strong sexual and aggressive feelings which are present at this time is gradually achieved by several means. Feelings are again put into words instead of acted out, and there is much fantasizing and playing out of trial solutions. Also, a reidentification with adults allows the adolescent to increasingly cope with the turmoil of this period.

While parents are held at a distance at least until the adolescent feels firmer in his/her sense of self, other adults are turned to for support and information. Coaches, teachers, and older neighbors or gang leaders become important resources in making this transition.

Usually the most explosive and painful part of the process of separation is over by age fourteen or fifteen. As the midteens arrive, parents and child have hopefully arrived at a new comfortable distance with each other. By late adolescence the child may even begin to communicate again about concerns on a new level of maturity and equality. The move to independence and autonomy is also aided by having a job outside of the home setting. In our culture, the final steps of achieving job skills and full economic independence may be drawn out over many years of continued education.

A new level of mastery either in or out of the school setting is greatly assisted by another major move in thinking capacities. For the first time the child is capable of truly abstract, symbolic thought. (One thirteen-year-old said on starting school in September, "I hate the first day of school. It's not really today I hate," he said in a reflective tone, "it's what it symbolizes.") This allows subjects such as math, physics, and chemistry to be introduced into school curricula. For the first time a teenager can understand that just as 6 plus 4 equals 10, 10 minus 6 equals 4. Reality at this age finally takes precedence over fantasy as a source of truth—though this must be with the qualification that the emotions are not too high. When they are not, a new kind of objectivity is possible.

In midadolescence (age fourteen to sixteen) the brain-mind development now progresses to the point where the child has the full capacity for abstract thought and an adult sense of time. An adult sense of time with the capacity to understand past, present, and future allows a new comprehension of the concept of death, and gives a new meaning to life and human relationships.

Sexual development associated with puberty is occurring about four months earlier every ten years. Black children achieve sexual maturity somewhat earlier than whites. Puberty occurred for girls at age seventeen in 1833, and in contrast it now begins at age nine or ten.

As ovaries produce increased level of female sex hormones, breast buds form and are present by age eleven. Menstruation begins between ages ten and thirteen. Boys enter puberty approximately two years later than girls, at age twelve. First there is enlargement of the testes and scrotum. Ejaculation is typically present by age thirteen or fourteen. Increased production of hormones causes great changes in the body shape and size.

From birth to the school years the areas of predominant body pleasure undergo shifts. In the first year stimulation of the skin and mouth are predominantly sought. In the second year awareness of pleasure located in the anal area appears. The nerve supply to this area is the same as that to the genital area, which is the next area of body pleasure. At puberty with the increase in sex hormones and subsequent body changes there is an increased awareness of pleasure associated with the genital area. How this pleasure is sought and satisfied will depend upon the culture and the course of sexual identity set in childhood. A homosexual experience at this age cannot make a person homosexual; this course will have been set much earlier in the child's life. It may, however, provide an opportunity for an awareness of homoerotic feelings and behaviors.

Initial steps in the process of developing sexual relationships frequently involve exploration of the newly developing sexual self in the safe presence of groups of the same sex. Talking, looking, and imagining precede explorations and behaviors, which are best initiated by a person at the time he/she feels ready. Turning away from family in the sexual context means the choosing of a special girl- or boyfriend. Reproductive maturity precedes psychological maturity. If pregnancy should occur before psychological separation from the family and establishment of a clear identity, an extremely important development process is interrupted and there is serious disequilibrium.

Notes

1. McLaughlin, *The Black Parent's Handbook.*
2. Klaus and Kennell, *Maternal-Infant Bonding.*
3. *Ibid.*
4. *Ibid.*
5. Martin, *The Abused Child.*
6. Mahler, Pine, and Bergman, *The Psychological Birth of the Human Infant.*
7. Blos, Peter, Jr., in Gellert, *Psychosocial Aspects of Pediatric Care.*

Appendix A(2)

Functional Tasks of Child Development

Judith Kleinman

In evaluation and treatment in cases of child abuse and neglect, it is often important to assess the status of the child involved. To do this, it is important to have a basic understanding of issues of child development. For this purpose, I will review tasks in emotional development which children usually accomplish during their childhood. I am categorizing this discussion into areas of psychological functioning rather than using one of the more traditional frameworks for discussing development, because I believe that the clarity of the evaluation is helped by keeping in mind the trends of development and their results in adult psychological functioning. I have chosen functions most affected by abuse and neglect.

In brief outline, the areas of psychological functioning which I will be discussing are:

Intense feelings and increasing ability to handle them
Sense of self and others
Self-esteem
Conscience

Intense Feelings and the Increasing Ability to Handle Them

It is difficult to discuss specific feelings of early infancy since there is little evidence that for the first few months infants are experiencing what we would generally describe as affect or feeling. Rather, they usually alternate between periods of equilibrium or contentment, sometimes described as a steady state, and periods of tension. These periods of tension are characterized by psychological disequilibrium with behavior such a crying and diffuse motor activity. Such periods of tension are a response usually to some physical need and are generally the same response whether the need is hunger, pain, or cold. Gradually during the first year of life, however, these global and general states are replaced by more specific expressions of what appears to be genuine feeling or affect. During the first year, we could categorize the feelings which do emerge as anger or rage, love, sadness, fear, and anxiety. Rage emerges in the latter half of the year and is global and usually overwhelming to the child. It is a reaction to frustration. Love also emerges as the infant begins to attach to specific people, and is expressed as happiness and contentment from being with a specific, important person. Sadness, at least in its early roots, also appears during this time when such behavior as withdrawal, a sober expression, and lack of response indicates the absence of a special person. Fear also emerges as a reaction to threatened danger, again later in the first year of life. Fear is closely related to anxiety, which is a general state of tension, alertness, and unease and is a signal of internal or external danger. Anxiety probably emerges before fear. In the first year of life, anxiety is most frequently seen in reaction to loud noises, overstimulation, and the presence of strangers or unfamiliar people.

These early evidences of feelings expand to the full range of affects through the following years of childhood and become more specific to specific situations, specific frustrations, and specific contentments, attachments, and pleasures. As they emerge, the child needs to learn ways of expressing the feelings, channeling them, or blocking them when necessary. The modes of expressing and coping with intense feelings tend to be carried out in two ways, physical and verbal. Early in childhood what one frequently finds is that a child will tend to find one mode more natural than the other for expressing feelings. For example, a child who shows precocious verbal ability will frequently find it quite easy to express, channel, and handle affects verbally. On the other hand, children who tend to be active physically frequently are a little later in the development of verbal skills and tend for a longer time to express feelings in a physical way. Through the course of development the child increasingly expresses intense feelings through words and other symbols and modifies or channels them when they become problematic. The negative feelings such as anger and rage are frequently the most problematic, and there is the most pressure for learning to mute and channel these feelings. However, pleasurable feelings can also become problematic if they become overtly sexual and are not contained. Early in childhood these feelings have primitive open expression, and there is only external pressure to modify them. Gradually this is changed throughout childhood and adolescence to an internal pressure—the motivation of the child him/herself to divert, channel, or express appropriately the feelings. This shift to an internal mode occurs first by identification with the parent who has been providing this limitation and structure, then by fear of loss of love of the loved parents or parenting people, and finally by wanting to live up to an inner self-expectation.

In order for this area of psychological functioning to be developed optimally through childhood, the environment needs to provide certain factors to facilitate handling intense feelings. It is important that the environment provide adult models of appropriate expression and diversion of such feelings and consistent limit setting for the children. If the parents themselves are impulsive and violent, for example, in expression of aggressive impulses and feelings, it is hard for the child to learn constructive handling of these feelings. In addition, the environment needs to provide loving, parenting persons who are also the limiting people, so that the negative feelings become modified by love. One of the most important modes of modifying aggressive feelings is their neutralization by the love and caring that the child has toward the same person. If the bonding and the loving between these people do not develop optimally, then there is less normal fusion of love and anger to mute and modify anger than is optimal. Another important quality that the environment needs to provide, particularly when the children are quite young, is persons who can sense when any of these feelings are becoming so intense they are overwhelming to the child and can step in and protect the child from them. This provides the child with the reassurance that these intense feelings are not dangerous and need not be overwhelming in their impact.

There are two common constellations seen in serious abusive or neglectful families around the handling of intense negative affect or impulses. Frequently, such parents deal with anger by repressing it rigidly until they are overwhelmed; they then have no alternative means of coping with anger except impulsive expression. Unless a child is exposed to alternatives in other settings, living with parents who have this style tends to create similar modes of defense in the child: rigid suppression and denial and impulsive aggression when the anger is intense.

The other commonly seen characteristic in abusive and neglected families is adults who have even less control, in whom aggressive outbursts are more common and arise under a minimum of frustration and anger. Children raised in this setting will also tend to take on a similar style of defense and become impulsively aggressive with frustration and anger.

Sense of Self and Others

A child's emerging sense of him/herself, sense of other people as real other people, and sense of trust in others is accomplished over several years beginning early in infancy. This accomplishment is dependent on a series of psychological steps which have been labeled psychological attachment followed by separation and individuation. This process begins when the infant first begins to experience itself and the other people caring for it as continuous. Very early in infancy a young child experiences itself and the other people around it much as a slow-speed motion picture, that is, as each event and interaction being separate and not continuous with the next. Gradually, by repeated and consistent experiences and maturation of the central nervous system, the infant gains a memory of past events and a concept emerges of both itself and other people being permanent and continuous over time. As this becomes a reality for the infant, there emerges the psychological attachment with the parent or parenting people. This heightens around five or six months of age, and through this process the infant emotionally attaches to a certain person or persons as specific primary objects. For an adult to become an infant's primary object, it is important that she/he be present consistently and involved in its care. As this "symbiotic" relationship emerges, it is experienced by the infant as a sense that its well-being and comfort are dependent on this other person's presence. The behavioral expressions of this emerging symbiotic relationship are such cues as the infant seeking out eye contact with this person or people, the infant looking for the person when it hears this person's voice, the infant reaching up to be held and snuggled by this person. Around eight months another behavioral manifestation emerges—stranger anxiety. By that is meant the infant's viewing anyone who is unfamiliar or who is not the primary caretakers with some distress, either seriousness and nonresponsiveness or overt crying. This behavior is calmed immediately by the primary object's arrival and is an expression of the infant's increasing awareness that the primary objects are the important, dependable people. Also around this time and even more intensely around fourteen or fifteen months of age a young child will become somewhat more sober, if not distressed, when the primary objects are not in view or in the same room. The infant at this point needs to check periodically on this person to be sure that she/he still is there and has not been lost.

After this period of maximum psychological attachment there begins a gradual process of separation-individuation over the following year and a half to two years. What gradually emerges is the accomplishment by the child of perception of itself as a whole integrated person separate from important others. Another way of describing this phenomenon is the emerging ability to feel separate and yet be related to important other people in an intimate way. This process continues through adolescence and often through some of adulthood, but the critical beginnings of it are from six months to three years.

Margaret Mahler has been the person who has most carefully described the process of differentiating following the symbiotic relationship. She has labeled the period from twelve to eighteen months as the beginning of the differentiation period and calls it the practicing period. During this stage, the child becomes a toddler and develops the physical ability to be mobile and to leave behind its important adult people. Children physically practice separation and autonomy but usually want to be near the mother at the same time. This is the age at which a child may toddle off through the house, suddenly realize it is far away from mother, become panicked, and cry out in great distress until she comes. It is also a period of the greatest self-love and enthusiasm in exploration of the child's surrounding world. Around eighteen to twenty-four months begins a period which Margaret Mahler labels "rapprochement." What she addresses with this term is that the child goes through a period during which she/he is suddenly becoming aware of her/his independence and becomes frightened. What emerges in behavior is that the child again becomes more distressed at separation from the important adults. Frequently parents will say that a child who earlier was quite happy and content to toddle around the house suddenly never wants the mother out of its sight, has trouble going to sleep, and does not want to be left by the parents. Again there are ups and downs and changes day to day in a child of this age in its comfort with separation. What emerges at the end of this stage is a better sense of comfort with being a separate individual and having needs which are different from those of the adults around him/her. The following period from twenty-four to thirty-six months is a period of consolidation, with similar but less intense ups and downs as the child tests out the significance and emotional responsiveness of the caring people as well as its own separation from those people. If all goes well during this stage, very important psychological groundwork is accomplished. The psychological functionings dependent on the emotional development of the attachment and then differentiation are a confident sense of a separate self, an ability to be autonomous but also rely on and give to others, an ability to see and relate to others as separate individuals, empathy, and a tolerance for love and anger toward the same person.

The difficulties in older children and adults for whom these early years have not provided adequate attachment and then separation and individuation range from subtle to crippling.

One area where conflict is commonly seen is dependence versus independence, where one expects a gradual progression from adequate nurturance from adults to predominate self-nurturance by adulthood. If a child is inadequately nurtured or if its moves toward autonomy and self-nurturance are not supported, the child will grow up experiencing him/herself as helpless and needing other people in order to function adequately.

Another major difficulty which emerges when these functions have not been adequately developed is an incomplete sense of self. This is most easily defined by the pathology frequently called narcissistic character disorder or "as if" personality. Persons with this disorder experience themselves as incomplete, empty, hollow unless they are with another person. "As if" personalities derive sense of wholeness from other persons and not from their own actual personality. They see other people as extensions of themselves. The effect of this is that relationships with others are shallow but a loss of a relationship can be quite devastating because the narcissistic character disorders have nothing left. Furthermore these people will literally change personality with different people and have a "chameleon personality." Thus a mother may seem intact in an evaluation but be quite different with her boyfriend who is aggressive and violent.

The final effects I would mention are the inability to trust, the inability to empathize, and the inability to love and hate the same person (splitting), all effects evolve from unsuccessful attachment and separation—individuation. These qualities—trust, empathy, and ability to tolerate ambivalence—are very important to adequate parenting.

These difficulties are present in many parents who have abused or neglected their children, and they will frequently emerge in children who have been abused or neglected in a way which affects attachment and separation, or individuation.

Self-Esteem

This function is interwined with the sense of self, and in fact some of the emotional groundwork is in the same process of symbiosis and then separation. The most important roots for sound self-esteem lie in two areas. First, in very young infancy a child's sense of being a worthy person who is lovable is dependent upon repeatedly experiencing loving, caring, and relief of tension by the adults caring for the infant. It is of course difficult to know what is going on in a child's mind during this stage. What we do know is based on evaluation of older children and adults who have had difficulties during these very early months of infancy, which may not have been related at all to the emotional ability of a parent to parent. Frequently the difficulties are related to a physical problem for which there is no relief. Children and adults who experienced frequent physical distress with no relief for prolonged periods early in infancy have a core sense of being unworthy and unlovable and a potential for severe depression which often never totally disappear no matter how good the subsequent experiences. There is, then, this core sense of self-esteem which is laid very, very early in infancy and has a physical basis.

A second root of self-esteem lies in the separation and individuation process. Self-esteem is dependent on acceptance and love of the toddler's autonomy and actual personality characteristics. When there is inadequate support for separation and individuation, an older child or adult will feel unsure of him/herself, will have a limited or pervasive sense of being an unworthy, unlovable person which is usually related to specific characteristics and which usually is relieved by a close and accepting relationship.

Both the sense of self and the sense of self-esteem require similar qualities from the environment of the child to be accomplished optimally. First, consistent and predictable nurturing persons who are present over the three years are needed. These developmental processes can be devastated and at times permanently damaged by the loss of the people to whom the child is attached. The effect of this will vary with the quality of the attachment, the stage of development, and the totality of the loss. The effect is most devastating with the total disruption of good attachments during the period of six to eighteen months of age.

Also needed for self-esteem early in infancy is the capacity of the infant to respond to efforts to calm and comfort by the caring people. Later, permission to separate, acceptance of the toddler's own needs, and tolerance of both separateness and neediness from the child are important.

Conscience

The psychological function of conscience or superego in adults has its roots in very young childhood in the relationship with the important caretaking people. The development of the superego as a more autonomous function, however, reaches ascendancy in the years of five to seven, a bit after the consolidation of separation. It is not a solid internally functioning quality until late in adolescence, but the important roots are laid in the years five to seven. Conscience evolves from taking in the morality and ethics of people who are important to the child, that is, the primary objects or the important caretakers. It is dependent on first experiencing externally consistent limits and then gradually internalizing these and indentifying with the parent. The roots of conscience lie first in the fear of punishment by people who are taking care of the child and whom the child loves, later in fear of loss of the love, and finally in internalized self-expectation.

From the environment the child needs to have consistent limits that are followed by all in the family as well as imposed on the child by the emotionally important people. The effect of unpredictable adults who do not live within the limits that they set for the children is an ineffective conscience. If a child sees its parent violating the guidelines of moral and ethical behavior or receives unspoken permission to behave against these limits, the child will often take on what is implicitly permitted rather than what is explicitly required. The evolution of conscience is also facilitated by the limits coming from someone who also loves and cares about the child and in return is admired and loved by the child. If conscience is founded only on fear, it will be brittle, rigid, and ineffective in helping a growing child and later an adult deal with his/her own impulses and the surrounding world.

Appendix B

Social History Outline

This outline is suggestive of categories to be included: The worker need not cover everything when completing a social history; rather, areas covered should be germane to the case.

I. Family members

   A. Full names
   B. Ages
   C. Relationships to head of household

II. Presenting problems and source of referral

III. Individual household members — background to present functioning

   A. Adults (i.e., father, mother, stepmother, stepfather, grandparents, mother's live-in partner, other relatives, friends) living in household

      1. Education
      2. Occupation
      3. Ethnic identification
      4. Religious background
      5. State of health
      6. Illness
      7. Work history
      8. Recreation interests
      9. Alcohol or drug history
      10. Marital history — Psychosexual functioning
      11. History of family of origin
      12. Intellectual functioning
      13. Personality

         a. Mood
         b. Impulse control
         c. Interpersonal relationships
         d. Capacity to parent
         e. Evidence of psychopathology or adjustment

B. Children

1. Early development—pregnancy, delivery, problems such as prematurity, and birth anomalies
2. Neonatal—feeding, sleeping, bowel patterns, illnesses, hospitalizations
3. Infant-toddler—unusual behavior, head banging, rocking
4. Developmental milestones—when rolled over, sat up, walked, talked, fed self; toilet training; separation
5. Special problems
    a. Enuresis
    b. Encopresis
    c. Tantrums
    d. Feeding difficulties
    e. Nightmares
    f. Sleeplessness
    g. Problems with peers
    h. Learning difficulties
    i. Physical problems—illnesses
6. Schooling
    a. Day care
    b. Schooling history—kind of school or classroom; overall school performance; attitude toward school; special achievements, interests
    c. Present grade and school functioning—grades
    d. Future plans
    e. Career
7. Sexual history
8. Work history
9. Role in family
    a. Relationship to sibs
    b. Relationship to parents
10. Personality

IV. Current family functioning

A. Living situation—adequacy; sleeping arrangements
B. Source of family income
C. Social supports
D. Agency and professional contacts
E. Current stresses and problems

V. Impressions (should contain no facts not presented in I through IV)

VI. Recommendations and/or plan (if indicated)

Appendix C (1)

Scan Protocol Short Form

1. It is State law and hospital policy that all suspected child abuse and/or neglect shall be reported to Protective Services. (See SCAN Folder Section 1.1-1.6.)

2. Notify SCAN person— days call SCAN Office at 3-0215; nights and weekends call SCAN person on call sheet located inside front cover of SCAN Folder. (SEE SCAN Folder, Section 2.1-2.4.)

3. Call Protective Services immediately—994-1882 day or night. (See SCAN Folder, Section 3.3.)

4. Inform family—"I am required by law to make a report to Protective Services whenever I see a child whose injuries (condition) concern me." (See SCAN Folder, Section 1.7-4.)

5. File 3200 Form—Within 72 hours file a written report; forms located inside front cover of SCAN Folder. Send the completed form directly to the SCAN Office. (See SCAN Folder, Section 3.3.)

6. IN ANY CASE WHERE YOU FEEL THE CHILD IS AT RISK IF RETURNED HOME, HOSPITALIZE THE CHILD UNTIL A FULL EVALUATION CAN BE MADE.

7. *Medical Evaluation*
   History: "Tell me what happened." Narrative of how injury occurred as stated by parents. Determine if others (adults or children) were involved in the injury. Determine when the injury occurred. Carefully examine for other injuries or for internal injuries. Check funduscopic for retinal hemorrhages, mouth, abdomen, genitals. (See SCAN Folder, Section 3.4.)

Skin Survey:	Document all skin injuries or scars on Skin Map. Describe size in mm, color of each lesion. (Skin maps in SCAN Folder.)
Photos:	Call Medical Photography (days). Use SCAN camera nights or weekends or if photos are needed immediately for affidavit. Include tape with case number and date in each field; sign each photo. (See SCAN Folder pg. 5.)
Bone Survey:	In children under two with unexplained injuries or nonaccidental injuries. In older children, obtain specific films of tender sites.
Coagulation Screen:	If bruises present or history of easy bruising.
Social Work Evaluation:	The Social Work Office should be notified of all child abuse and neglect cases seen in the hospital.
GYN Consult:	If rape (assault by outsider). Not for incest or assault by family member.
Psychiatry Consult:	If parent is highly disturbed. If child is sexually assaulted or raped.

November 1977

"Was That Child's Injury an Accident?" (Cues for the physician)

History

"Tell me what happened."

"When did it happen?"

Accidental injury—response fits injury, no delay.

Preventable accident—response fits injury and no delay, but frequency of injury or child-child injuries suggest *inadequate supervision.*

Non-accidental injury—response does not make good sense or seems fishy; delay in seeking medical help (maybe it will get better and nobody will know).

Physical exam—child under 6 years completely disrobed

Accidental injuries—mostly lacerations with or without bruises over bony prominences—extremities, crown, periorbital bony ring, chin

Preventable injuries—similar distribution to accidental injuries, repeated injuries, burns, toxic ingestions

Nonaccidental injuries

Bruises with or without lacerations, abrasions, linear parallel (belt), loops (cord), multiple linear (switch)

Over soft tissue areas—buttocks, back, upper thighs and arms, cheeks and ears, neck, genitals

Burns
Fracture in child under 2 years

Hospitalize
Nonaccidental injuries in child under 2 years
Home not safe
Unexplained injuries
Infant with history of "spells," vomiting, parents inappropriate

Reporting
Child Protection Law, Act No. 238, Public Acts of 1975, Michigan Compiled Laws. "A physician, coroner, dentist, medical examiner, nurse, audiologist, certified social worker, social worker, social work technician, social administrator, school counselor or teacher, law enforcement officer, or duly regulated child care provider who has reasonable cause to suspect child abuse or neglect immediately, by telephone or otherwise, shall make an oral report, or cause an oral report to be made, of the suspected child abuse or neglect to the department (Protective Services)."
Key Statements
"It looks like you have had some trouble with your child."
"I am required by law to make a report to Protective Services whenever I see a child whose injuries (condition) concern me."
"A social worker from Protective Services will visit your home in the next few days."
Failure to identify or act (report)
Prohibits intervention or treatment.
Allows subsequent injury, disability, or death.
Makes nonreporter liable for proximal damages.
Is irresponsible or neglectful to the child.
Reasons (rationalizations) given for not reporting
System does not work.
Destroys therapeutic relationship.
Infringes on parental rights.
Don't wish to get involved in time-consuming social-legal problems.
Did not recognize abuse—incomplete history, exam.
Don't wish to offend patient; he might sue.

Referral
Hospital or community SCAN consultant.
Social work evaluation *essential* for adequate evaluation, management.

Photographs
Polaroid SX-70 ideal.
Identify patient's number, date in field.
Part of routine medical evaluation of this specific problem—could you manage fractures without x-rays?

These materials have been developed by the University of Michigan Hospital Child Protection Team for use in medical evaluation of Suspected Child Abuse and Neglect (SCAN).

Appendix C (2)

Skin Maps

INJURY SKIN MAP

COMMON SITES OF INFLICTED INJURY

COMMON SITES OF ACCIDENTAL INJURY

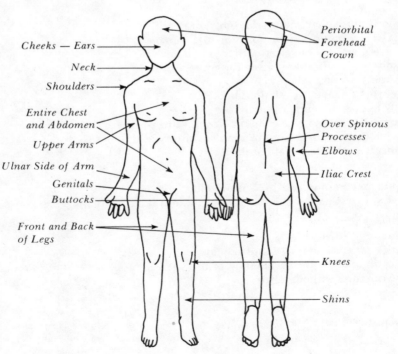

Cheeks — Ears
Neck
Shoulders
Entire Chest and Abdomen
Upper Arms
Ulnar Side of Arm
Genitals
Buttocks
Front and Back of Legs

Periorbital
Forehead
Crown
Over Spinous Processes
Elbows
Iliac Crest
Knees
Shins

Skin Maps

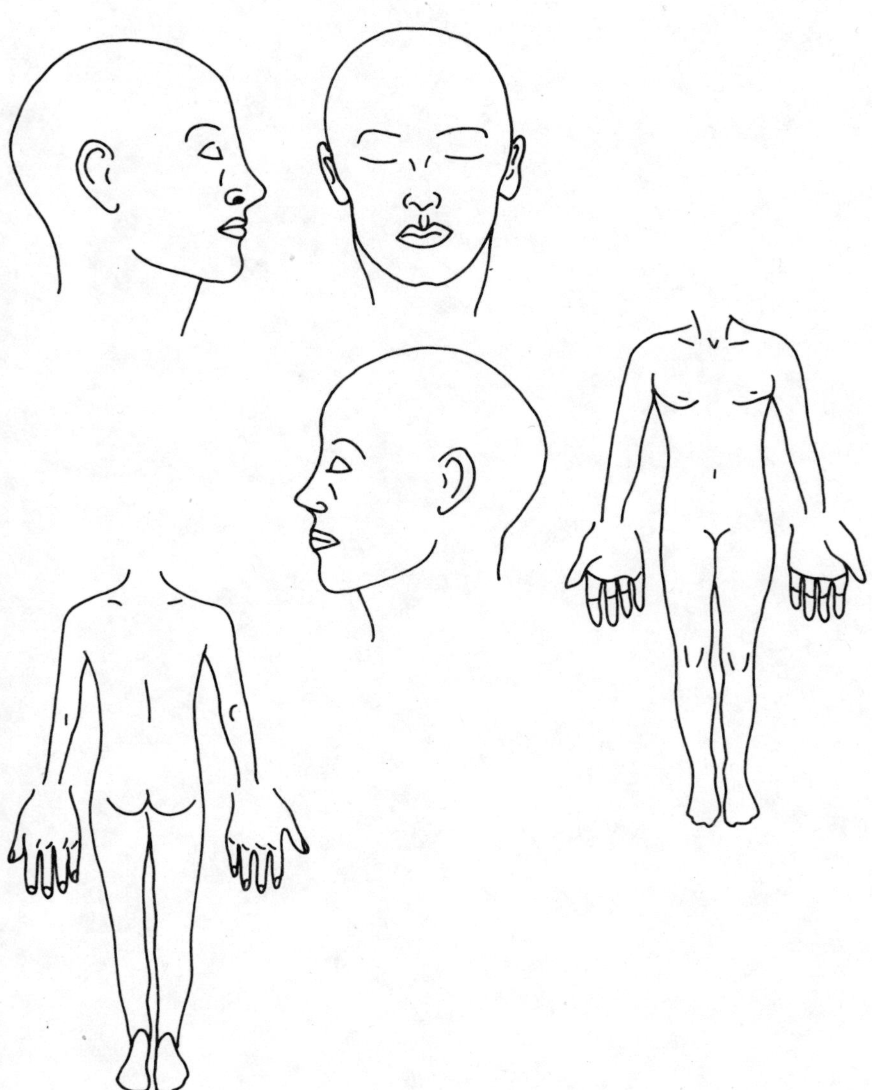

References

American Humane Association

1980 *Highlights of the 1978 National Reporting Data* (Englewood, Colo.: AHA).

1978 *National Analysis of Child Abuse and Neglect Reporting* (Englewood, Colo.: AHA).

1976 *Analysis of the Official Child Abuse and Neglect Reporting* (Englewood, Colo.: AHA).

Anastasi, A.

1968 *Psychological Testing*, 3rd ed. (New York: Macmillan).

Bagley, Christopher

1969 "Incest Behavior: The Incest Taboo," *Social Problems, 16*, 505-519.

Baher, E., et al.

1976 *At Risk: An Account of the Work of the Battered Child Research Department* (National Society for Prevention of Cruelty to Children). (London, Eng.)

Baldwin, J. A., and Oliver, J. E.

1975 "Epidemiology and Family Characteristics of Severely Abused Children," *British Journal of Preventive Social Medicine, 29*, 205-221.

Bates, Robert P.

1977 Paper presented at Conference on Domestic Violence of the International Conference of Law. (Wash., D.C.)

Besharov, Douglas J.

1974 *Juvenile Justice Advocacy, Practicing Law Institute.*

Caffey, John, M. D.

1946 "Multiple Fractures in the Long Bones of Children Suffering from Chronic Subdural Hematoma," *American Journal of Roentgenology, 56*, 163.

References

CHESS, S., AND THOMAS, A.

1977 "Temperamental Individuality from Childhood to Adolescence," *Journal of the American Academy of Child Psychiatry, 16,* 218-225.

CHILDREN'S DEFENSE FUND

1978 *Children Without Homes* (Washington, D.C.: Children's Defense Fund).

CITIZENS' BOARD OF INQUIRY INTO HUNGER AND MALNUTRITION IN THE UNITED STATES

1968 *A Report* (Wash., D.C.: New Community Press).

CODE OF FEDERAL REGULATIONS PART 231.1

See also Michigan Compiled Laws 722.622.

COHN, ANN HARRIS

1979 "Effective Treatment of Child Abuse and Neglect," *Social Work*, November.

COLORADO STATUTES, ARTICLE 13. CRIMINAL CODE.

COPAISS, STUART, et al.

1979 "The Stresses of Treating Child Abuses," *Children Today*, January-February.

DEFRANCIS, VINCENT

1970 *Child Abuse Legislation in the 1970's,* (Denver, Colo.: Children's Division, American Humane Association).

1966 *Child Victims of Incest* (Denver, Colo.: Children's Division, American Humane Association).

DELANEY, JAMES J.

1976 "New Concepts of the Family Court," in Ray E. Helfer and C. Henry Kempe (eds.), *Child Abuse and Neglect: The Family and the Community* (Cambridge, Mass.: Ballinger), p. 350.

DOWNS, S.

1979 "Guardian ad Litem Program in Seattle," *Case Record*, Portland State University (Portland, Oregon), pp. 1-3.

ELMER, ELIZABETH

1977 *Fragile Families and Troubled Children* (Pittsburgh: University of Pittsburgh Press).

ELMER, ELIZABETH

1977 "Follow-up Study of Traumatized Children," *Child Abuse and Neglect: The International Journal*, VI, 105-109.

ERICKSON, ERIK H.

1950 *Childhood and Society* (New York: Norton).

FANSHEL, DAVID, AND SHINN, EUGENE

1978 *Children in Foster Care: A Longitudinal Investigation* (New York: Columbia University Press).

References

FINKELHOR, DAVID

1979 *Sexual Victimization of Children* (New York: Free Press).

FRASER, BRIAN

1973 *The Legislative Approach to Child Abuse: A Current Compilation of Our States' Statutes,* (Denver, Colo.: National Center for the Prevention & Treatment of Child Abuse & Neglect).

FREUD, ANNA

1965 *Normality and Pathology in Childhood* (New York: International Universities Press).

GALDSTON, R.

1971 "Violence Begins at Home: The Parents' Center Project for the Study and Prevention of Child Abuse," *Journal of the Academy of Child Psychiatry, 10,* 336–350.

GARRIETTO, HENRY

1979 "Sexual Victimization of Children; Trauma, Trial, and Treatment," conference presentation, Washington, D.C., November-December.

1976 "Humanistic Treatment of Father-Daughter Incest," in Ray E. Helfer and C. Henry Kempe, (eds.), *Child Abuse and Neglect: The Family and the Community* (Cambridge, Mass.: Ballinger).

GELLERT, ELIZABETH (ed.)

1978 *Psychosocial Aspects of Pediatric Care* (New York: Grune).

GELLES, DAVID

1973 "Child Abuse as Psychopathology: A Sociological Reconstruction," *American Sociological Review, 38,* 611–621.

GELLES, RICHARD

1978 Conference presentation, 3rd National Congress on Child Abuse and Neglect, New York, April.

Results of NIH commissioned survey, presented at Philadelphia Conference on Child Abuse and Neglect, November.

GIL, DAVID

1973 *Violence Against Children* (Cambridge, Mass.: Harvard University Press). Second edition.

1970 *Violence Against Children: Physical Abuse in the United States* (Cambridge, Mass.: Harvard University Press).

GIOVANNONI, JEANNE M.

1970 "Parental Mistreatment: Perpetrators and Victims," *Journal of Marriage and the Family, 11,* 649–657.

GIOVANNONI, JEANNE M., AND BECERRA, ROSINA

1979 *Defining Child Abuse* (New York: Free Press).

GOLDSTEIN, JOSEPH

1977 Remarks in workshop at Conference on Domestic Violence of the International Society on Family Law, Montreal, Canada.

GOLDSTEIN, JOSEPH, FREUD, ANNA, AND SOLNIT, ALBERT
1973 *Beyond the Best Interests of the Child* (New York: Free Press).

GORDON, THOMAS
1970 *Parent Effectiveness Training* (New York: Peter Wyden).

GREEN, A.
1978 "Psychopathology of Abused Children," *Journal of the American Academy of Child Psychology, 17*, 92–103.

HANSON, DONALD, AND HILL, REUBEN
1964 "Families Under Stress," in Harold T. Christensen (ed.), *Handbook of Marriage and the Family* (Chicago: Rand McNally), pp. 787–792.

HELFER, RAY E.
1969 "The Special Problem of Failure to Thrive," in Helfer, *The Diagnostic Process and Treatment Programs*, U.S. DHEW publication (OHD) 75-69 (Wash., D.C.: Government Printing Office).

HELFER, RAY E., AND KEMPE, C. HENRY
1968 *The Battered Child* (Chicago: Univ. of Chicago Press).

HELFER, RAY, AND KEMPE, C. HENRY
1980 *The Battered Child Revisited*, 3rd ed. (Chicago: University of Chicago Press).

HELFER, RAY E., AND KEMPE, C. HENRY (eds.)
1976 *Child Abuse and Neglect: The Family and Community* (Cambridge, Mass.: Ballinger).

HERRENKOHL, ROY
1978 "Research in Progress," paper presented at the 3rd National Conference on Child Abuse and Neglect, New York, April.

HOLMES, SALLY, et al.
1973 "Working with the Parent in Child-Abuse Cases," *Social Casework, 56*, 3–12.

HOPWOOD, NANCY, AND BECKER, DOROTHY
1978 "Psychosocial Dwarfism: Detection, Evaluation, and Management," paper presented at the 2nd International Congress on Child Abuse and Neglect, London, England.

INSTITUTE OF JUDICIAL ADMINISTRATION–AMERICAN BAR ASSOCIATION
1977 Juvenile Justice Standards Project, *Abuse and Neglect* (Cambridge, Mass.: Ballinger).

ISAACS, J. L.
1972 "The Role of the Lawyer in Child Abuse Cases," in C. H. Kempe and R. E. Helfer (eds.), *Helping the Battered Child and His Family* (Philadelphia: Lippincott).

JOHNSON, B., AND MORSE, H.
1968 "Injured Children and Their Parents," *Children, 15*, 147–152.

Jones, Carolyn Okell
1978 Paper presented before the Family and Children's Services Child Abuse Workshop, London, Ontario, May.
"The Predicament of Abused Children," in Constance Lee (ed.), *Child Abuse: A Reader and Sourcebook* (Milton Keynes, England: The Open University Press, 1978).
1977 "The Fate of Abused Children," in A. White Franklin (ed.), *The Challenge of Child Abuse* (London: Academic Press).

Justice, Blair, and Justice, Rita
1976 *The Abusing Family* (New York: Human Sciences Press).

Kadushin, Alfred (ed.)
1978 *Child Welfare Strategy for the Coming Years*, U.S. DHEW publication (ODHS) 78-30158 (Wash., D.C.: Government Printing Office).

Katz, Sanford, et al.,
1975 "Child Neglect Laws in America," *Family Law Quarterly, 9*, 40-41.

Kempe, C. Henry, Silverman, Frederic N., Steele, Brandt, Droegemueller, W., and Silver, H.K.
1962 "The Battered Child Syndrome," *Journal of the American Medical Association, 181*, 17-24.

Keniston, Kenneth, and the Carnegie Council on Children
1977 *All Our Children: The American Family Under Pressure*, New York: Harcourt Brace Jovanovich.

Kinnard, M.
1978 "Emotional Development of Abused Children: A Study of Self-Concept and Aggression," doctoral dissertation, Brandeis University. Ann Arbor, Mich., University Microfilms, no. 7821706.

Klaus, Marshall H., and Kennell, John H.
1976 *Maternal-Infant Bonding* (St. Louis: Mosby).

Korbin, Jill
1977 "Anthropological Contributions to the Study of Child Abuse," *Child Abuse and Neglect: The International Journal, 1*, 7-24.

Lourie, Ira
1978 "Family Dynamics and the Abuse of Adolescents: A Case for a Developmental Phase Specific Model of Child Abuse," paper presented at the 2nd International Congress on Child Abuse and Neglect, London, England, September.

Mahler, Margaret S., Pine, Fred, and Bergman, Anni
1975 *The Psychological Birth of the Human Infant: Symbiosis and Individuation* (New York: Basic Books).

Martin, Harold P.
1976 *The Abused Child: A Multidisciplinary Approach to Developmental Issues and Treatment* (Cambridge, Mass.: Ballinger).

MARTIN, HAROLD P., AND BEESLEY, P.
1977 "Behavioral Observations of Abused Children," *Developmental Medicine and Child Neurology, 19*, 373–387.

MCLAUGHLIN, CLARA
1976 *The Black Parent's Handbook* (New York: Harcourt Brace Jovanovich).

MEAD, MARGARET
1970 *Culture and Commitment: A Study of the Generation Gap* (Garden City, N.Y.: Natural History Press).

MEIKAMP, KATHIE D.
1978 "The American Way of Life," *Midwest Parent-Child Review, III* (3).

Michigan Child Cruelty Statute

Michigan Child Protection Law

Michigan Compiled Laws
Juvenile Court Rules

MICHIGAN STATE DEPARTMENT OF SOCIAL SERVICES
1970 *Services Manual: Protective Services*, revised (Lansing: Michigan State Department of Social Services).

MORRIS, M., AND GOULD, R.
1963 "Role Reversal: A Necessary Concept in Dealing with the 'Battered Child Syndrome,' " *American Journal of Orthopsychiatry, 33*, 14–17.

MORSE, C. W., SAHLER, O. J., AND FRIEDMAN, S. B.
1970 "A Three Year Follow-up Study of Abused and Neglected Children," *American Journal of Diseases of Children, 120*, 439–446.

MURPHY, L.
1976 *Vulnerability, Coping and Growth from Infancy to Adolescence* (New Haven, Conn.: Yale University Press).

NEWBERGER, ELI H., AND BOURNE, RICHARD
1977 Paper presented at the Conference on Domestic Violence of the International Society of Law (Montreal, Can.).

ORR, DAVID
1978 "Limitations of Emergency Room Evaluations of Sexually Abused Children," *American Journal of Diseases in Children, 132*, September, 873–875.

PELTON, LEROY H.
1978 "Child Abuse and Neglect: The Myth of Classlessness," *American Journal of Orthopsychiatry*, 48(4), 608–617.

POLANSKY, NORMAN, CHALMERS, MARY ANN, BUTTENWEISER, ELIZABETH, AND WILLIAMS, DAVID
1978 "The Isolation of the Neglectful Family," unpublished manuscript.

POLANSKY, NORMAN, DESAIX, CHRISTINE, AND SHARLIN, SCHLOMO
1972 *Child Neglect: Understanding and Reaching the Parent* (New York: Child Welfare League of America).

ROLDE, E. J.
1977 "Negative Effects of Child Abuse Legislation," *Child Abuse and Neglect: The International Journal, 1*, 167-171.

SCHMITT, BARTON D.
1978 "The Physician's Evaluation," in Barton Schmitt (ed.), *The Child Protection Team Handbook* (New York: Garland STPM Press).

SCHNEIGER, FRANK
1977 Introduction, in "Child Abuse, Neglect and the Family Within a Cultural Context," *Protective Services Resource Institute Report, 2*(1) (Piscataway, N.Y.).

SCHULTZ, LEROY
1980 *The Sexual Victimology of Youth* (Springfield, Ill.: Thomas).

SHEPARD, R. E., JR.
1965 "The Abused Child and the Law," *Washington and Lee Law Review, 22*, 182-184.

SMALL, WILLIE V.
1977 "The Neglect of Black Children," in "Child Abuse, Neglect and the Family Within a Cultural Context," *Protective Services Resource Institute Report, 2*(7) (Piscataway, N.Y.).

SMITH, PATRICIA
1977 "Towards a New Perspective," *Midwest Parent-Child Review, ii*, no. 2.

SMITH, S. M., AND HANSON, R.
1974 "134 Battered Children: A Medical and Psychological Study," *British Medical Journal, 3*, 666-670.

SPINNETTA, JOHN, AND RIGLER, DAVID
1972 "The Child Abusing Parent: A Psychological Review," *Psychological Bulletin, 77-7*, 296-314.

STEELE, BRANDT
1970 *Working with Abusive Parents from a Psychiatric Point of View*, U.S. DHEW publication (OHD) 76-30070 (Wash., D.C.: Government Printing Office).

STRAUS, MURRAY
1978 "Family Patterns and Child Abuse in a Nationally Representative American Sample," paper presented at the 2nd International Congress on Child Abuse and Neglect, London, England, September.

STRAUS, MURRAY, GELLES, RICHARD, AND STEINMETZ, SUZANNE
1980 *Behind Closed Doors: Violence in the American Family* (New York: Anchor Press).

Straus, P., and Girodet, D.
1977 "Three French Follow-up Studies of Abused Children," *Child Abuse and Neglect: The International Journal, 3*, 555-563.

Summit, Roland, and Kryso, Jo Ann
1978 "Sexual Abuse of Children: A Clinical Spectrum," *American Journal of Orthopsychiatry, 48*, 237.

Sussman, E.
1974 "Reporting Child Abuse: A Review of the Literature," *Family Law Quarterly, 8*: 245-248.

U.S. Department of Health, Education, and Welfare, National Center on Child Abuse and Neglect
1978 *Excerpts from Child Abuse and Neglect State Reporting Laws*, Publication (OHD) 80-30265 (Wash., D.C.: Government Printing Office).

U.S. Department of Health, Education, and Welfare, Children's Bureau
1977 *Model Child Protection Act with Commentary* (Draft) (Wash., D.C.: Government Printing Office).

U.S. Department of Health, Education, and Welfare
1977 *A Guide to Protective Services for Abused and Neglected Children and Their Families*, Publication (OHD) 77-02003 (Wash., D.C.: Government Printing Office).
1975 *Child Abuse and Neglect: The Problem and Its Management*, 3 vols., Publication (OHD) 75-30075 (Wash., D.C.: Government Printing Office).

Wald, Michael
1976 "State Intervention on Behalf of 'Neglected' Children: A Search for Realistic Standards," *Stanford Law Review, 27*, 985-1040.

Walters, James, and Stinnett, Nickolas
1970 "Parent-Child Relationships: A Decade Review of Research," in Carlfred Broderick (ed.), *A Decade of Family Research and Action*, 1960-69 (Minneapolis: National Council on Family Relations), pp. 99-140.

Wiltse, Kermit
1978 "Current Issues and New Directions in Foster Care," in Alfred Kadushin (ed.), *Child Welfare Strategy in the Coming Years*, U.S. DHEW publication (OHDS) 78-30158.

Zaphiris, Alexander G.
1978 *Incest: The Family with Two Known Victims* (Denver, Colo.: Children's Division, American Humane Association).

Index

Index

Index